EXPERIENCE GRACE IN ABUNDANCE

Books written by Johnnette S. Benkovic:

The New Age Counterfeit

Full of Grace: Women and the Abundant Life

Grace-Filled Moments

Living Life Abundantly:
Stories of People Who Have Encountered God

Experience Grace in Abundance:
Ten Strategies for Your Spiritual Life

Visit *www.lhla.org* for more information on these titles.

EXPERIENCE GRACE IN ABUNDANCE

Ten Strategies for Your Spiritual Life

JOHNNETTE S. BENKOVIC

OUR SUNDAY VISITOR PUBLISHING DIVISION
OUR SUNDAY VISITOR, INC.
HUNTINGTON, INDIANA 46750

Nihil Obstat
Reverend Craig A. Doty, J.C.L.
Censor Deputatus

Imprimatur
Most Reverend Fabian W. Bruskewitz, D.D., S.T.D.
Bishop of Lincoln
November 6, 2002

The *Nihil Obstat* and *Imprimatur* are official declarations that a book or pamphlet is
free from doctrinal or moral error. No implication is contained therein that those who
have granted the *Nihil Obstat* and *Imprimatur* agree with the contents, opinions, or
statements expressed.

To my parents, Willis and Johnnette Simon.
In grateful appreciation for the life you gave me,
the love that nurtured me,
and the Catholic faith that sustains me.
I love you.
May God bless you abundantly today and forever.

Blessed Brother André, pray for us.

CONTENTS

ACKNOWLEDGMENTS

I am most grateful for the help and assistance of many individuals and organizations whose generosity and kindness assisted in the writing and publishing of *Experience Grace in Abundance: Ten Strategies for Your Spiritual Life*. It is with sincere gratitude that I thank the following:

Thank you to Our Sunday Visitor Publishing, which believed in this project from the beginning. And thank you for giving me permission to use Peggy Eastman's story, "Please Don't Touch," from her book *Godly Glimpses: Discoveries of the Love that Heals*. Thank you especially to Michael Dubruiel, my editor, whose patience, understanding, encouragement, and keen insight guided me throughout. Thank you, also, to George Foster for a careful read.

Thank you to Father Craig A. Doty, J.C.L., for his helpful suggestions and thorough read, and to Bishop Fabian W. Bruskewitz, D.D., S.T.D., for his imprimatur and the use of his "keys" to a happy marriage, from his book *A Shepherd Speaks*.

Thank you to Father Edmund Sylvia, C.S.C., theological consultant for this book. As always, your friendship, advice, and counsel have been invaluable to me.

Thank you to Marietta Jaeger-Lane for sharing with the world her powerful testimony of forgiveness. From your pain, Marietta, so many have come to wholeness and hope. You are a guiding light through whom God's love shines. May God bless you.

Thank you to The University of Wisconsin Press for giving me permission to use the excerpts of Marietta's story from the book *Exploring Forgiveness*, edited by Robert D. Enright and Joanna North (copyright © 1998). Thank you also to Robert D. Enright and Richard P. Fitzgibbons, M.D., for their outstanding work in the area of forgiveness therapy and for use of their work *Helping Clients Forgive: An Empirical Guide for Resolving Anger and Restoring Hope*.

Thank you, also, to Lee Sayne for permitting me to share his story of forgiveness. I am privileged to offer it to my readers. Lee, you show us all how to forgive even when racked by the pain of loss. I know that you will inspire many to walk the road of forgiveness.

Thank you to the staff members of *Living His Life Abundantly* ® *International, Inc.* for their help and support as I worked on this project. And thank you also for your many prayers. They sustained me more than you could know.

Thank you always to my friend Anne, whose witness of faith brought me back to the Catholic faith.

But most especially, thank you to my husband, Anthony. You have given me the love, understanding, flexibility, and generosity to write this book, and many of these "strategies" we have experienced together. Spending my life with you has been my greatest gift.

If there are any omissions or errors in this book, they are all my own.

PREFACE

Experience Grace in Abundance: Ten Strategies for Your Spiritual Life offers strategies to help us fulfill our fundamental vocation in life: to grow in holiness and to be conformed to the image of God. Each strategy leads us along the continuum of transformation by giving us a deeper understanding of the spiritual principles that mark the interior life and practical ways of implementing them in our daily lives. An opportunity for "Working the Strategy" is offered at the close of each chapter to encourage spiritual growth. In addition, placed throughout the book are seven more "spiritual essentials," which are neatly formulated according to the acronym "S.U.C.C.E.S.S." These "tips" offer still other means of living the abundant life of Jesus Christ and sharing it with others.

Today, the world needs "new saints" and "new evangelizers." It is my prayer that all of us who read this book will not only grow to a deeper appreciation of our life in Jesus Christ and the rich treasure of our Catholic faith, but also that we will be challenged to live our faith with holy zeal through word and deed.

If any of this should be accomplished, it will be my great joy. For, in each and every case, it will be the irrefutable reality that the Holy Spirit has been at work in us. May lives be changed, may hearts be healed, and may souls be saved! Thus will we experience grace in abundance!

Johnnette Simon Benkovic
October 28, 2002
Feast of Sts. Simon and Jude, Apostles

Part One

OUR RELATIONSHIP WITH GOD

❧

STRATEGY ONE

Believe the Truth About Yourself

❦

ANGELA'S STORY

The young woman's eyes filled with tears as the counselor spoke the truth to her. Angela had been raised in a two-parent family and had attended private schools through all twelve years. She and her older brother were the only children. While family life seemed well grounded and apparently stable, parental approval came at a high price.

Angela couldn't remember a time when she had been told that she had worth and value in and of herself. She was always measured against her performance — good grades, proper behavior, the "right" friends, and extracurricular accomplishments. When she did well, she received affection and encouragement. When she did not, her parents voiced their disappointment and became emotionally distant. The reality was that Angela failed the "test" more often than she passed it. Throughout her life, the thought haunted her that she could never get it quite right and, therefore, was unlovable.

That's what had brought her to the counselor in the first place. She had sought the love and affection she missed in all the wrong places. Her seeking had led her into and out of the arms of many lovers. All through high school, she gave herself away, searching for an intimacy she never quite found. Urged on by her unfulfilled need, Angela's promiscuous behavior followed her into her twenties. Now, she was paying the price — again.

Angela sat before the crisis-pregnancy counselor with tears in her eyes. She was hearing words that promised freedom and new life, and these words were a soothing balm to her aching heart. The counselor was telling her that she, Angela, was precious, that God loved her, and that nothing she could do or had done could change that fact — not even her two prior abortions. The counselor was telling her there was a way back. There was a way to restore what the locusts had eaten (Joel 2:25). There was hope. And it began by Angela coming to know the truth about herself.

Perhaps you can relate to some of the details in Angela's story. You may not have had the same kind of relationship with your parents. You may never have had an abortion. And you might not even be a woman. But, like Angela, you need to know you are loved. You need to know you have worth and value. And you need to know that God has a plan for you — in spite of the mistakes you have made, the sins you have committed, and the decisions of your past. Like Angela, you need to know the truth about yourself. And, you need to believe it.

Believing the truth about yourself is absolutely essential for growth in the spiritual life. Without knowing the truth and then believing it, you simply cannot grow in your relationship with God.

But what *is* that truth? Scripture passages give us the answer. Let's take a look at Genesis 1:26-27, Ephesians 1:4, Genesis 3:15, and John 3:16. These passages tell us much about ourselves and the God who gave us life.

CREATION

The first chapter of Genesis recounts the creation of the world. It is a beautiful chapter, rich in meaning and revelation, which leads us into a prayerful consideration of the awesome nature of our God: only an omnipotent (all-powerful) God can create everything out of nothing; only an omniscient (all-knowing) God can know exactly what to create and for what purpose; and only an omnipresent (all-present) God can uphold and sustain the entirety of creation by His divine existence.

The first chapter of Genesis shows us that God created the world in an orderly fashion, and that the order itself reveals His intention and purpose. In Verse 1, we learn that when God created the earth it was without form, it was void, and it was dark. God separated the earth from the heavens and He said, "Let there be light" (1:3). And there was light. Then God gathered the waters under the heavens into one place and the dry land appeared. Next, He created vegetation, plant life, and fruit-bearing trees. He created the sun, the moon, and the stars in the heavens. He created the creatures of the sea, the birds of the air, and the living creatures of the earth. All of this He created, and all of this reflected His glory and His majesty. It reflected His power and His supreme intelligence. And all of it was good.

However, God was not finished. Everything that He had brought into existence thus far seemed to anticipate a creature that would be the pinnacle of His creation. The very order in which He executed His plan of creation indicated as much. Moving from the inanimate to the animate, and from primitive life forms to more complicated species, suggested a reasoned, intentioned, and well-ordered approach. Indeed, it seemed God had "arranged all things by measure and number and weight" (Wisdom 11:20).

In addition, everything was in place for a creature that could benefit by what God had created. There were plants to eat, water to drink, animals to enjoy, beauty to appreciate, sun for light, and darkness for rest.

But one thing more seemed to suggest a masterpiece to God's creation. While the whole of creation reflected aspects of God's nature — His glory, His majesty, His power, and His intelligence — nothing thus far communicated His essence. Nothing spoke to the truth of who God is.

GOD IS LOVE

Who is this God of creation? Implicit in Sacred Scripture and explicit in the teachings of the Catholic Church is the discovery that God is a Trinity of Persons: God the Father, God the Son, and God the Holy Spirit. Though each Person is separate and distinct, the Divine Persons are "one in being" and exist as a "communion of Persons."

The defining feature of the Triune God is love. In fact, theologians tell us that so great is the love of God the Father for God the Son, and so great is the love of God the Son for God the Father, that Their mutual love "spirates" the Third Person of the

Blessed Trinity, the Holy Spirit. Thus, love itself becomes a Person, a Divine Person. Capturing this interior reality of God, St. John the Evangelist sums it up neatly by simply saying, "God is love" (1 John 4:16).

(According to *A Catholic Dictionary*, edited by Donald Attwater, "spirate" is the mode in which the Third Person of the Trinity has His origin from the other two. "Spiration" is a word that indicates the act of loving, and denies the procession by generation which is proper to the Son. The Catholic faith teaches that the Holy Spirit proceeds from the Father and the Son.)

But what is love, and what are its characteristics? While the world offers many definitions of love and many pseudo-manifestations of it, the world most frequently fails to capture the essence of true love. Love is a **dynamic** reality. Love cannot be contained. Love seeks an outward expression. Love, by its very nature, must be shared. But how is it to be shared? Love is a **self-donating** reality. Love seeks to give completely and totally, without reservation and without condition. Love desires to ignite the heart of another, who in turn will love back freely in a corresponding act of self-donation. And when this happens, love reflects the Divine Love and achieves its true purpose: Love becomes a **life-giving** reality.

A REFLECTION OF GOD

Though the heavens and the earth, and the plant and animal kingdoms, were resplendent with God's glory and majesty, and reflective of His power and intelligence, love was the essence of God's nature that creation still did not communicate. In order for it to do so, a creature would need to exist that would be categorically different from everything God had already created. This creature would need to have attributes that would make it capable of love and relationship. This creature would need the ability to think (intelligence). It would need the ability to reason (rationality). It would need the ability to *know* itself and others (consciousness). And it would need to have free will (freedom to decide for itself). These were attributes of God himself, attributes of His *Personhood*, and no other creation on earth had been endowed with these gifts.

To share His love with His creation, God would create a *person* who could receive His love.

And so, in an act of self-donation, manifested in a dynamic and life-giving moment, God determined that He would create such a creature. He would create a person who was capable of receiving love and giving love, a creature who would be a reflection of himself: "Let us make man in our image, after our likeness," He said, "and let them have dominion over the fish of the sea, and over the birds of the air, and over the cattle, and over all the earth, and over every creeping thing that creeps upon the earth." Scripture continues, "So God created man in his own image, in the image of God he created him; male and female he created them" (Genesis 1:26-27). God breathed life into the nostrils of man (Genesis 2:7), and man became a person who imaged the likeness of God. Through the gift of personhood, man could receive God's love, and he could love God in return. Man and his Creator could be in relationship with each other.

But that is not all. God determined that man should have one like himself to love as well. And in His divine plan, they would become a sign and an image of the love between the Divine Persons of the Trinity, and participate in God's most sublime role as Creator. How would this come to be?

A REFLECTION OF THE TRINITARIAN LIFE

The Scripture passage says that God created man "male and female," and with these words the plan of God unfolds. This phrase is stunning in what it communicates. First, every human being, by virtue of his or her personhood, is made in the image and likeness of God. Second, by creating two genders, God expresses the dynamic reality of love. Not only will each person receive His love, but also each person will communicate His love to another. Third, the two genders will express the self-donating dimension of God's love, and they will do this through their bodies.

Fourth, this self-donating dimension of man and woman, expressed by their physical coming together, will be life-giving: "Be fruitful and multiply," God says to them (Genesis 1:28). Just as the mutual love of the Father and the Son spirates the Holy Spirit — the personification of that love — and just as the Trinity reveals its loving nature through the creation of man, so too will the union of man and woman bring forth a new life — a personification and outward manifestation of their love for each other.

Fifth, this "communion of persons," witnessed by the self-donating love of man and woman, becomes a sign and an image of the Trinitarian life. This elevates their loving union to the status of a sacrament, the Sacrament of Matrimony. As such, it is an outward sign instituted by God, through which divine life — grace — is experienced.

Sixth, this sacrament is a sign in the world and, therefore, should be a godly influence. It is meant to "fill the earth and subdue it" (Genesis 1:28) by bringing all creation, and all who people it, into union with God through love. In "Strategy Three: Make Use of the Sacraments," we will gain even deeper insights into the beautiful gift of the Sacrament of Matrimony.

MADE FOR LOVE

The creation of man was no whim of God. Scripture tells us that He intentioned man's creation before the foundations of the world were laid in place (Ephesians 1:4). It is important to note that God did not need to create man. God is total and complete in and of himself, and therefore He needs nothing. Rather, God loved man into life and desired to share with man His eternal beatitude. This is true to God's nature, true to being a God who is love.

The *Catechism of the Catholic Church* (CCC) reaffirms this truth. It says that "God is love: Father, Son, and Holy Spirit" and that He "freely wills to communicate the glory of his blessed life" upon "his sons" whom "he destined . . . in love . . . before the foundation of the world." This is the "plan of his loving kindness," and this loving kindness stems "immediately from Trinitarian love" (no. 257). Thus, God created man in love that man might know love; that man might give love; and that man, like God, might *be* love. The mystery of the Most Holy Trinity is, therefore, the "central mystery of Christian faith and life" (no.

234) and the animating principle of every human person. Only through loving union with the Triune God does man find his ultimate purpose, achieve true fulfillment, and experience the abundant life. And only through this loving union can man love others as God loves.

A PERSONAL REVELATION

As she sat with the crisis-pregnancy counselor, it was this deeper understanding of God's love that brought tears to Angela's eyes. Man was not the result of some random act of nature. Nor was he the result of some big bang. No, an intelligent, rational, and loving God determined that man would have life, all for the purpose of entering into relationship with Him and experiencing His love.

"What are the implications of this in my own life?" Angela wondered. When she asked the question aloud, the counselor shared something with her that began a life-changing process. The crisis-pregnancy counselor referred, once again, to Ephesians 1:3-4:

> Blessed be the God and Father of our Lord Jesus Christ, who has blessed us in Christ with every spiritual blessing in the heavenly places, even as he chose us in him before the foundation of the world, that we should be holy and blameless before him.

Here, Angela began to discover the remarkable truth about herself. She, too, had been specifically chosen by God to have life. Angela discovered that God had been in love with the very thought of her before He had laid the foundations of the world in place. She was His daughter whom He had loved into being. Therefore, Angela was lovable in and of herself, and her very existence was proof of it. Angela discovered that God had destined her to be *holy and blameless* before Him. In this way, she could experience the depths of His love for her, and she, in turn, would then be able to share His love with others.

These words had a profound effect upon Angela. The light of truth was permeating her mind and the shackles of misunderstanding were beginning to loosen their grip. God had always loved her, and He would love her forever!

But she was confused. What about her life? What about the choices she had made? What about her two abortions? What about her promiscuous behavior? Wasn't God's love somehow tied to her performance — if she did the right things, she got His love; if she didn't do the right things, she didn't get His love? Didn't God's love depend upon her actions and her decisions? She knew one thing — her relationships with men certainly did not fulfill the beautiful reality of His Trinitarian life. Her relationships were not sacramental. They were outside of the marital covenant. She was not holy or blameless. What about that?

Angela's questions were good questions — and ones the crisis-pregnancy counselor was waiting to answer. Now Angela was ready to hear the really exciting part of God's love for man: that even while man was in the midst of sin, God was about the business of making provision for him.

IN THE GARDEN

One of the most remarkable passages in Scripture is Genesis 3:15. The third chapter of Genesis recounts the fall of man, and the fifteenth verse speaks of God's provision for man after man's fall. Let's take a moment and review the story.

God had made man in His image and likeness. This meant that man had intelligence, rationality, consciousness, and free will. The man, who was called Adam, and the woman, who was called Eve, lived in the Garden of Eden and enjoyed all that God had provided for them. But they enjoyed more as well. God had created Adam and Eve for a supernatural destiny, and He had raised them to a supernatural state through grace. It was His intention that they transmit this state of grace to their children and to their progeny. This was God's plan for mankind.

Through this supernatural state of grace, man's free will was conformed to God's will, and this conformity created a loving union between God and man. Thus, man lived in abiding peace. At peace with God, man was at peace with himself; at peace with himself, man was at peace with the rest of creation. Spiritual writers call this supernatural state of peace the "triple harmony": Man's harmony with God produced harmony within himself, which produced harmony between himself and the rest of the world. This was the initial experience of Adam and Eve.

God had placed one stipulation upon Adam, however. He could not eat of the fruit from the tree of the knowledge of good and evil. While he had free access to everything else in the Garden of Eden, the fruit of this tree was off-limits. In fact, eating the fruit of the tree carried a great penalty. God told Adam, "Of the tree of the knowledge of good and evil you shall not eat, for in the day that you eat of it you shall die" (Genesis 2:16). It was a small condition, and for a time Adam perfectly conformed to God's will.

But one day the most subtle and wild of all the creatures, the serpent, approached the woman, Eve. He tempted her by saying that the fruit of the tree of the knowledge of good and evil would not cause her to die. Rather, the tree's fruit would make her like God: "For God knows that when you eat of it your eyes will be opened, and you will be like God, knowing good and evil" (Genesis 3:5).

Poor Eve. She did not realize she was already "like God" through grace. She fell prey to the serpent's temptation and used her gift of free will to sin against God. Disobeying, Eve took of the tree's fruit and gave some to her husband, who also ate of it. "Then the eyes of both were opened, and they knew that they were naked; and they sewed fig leaves together and made themselves aprons" (Genesis 3:7).

What effect did the sin of disobedience have on Adam and Eve, and subsequently on the whole of mankind? Genesis 3:7-13 tells the tale. At Verse 7, Adam and Eve lose their innocence, discover their vulnerability, and experience shame. They also discover a new temptation — concupiscence of the flesh, the temptation to lust. Their unselfish, unencumbered relationship is compromised. Harmony between them becomes strained.

Verses 8-10 show that not only have Adam and Eve experienced a fracturing of their relationship, but their friendship with God has also been broken. When God calls them to come to Him, they run and hide instead. Fear, the bitter fruit of disobedience, has taken root in them. And, almost immediately, fear produces more bad fruit. When God questions Adam and Eve about their actions, Adam blames Eve, and then Eve blames the serpent. They blame circumstances and others for their disobedience rather than themselves. They do not repent.

Adam and Eve's actions reveal something to us about the effects of sin. All sin ruptures man's communion with God (CCC, no. 1440), it wounds man's nature (CCC, no. 1872), and it severs human solidarity (CCC, no. 1872). In so doing, sin has a devastating impact on the whole moral order. When sin is not repented, its consequences can be staggering. Immediately, God, in His justice, tells Adam and Eve that their sin merits a stiff penalty, not the least part of which is death.

GOD'S PROVISION

Angela understood the story well. She could see how closely her own life paralleled what the crisis-pregnancy counselor was sharing. She knew the devastation of sin. She certainly was not at peace with God. She wasn't at peace with herself. Her interior dissatisfaction had caused distress in her relationships that ultimately culminated in her abortions, and true happiness eluded her. What she thought would bring her fulfillment had brought her misery instead, and the penalty of her sin hung heavy about her. Lack of repentance had brought her unspeakable heartache, and now she desperately wanted to make things right. She knew she couldn't change the past, nor could she bring her two babies back to life. But could she change the present? Could she change the future? Was there a way to do this?

Genesis 3:15 provided Angela with the answer she was seeking. Here, God metes out to the serpent its punishment. The serpent symbolizes the devil, Satan, the father of lies. His identity, history, and fate are revealed in Revelation 12:7-9:

> Now war arose in heaven, Michael and his angels fighting against the dragon; and the dragon and his angels fought,

but they were defeated and there was no longer any place for them in heaven. And the great dragon was thrown down, that ancient serpent, who is called the Devil and Satan, the deceiver of the whole world — he was thrown down to the earth, and his angels were thrown down with him.

Throughout time, the devil, an angel who became evil through his own doing (CCC, no. 391), has sought to frustrate the plans of God and draw men into sin and damnation. This was his intention in the Garden of Eden, and it remains his intention today.

Because the serpent, too, had played a part in the sin of Adam, it would share in the consequences. Because of its actions, God tells the serpent that it will be cursed above all the wild animals, and that it will crawl upon its belly and eat dust all the days of its life. And God tells the serpent something more as well. God proclaims that the battle between man and the serpent is not over. No, man and evil will battle again, and in the end man — though not just any man — will win the war. God says:

> "I will put enmity between you and the woman, and between your seed and her seed; he shall bruise your head, and you shall bruise his heel." — GENESIS 3:15

These are important words indeed. Through them, God is announcing that there is a way back. He is proclaiming that redemption is possible. He is telling the serpent and Adam and Eve — and us as well — that He has already made a provision for man. And this provision involves *the woman* and *her seed*. Who is this woman and who is her seed?

The Catholic Church has always taught that the woman is the Blessed Virgin Mary, and that her seed is Jesus Christ, the Son of God, the Redeemer and Savior. While Eve's disobedience to God bore the fruit of sin and death, Mary's obedience to Him will bear the fruit of salvation and life. Though God says that the serpent will mount an offensive against the Redeemer, striking at his heel, the Redeemer will crush the serpent's head, dealing him a mortal blow. Mary's seed, Jesus Christ, will be victorious. He will bring redemptive grace, and He will conquer sin and death.

What a stunning example of God's mercy and unconditional love this passage provides! In the midst of man's sin and depravity, God is already about the business of restoration and redemption. He will send His Son, born of Mary, to save mankind. Why? Why would He do such a thing even as man stubbornly stood in opposition to His divine will?

John 3:16 provides the answer: "For God so **loved** the world that he gave his only Son, that whoever believes in him should not perish but have eternal life" (emphasis added). It is because of *love* — God's *love*, which is unconditional; God's *love*, which is everlasting. In *love*, God makes a way for man to regain that which was lost. God's love, given to us through His Son, Jesus Christ, restores what the locusts have eaten (Joel 2:25). We have only to accept His Son, receive His love, repent of our ways, and enter into loving union with Him once more.

This was the truth the crisis-pregnancy counselor shared with Angela, and this was the truth that began to set her free. Angela left the crisis-pregnancy center with hope in her heart and conviction in her spirit. She would have this child whom she carried in her womb. And this child would be a daily reminder of God's love for her. Angela stopped at the first Catholic church she saw and asked that a priest hear her confession. She repented of her sins, and through the Sacrament of Reconciliation she received grace to amend her life. That day, Angela became a new creation through the love of God, who reconciled himself to us through Christ Jesus, His Son (2 Corinthians 5:17-18).

YOUR TRUTH, TOO

Angela's story is a story for all of us. Our circumstances may be different, our lives may have followed a different route, but each of us shares much in common with her. God has loved each one of us into life. And He desires that each of us experience grace in

A Tip for Spiritual
S.U.C.C.E.S.S.

Overview

*T*he world would have us measure success by our monetary status, the title of our position, the number of degrees we hold, or the name of the club to which we belong. But in the spiritual life, these things matter not. A beggar can be a king; a pauper can be a saint; an illiterate can be the wisest of men; and the most humble of servants can be the greatest of all. To be successful in the spiritual life requires one thing and one thing alone: love. It requires that we come to know the One who is Love, that we receive His love, that we conform to His love, and that, in the end, we become His love. This is the stuff of saints, this is the stuff of sanctity, this is the stuff of grace in abundance.

Throughout this book, the acronym "S.U.C.C.E.S.S." provides us with "spiritual essentials" that lead us along the path of holiness and sanctity. They show us how we can grow in God's love and how we can become a source of God's love in the world. These spiritual essentials are not for the faint-hearted! Their demands are great! They insist upon perseverance and fortitude, faithfulness and patience, humility and sacrifice. But through them, God's own love is found. And through God's love, heaven is experienced on earth. Let us find the way to spiritual S.U.C.C.E.S.S. The Blessed Virgin Mary will be our guide.

❧

abundance. But, like Angela, each of us has sinned. We all have fallen short of the glory of God.

Through His Son, Jesus Christ, God offers us a way back. He extends to us the grace of reconciliation so that we might enter into loving relationship with Him and discover the abundant life He longs to give us. All He asks is that we repent of our sin, amend our lives, and return to Him.

This does not mean that we will not be tempted to sin again. The evil one still desires to thwart God's plans for us, and the consequences of original sin have left us with a predilection to sin. But it does mean that we will have all the heavenly aid we need to wage a holy war against the wiles and tactics of the devil.

Our baptism in Christ has promised us this, as have the sacramental graces received through Penance, Eucharist, Confirmation, and any other sacrament we have received. Our job is to make use of these graces to overcome our natural inclination to sin and our own human weakness that works against our holy call. By so doing, we will achieve the purpose for which we were created: loving union with the Blessed Trinity, a union so profound that it will become a life-giving force for us and for others.

This is the truth about ourselves, and this is the truth we need to believe if we are to grow in the spiritual life. That is why it is the first strategy we employ to experience grace in abundance.

However, it is only a beginning. Once we know that we have been created for a supernatural destiny, everything in our life must become ordered to it. The natural must yield to the supernatural, the worldly to the spiritual, and the temporal to the eternal. This requires a new vision, a supernatural perspective through which we see ourselves, others, and the circumstances of our lives. It also requires that we cooperate with the grace God gives us as we seek to conform our will to His. The way we do this is through prayer, the next strategy in our quest to experience grace in abundance.

WORKING THE STRATEGY

Believe the Truth About Yourself

1. Angela lived and acted under the misconception that she was unlovable. Do you live and act under any misconceptions or misperceptions about yourself that have been part of your upbringing, the culture in which you live, or experiences you have had? What in this chapter has spoken the most to your misconception? What new truth about yourself do you now see? How can you begin to believe the truth about yourself as it has been presented to you in the previous pages?

2. Angela needed to repent of her sins and amend her life. Are there sins from which you need to repent? What prevents you from doing so? Read the following teachings from the *Catechism of the Catholic Church* — nos. 982, 1450-1458, and 1468. What new insights have you gained from these teachings?

3. The crisis-pregnancy counselor became a "conduit of God's grace." She helped Angela to see the truth about herself. Who have been "conduits" for you in your life? How did God use them? For whom can you be a "conduit of grace"?

STRATEGY TWO

Engage in Prayer

❧

When I was a child, my instruction in the Catholic faith came through the zealous tutelage of the Vincentian Sisters of Charity. Like most children of my era, our primary text was the Baltimore Catechism, a primer of Catholic teaching that posed a catechetical question, which was followed by a concise but theologically accurate answer. While some have criticized the Baltimore Catechism for its method of rote memorization, many of us can still recite both the questions and the answers — a testimony to our teachers and to the method.

One question I remember was "Why did God make me?" The answer was characteristically simple and to the point: "God made me to know Him, to love Him, and to serve Him in this life, and to spend all eternity with Him in heaven." This short but profound statement sums up the purpose and substance of the Christian life. As the *Catechism of the Catholic Church* puts it, "The whole Christian life is a communion with each of the divine persons. . . . The ultimate end of the whole divine economy is the entry of God's creatures into the perfect unity of the Blessed Trinity" (nos. 259-260). It is through this "entry" into the Trinitarian life that we experience grace in abundance. How, then, do we come to *know* God, to *love* God, and to *serve* God in this life so that we can spend all eternity with Him in heaven? As Mother Teresa of Calcutta would say, "Everything starts from prayer."

PRAYER AND THE CHRISTIAN LIFE

For the Christian — one who is serious about who he really is — prayer is not optional; it is essential. As lungs are to physical life, prayer is to spiritual life. Without it, the spiritual life languishes, suffers, and dies; and though life may remain in the body, lost is the central purpose for living at all: communion with God. That is why Pope John Paul II reminds us:

> Prayer is not one occupation among many, but is at the center of our life in Christ. It turns our attention away from ourselves and directs it to the Lord. Prayer fills the mind with truth and gives hope to the heart. Without a deep experience of prayer, growth in the moral life will be shallow.

As the Holy Father's words suggest, prayer is to be the major occupation of our life. It is not to be a sideline event, nor an activity reserved only for serious problems or Sunday mornings. Rather, prayer is meant to hold center stage. It is meant to be the "breath" of our existence. And this is for good reason: Prayer is the means by which we communicate with God and God with us. As St. Francis de Sales tells us, "The chief exercise of prayer is to speak to God and to hear God speak in the bottom of your heart." Cardinal John Henry Newman puts it this way: "As speech is the organ of human society, and the means of human civilization, so is prayer the instrument of divine fellowship and divine training."

Prayer, then, is the gateway to intimacy with our Creator and our Lord. Through it, we dialogue with God, we find fellowship with Him, and we are trained in His ways. What effect does such interaction have?

The Holy Father's words suggest that prayer has at least three effects. First, prayer *informs*. As the Pope states, prayer "fills the mind with truth and gives hope to the heart." Second, prayer *reforms*. It "turns our attention away from self and directs it to the Lord." Third, prayer *transforms*. It deepens our moral life by taking it from a shallow state based primarily upon the sensate world to an increasing experience of grace leading us to union with God. Through prayer, our mind is renewed, our soul is purified, our heart is converted, and we radiate "the perfect unity of the Blessed Trinity" (CCC, no. 260).

Indeed, prayer is effective. In prayer, we come to know God, and knowledge of Him informs us of His love. Through prayer, we come to love God, and love of Him reforms our life. With prayer, we come to serve God, and service in Him transforms our hearts. By prayer, we achieve the purpose of our existence even as we attain to eternal life. In knowing God, loving God, and serving God, we are informed, reformed, and transformed. And, ultimately, prayer becomes a conforming agent, causing us to reflect more clearly the image and likeness of God.

A MEETING WITH JESUS: JOHN 4:1-30

A story from Sacred Scripture dramatically illustrates the effects of prayer. Jesus was on His way to Galilee from Judea. Though there were two possible routes for the journey, Jesus chose the one that took Him through Samaria, a region in Palestine. This was the shorter and more frequented of the two routes, but it posed its own challenges. For one thing, the hostility between the Jews and the Samaritans was legendary. It was likely to be an unfriendly sojourn for Jesus and the disciples. However, Our Lord had more on His mind that day than a pleasant journey. Perhaps He saw the trip through Samaria as an opportunity to preach.

The band reached an outlying area of Samaria near the small city of Sychar. They neared the field that Jacob had given to his sons, not far from Jacob's well. It was near noon, and they were tired and hungry from their travel, so they decided to stop for a while. The disciples headed off into the town to buy food, and Jesus sat down beside the well to rest.

Soon, He saw a Samaritan woman approaching the well. She carried a large water jar, and she was alone. This, coupled with the time of day, indicated something about her. It was customary for women to group together to go to the well. It was safer that way and made them less vulnerable. Their usual times for drawing water were morning and early evening, not the middle of the day. It was obvious that this woman came to the well at a time when she expected to be alone. These facts added up to only one conclusion: She must be a social outcast, perhaps a woman of ill repute.

The sight of a strange man sitting by the side of the well may have provoked caution in the woman. She could see by his clothes that he was a traveler. Was he harmless? Why was he at the well without a water jar or any other vessel for drawing water? As she approached, Jesus lifted His head and she saw that He was a Jew. This provoked the woman's curiosity. What was a Jew doing in Sychar, a Samaritan city? What could be His purpose in coming there? Caution swept over her once more, but she needed the water, and this was her time to come to the well. Besides, her curiosity was getting the best of her. So, being no stranger to men, she drew nearer, finally arriving at the well, prepared to draw her day's supply.

Jesus was thirsty. "Give me a drink," He said to the woman. Now this was stunning. In the first place, Jews had nothing to do with Samaritans. The strain was over religion. Samaritans held only to the first five books of the Old Testament and discarded the rest. Moreover, they used their own version of the Pentateuch, which altered the Jewish text. By Jewish standards, this made the Samaritan religion seriously flawed and heretical. More importantly, Jews considered Samaritan women to be ritually impure. Therefore, Jews could not drink from a vessel these women had handled. For a Jew to ask for a drink from any Samaritan was unheard of. But for a Jewish rabbi to ask for a drink from a Samaritan woman — especially one of questionable background — was remarkable.

The woman expressed her astonishment: "How is it that you, a Jew, ask a drink of me, a woman of Samaria?" Jesus was quick to reply. "If you knew the gift of God, and who it is that is saying to you, 'Give me a drink,' you would have asked him and he would have given you living water."

The woman was intrigued. What did this man mean that He would have given her "living water?" He didn't have anything to use to draw the water out of the well, and the well was very deep. How could he give her any water, much less "living water?" And so, perhaps with some sarcasm, she asked Him, "Are you greater than our father Jacob, who gave us the well, and drank from it himself, and his sons, and his cattle?"

Jesus' answer intrigued her even more: "Every one who drinks of this water will thirst again, but whoever drinks of the water that

I shall give him will never thirst; the water that I shall give him will become in him a spring of water welling up to eternal life."

Jesus really had her interest now. The Samaritan woman knew one thing: She wanted this water. Carrying the water jar to the well, drawing the water, and hauling the heavy full jar home again was hard work. Besides, her lonely trips were unpleasant reminders of her sinful state and poor reputation. "Sir, give me this water, that I may not thirst, nor come here to draw," the woman exclaimed.

Jesus knew what she was thinking, and there was more He wanted her to know, so He confronted her with her situation. "Go, call your husband, and come here," Jesus told her. "I have no husband," the woman replied. Jesus said, "You are right in saying, 'I have no husband'; for you have had five husbands, and he whom you now have is not your husband; this you said truly."

The Samaritan woman was flabbergasted. Who was this man, this traveler, sitting at the well? How could he know all about her? He must be a special person, someone anointed by God! "Sir, I perceive that you are a prophet," she said to Him. "Our fathers worshiped on this mountain; and you say that in Jerusalem is the place where men ought to worship."

This was an issue that had long affected the relationship between the two peoples. The Jews claimed that worship could only take place in Jerusalem, while the Samaritans maintained that the shrine erected on Mount Gerizim was also acceptable.

Jesus used the Samaritan woman's question as an opportunity to teach her about the New Covenant that the Messiah would establish between God and man. He replied, "The hour is coming, and now is, when the true worshipers will worship the Father in spirit and truth, for such the Father seeks to worship him. God is spirit, and those who worship him must worship in spirit and truth." The woman's response showed her religious knowledge: "I know that Messiah is coming (he who is called Christ); when he comes, he will show us all things." With this, Jesus revealed to her His identity: "I who speak to you am he."

What could the woman have thought? What must have gone through her mind? Here, sitting beside her at the well, was the

Messiah, the Anointed One of God! The woman was overcome by this revelation. Leaving her water jar behind, she ran off into the town to announce to all who would listen that she had met the Christ. "Come, see a man who told me all that I ever did. Can this be the Christ?" she proclaimed. And, upon hearing her proclamation, the people came out of the town to find Jesus.

INFORMED + REFORMED + TRANSFORMED = CONFORMED

On one level, the story of the Samaritan woman at the well appears to simply relate a chance conversation between Jesus and a woman He met while traveling from one city to another. However, much more is going on than first meets the eye. No meeting with Jesus is ever by chance, and no conversation with Him is small talk.

Many Scripture scholars maintain that Jesus *planned* to meet the Samaritan woman. At John 4:4, the passage states that Jesus *had to go through Samaria*, even though there were two routes back to Galilee. Why did Jesus *have* to go through Samaria? What compelled Him to take that route?

Only one explanation suffices: He took that route intentionally to meet the Samaritan woman. Her eternal life depended on it. Wasn't He sitting at the well at the appointed time when she would come? Didn't He lead her into a deepening understanding of who He is? And wasn't this information effective in her life?

Jesus loved the Samaritan woman, and not even her sin could negate that love. He wanted her to experience the divine life, the "living water," that sets us free and draws us into union with Him. Jesus' journey that day was part of His divine mission. He went to Sychar in Samaria to save that which was lost.

Nor was the conversation between Jesus and the Samaritan woman coincidental. This conversation was life-changing, and it was laden with eternal implications. Every word that Jesus spoke to the woman carried a supernatural value. Every word led her closer to conversion. Every word drew her to know God, to love God, and to serve God. Every word moved her along the continuum of transformation.

The first words that Jesus speaks to the woman at the well are significant. "Give me a drink," He says to her. While Jesus is probably thirsty from traveling all morning, and while asking the woman for a drink also engages her in conversation, Jesus' words indicate much more. He is, after all, the Second Person of the Blessed Trinity. And, while He is thirsting for water in His humanity, in His divinity He is thirsting for something more.

These words remind us of another time when Jesus will acknowledge His thirst. Then, He will be hanging on a cross, offering His life for us. In that moment, His thirst will indicate His thirst for souls, a thirst that springs from infinite love. And here, too, sitting at the side of Jacob's well in the little town of Sychar, at the outskirts of Samaria, Jesus is thirsting for a soul, the soul of the Samaritan woman. God thirsts for all who are lost to Him through sin, and from those first words forward, the conversation between Jesus and the Samaritan woman is a conversation of conversion, a conversation that informs her, reforms her, and transforms her. It is a conversation that bids her to come into conformity with Him.

Though the woman is surprised that Jesus, a Jew, asks her for a drink, she responds. Her response, questioning though it is, indicates an opening of her heart to Him. This is true of every conversion. God appeals to us, and we respond to Him. He knocks, and we open. "Today, when you hear his voice, do not harden your hearts," says one Scripture passage (Hebrews 3:7-8); and yet another says, "Behold, I stand at the door and knock; if any one hears my voice and opens the door, I will come in to him and eat with him, and he with me" (Revelation 3:20). God will never trespass our free will. In love, He made us like himself: free. He will not take back the gift He has given. But when the gift is surrendered, He gives us infinitely more — He gives us a share in His divine life. This is what Jesus offers the Samaritan woman: "living water," the water of divine life.

The woman responds tentatively to Jesus, and this is also significant. She has not yet grown in trust. She has not yet tasted the living water, the supernatural life He is offering her. And so, she is skeptical. She questions Him. How can He draw water with no bucket? Where can He get this living water? Does He think He is greater than Jacob, who gave them the well in the first place?

The woman wants answers before she is willing to trust, and she wants proof before she is willing to believe. She has not yet discovered what happens when God's invitations are embraced rather than excused. She has not yet learned that the invitation is pregnant with true peace, abiding happiness, and real fulfillment. She has not yet learned that by embracing the invitation, she would experience what all other embraces had promised but could not fulfill.

Jesus is abundantly patient with her. He sees beyond her words into her heart. The fact that she remains in conversation with Him tells Him much. It indicates that deep inside she longs for the eternal life He holds out to her. And so, He meets her questions with greater explanation of the gift He is offering. He tells the Samaritan woman that the water He speaks of will slake her thirst forever. It is a "spring of water gushing up to eternal life" (John 4:14; NRSV).

Gradually, Jesus reveals to her the most profound of truths. He gives her light, a little at a time, so that her inner vision can adjust to the revelation. Too much, too soon would only blind her, and she would never see the great gift He offers her. Like a brilliant globe whose yellow beam proves irresistible to the flittering moth, so too does Jesus woo the Samaritan woman to himself, gently drawing her to the wellspring of divine life.

And then, the turning point comes. Jesus' words have captured the Samaritan woman. She is intrigued. She wants this water, and she asks for it: "Sir, give me this water." This is an important step: It is the woman's profession of faith. Though her motives are mixed with human concerns — she doesn't want to be thirsty anymore, nor does she want to come to the well again — she has nonetheless expressed belief in the One who sits before her. She believes that this man will do what He says. She believes that He will give her living water, the gift of eternal life. This is the step that Jesus has waited for, and He takes the woman at her word.

But there is still more for the woman to know. Now is the time for her to see the truth about herself and the truth about the One who sits beside her. Only in recognizing the chasm between ourselves and God, only in acknowledging our dependence on Him, and only in seeing our humble state in relation to His incomparable majesty can we truly enter into union with Him. And, for the woman, this moment has come. Our Lord asks her a question, and the question bids her to confront her sin. Can she bear it? "Go, call your husband, and come here," Jesus says to her.

How her guilt must burn within her. Even the water she has drawn cannot quench the sting of reproach that sears her conscience. Only the living water can do that, not the water that fills her bucket. "I have no husband," she answers, and Jesus replies, "You are right in saying, 'I have no husband'; for you have had five husbands, and he whom you now have is not your husband; this you said truly."

There is something profoundly attractive about the truth. It is the light of God it reflects, a light that leads us on into the Divine Mystery regardless of our state or condition. A light full of promise and full of hope. It illumines, and it reveals. It calls forth from us anything that is like itself so that it, too, may reflect the Divine Light and dispel our darkness.

It is a haunting light, this light of truth. It clings to us and holds us. It captivates us. It follows us and wrestles with us. It speaks to us. It provokes our conscience and tries our soul. And though we may wish to flee it because its brilliance is too much, this light compels, and we are willing to go as far as the light will take us.

This is how truth enchants the soul and bids it to the heights, even as it plumbs the depths of the Mystery whose depth is unfathomable. This is how truth draws us to the truth about ourselves and enables us to surrender that truth to the mercy of God. As St. Augustine exclaimed in his *Confessions*:

> O Lord, the depths of a man's conscience lie exposed before your eyes. Could anything remain hidden in me, even though I did not want to confess it to you? In that case I would only be hiding you from myself, not myself from you

. . . you are my light and the source of my joy. . . . I am thoroughly ashamed of myself: I have renounced myself and chosen you, recognizing that I can please neither you nor myself unless you enable me to do so.

The Samaritan woman saw the light that day. It radiated from the One who sat before her, for He himself was that Light. He himself was that Truth. And this Light spoke to her beyond the light of her understanding. This Light spoke to her heart, to her soul, to that part of her that longed to know beauty and truth, compassion and hope. It spoke to her spirit in Spirit-words that ignited the light of love in her soul and helped her reach beyond her sin to grasp the incomprehensible: the pure light of God's love, a love that could re-form her and re-shape her, a love that would transform her, a love that would make her new.

The woman knows that this is no ordinary man beside whom she sits, and initially she finds the purity of the Light too much. She squirms in its effulgence and tries to divert the conversation to a religious controversy, but the Light holds her fast, fascinating her with its beauty. And she remains engaged, basking in its purity and translucence. Like a flower that opens its petals to receive the penetrating warmth of the sun, so has she opened her soul, and the Son has pierced her darkness. The Spirit of Truth has entered her soul, so she can worship in spirit and truth, a true daughter of the New Covenant.

Did the Samaritan woman's mind comprehend what her spirit understood? Or would it take more?

She speaks words intuited by the Spirit of Truth, prophetic words that identify the One with whom she speaks and the purpose of His mission, a mission already being accomplished in her: "I know that Messiah is coming (he who is called Christ); when he comes, he will show us all things." Jesus sees the Spirit at work in her, and so He tells her who He is: "I who speak to you am he."

Now her mind understands what her spirit already knew. The One who sits with her at the well is the Messiah, the long-awaited

Savior, and He has already begun to show her "all things." The living water rises up within her, and the Samaritan woman realizes she has been set free. Grace floods her heart, and zeal surges within her soul. She must share this good news with others!

The Samaritan woman runs into town unencumbered. She has left her water jar behind. She has no need for it now — a spring of eternal life is gushing up within her. And no longer has she the sin and shame her water jar represented — this new spring has brought with it new life. Freed from the weight of sin, freed from the burden of guilt, the Samaritan woman proclaims to everyone who will listen, "Come, see a man who told me all that I ever did. Can this be the Christ?" Now she is no longer a woman of wanton ways. Now she is an evangelist, a proclaimer of the Truth. And like the One who is the Truth, like the One who is the Light, she now is a light, leading others to the well of Divine Life.

A METAPHOR FOR PRAYER

Our Lord's encounter with the Samaritan woman at the well provides us with a metaphor for prayer. It reminds us that, in its essence, prayer is, as St. Teresa of Ávila wrote, "friendly intercourse and frequent solitary conversation with Him who loves us." It reminds us that this dialogue is like no other: This dialogue is life-changing, heart-expanding, and soul-saving. This dialogue informs us, reforms us, and transforms us. This dialogue heals and soothes, convicts and forgives, unbinds and sets free. This dialogue brings light to our understanding and illumination to our soul. It can do all this and more, because this dialogue is conversation with God.

Each day Jesus sits at the well of our heart, waiting for us to come and converse with Him. He has journeyed there, outside of time and space, and is as surely present to us in that moment as He was to the woman at the well in Sychar two thousand years ago. He has come to bid us to drink from the eternal springs of everlasting life. He is there to save us, and to redeem each part of ourselves that has been lost through sin. He wants to attract us to the truth of who He is and to reveal to us the truth of who we are so that we might experience the new life He has in mind for us. He desires to engage us, to captivate us with His love, and to open the petals of our heart with tenderness and care. He wants to pierce our darkness with the light of His love. He desires to transform us.

This is what true prayer is all about. Prayer releases streams of grace into the dried and parched tributaries of our lives, imbuing all we do, indeed all we are, with the life of God himself. Prayer takes the mundane — like drawing water from a well — and makes it spectacular. It takes the traumatic — like seeing the reality of our condition — and makes it life-changing. It takes our pain and our sorrow — like broken relationships and unhappy decisions — and gives them eternal value. It takes our suffering — like rejection, betrayal, and misunderstanding — and fills it with joy. In the end, prayer takes us — weak as we are — and makes us instruments of light and truth by transforming us more nearly into the object of our desire: Christ himself.

THE DIVINE APPOINTMENT

The Samaritan woman's encounter with Jesus is a microcosm of the life of prayer. Note that she did not immediately exercise trust, nor did she originally understand the significance of Jesus' words. She did not become convicted of her sin at the outset, nor did she initially recognize with whom she was speaking. She did not open her heart to receive Jesus at the start of their conversation, nor did she experience the living water early in their dialogue. She did not taste the grace of transformation in the beginning, nor did she see herself as an instrument of the Lord. All of this happened as a process, as she spent time with Jesus, as she listened to His words, and as she accepted what He was saying. One could even go so far as to say that the woman only came to a full understanding of what Jesus offered her as she became *accustomed* to His voice, and *trained* in His ways.

So it is with us. Like the Samaritan woman, we must sit with Jesus. We must listen to His words. We must ponder what He tells us. We must accept what He says. We must grow accustomed to the sound of His voice. We must grow trained in the ways He interacts with us. As we do, our soul begins to receive, our mind begins to grasp, our heart opens wide, and we begin to experience grace in abundance. This is what prayer is all about; this is its process; and this is its transforming effect.

Throughout the ages, great men and women of prayer have shared their experiences of prayer with us. What they have written is helpful. It educates us, encourages us, and enlightens us. They tell us much about prayer, and all of them agree on this point: Prayer requires time. As was the case with the Samaritan woman, it is through regular and consistent interaction with Jesus that we come to understand Him, to recognize His voice and His ways. Prayer is a discipline that requires training through regularity and consistency. Ultimately, we must make time for prayer if we are going to reap its benefits and if its discipline is to have a defining effect on our life.

That is why the only way to pray well is to pray often. As one spiritual writer, Dom Chapman, says:

> The only way to pray is to pray; and the only way to pray well is to pray much. If one has no time for this, then one must at least pray regularly. But the less one prays, the worse it goes.

St. Teresa of Ávila says as much when she tells us that prayer is to be "*frequent* conversation with the One who loves us" (emphasis added). Regularity and consistency are important if the soul is to grow and develop. Therefore, we must schedule our day for a divine appointment — a time specifically set aside to converse with Our Lord and Savior. What are some of the features that should define this time of prayer?

Solitude

St. Teresa of Ávila tells us that not only is prayer to be "frequent" conversation, but she also tells us this conversation is to be a "solitary" endeavor. The type of prayer that Teresa outlines here is personal, private prayer. While there is a place in our prayer life for corporate prayer — prayer offered to God in a group setting such as a prayer meeting, the corporate recitation of the Rosary, or the Liturgy of the Hours — our prayer life must include time for private conversation with Our Lord.

Again, Jesus' interaction with the Samaritan woman gives us a good example. They are alone at the well, with no one else around. Jesus has the woman's full attention. There is little to distract her from the words He speaks. There seems to be no rush, no hurry. Solitude and silence pervade the atmosphere. Though the woman's understanding is dim, through the time they spend together, the light of truth penetrates her mind and pierces her heart, and she experiences the living water Jesus has come to bring her.

We, too, must come to our divine appointment with these same characteristics, and the setting we select for our time of prayer must lend itself to these attributes. First, we must choose a place that permits us to be alone with Jesus. It could be a room in our home, a back porch or peaceful place in the yard, a bench in the park, or a pew in our parish church. But it must be a place where we are unlikely to be disturbed.

This also applies to the time we choose for our appointment. It must be a time that is conducive to quiet, solitary prayer. It should not be at a time when family members need us, or when the duties of the day are pressing upon us. Prayer shouldn't be "squeezed" into our schedule; rather, our schedule should flow from our prayer. Ideally, the time we select should be an hour when we can devote time in a non-hurried, non-harried way. When given its space and time, our prayer becomes a conduit of grace that imbues all of our activities with the life of God.

Posture

God has created man, body and soul. We are an integrated union comprised of a physical reality and a spiritual reality. These two aspects of the human person must be suitably engaged to achieve a desired result. For example, we may desperately want to play tennis, but our goal will not be attained if we only desire it. We must get off the couch, go to the court, and engage in the game.

Moreover, the way in which we use our body on the court also helps us to accomplish that which we deeply desire — a good game of tennis. To stand on the court immobile for two hours, with our head hung low, racket dangling from our hand, will never do. We must extend the racket, connect with the ball, and send it whipping over the net (hopefully inbounds and neatly tucked in the far corner of our opponent's quadrant). And to keep the play in motion, we must adjust our position when necessary, now moving nearer the net, now running back, now to the left, now to the right, in our pursuit of the point. Obviously, the positions and postures we assume greatly help or hinder our ability to achieve our goal.

So it is with prayer. The posture we assume must be chosen with one criterion in mind: It should aid us in our time of prayer rather than hinder us. Kneeling, sitting, standing, walking — all are acceptable to the extent that they move us toward our goal to pray. We may even find it necessary to change our position or posture during prayer in order to remain focused and attentive. This is completely acceptable and a matter of common sense. Ultimately, our position for prayer should lead us to concentration rather than distraction. It should not overtire the body so that it grows fatigued, nor should it make the body so comfortable that the soul loses its ability to attend.

If a person suffers from back problems, for example, kneeling may so aggravate his physical condition that he may not be able to enter into prayer at all. On the other hand, one who is prone to laziness may benefit more by being on his knees at a prie-dieu rather than on his rump in a comfortable chair. The first posture may keep him alert, while the second may lull him to sleep.

Spiritual writer Father Franz M. Moschner, in his book *Christian Prayer*, puts it this way:

> The essential thing is always that our heart should not be diverted; that it should abide in God as quietly and recollectedly as possible. Any strain or stress, any will-power in the sense of a physical exertion is not good here; it obstructs the way, strains the nerves, makes us tired . . . and, finally, weary of everything, all because of a wrong method which could never reach the right end.

Pious Actions

Also useful in helping us to attain our goal of prayer is the piety we exhibit during it. Holy actions can remind us of our purpose and the One to whom we direct our prayers. Making the Sign of the Cross with the deliberate intention to pray the words as we sign ourselves, folding our hands or lifting them to the heavens, extending our arms crosswise over our chest, or keeping our hands opened face-up in our lap — all help us to focus on the reality of what we are about: conversing with Our Lord. One word of caution, however: Pious actions should never be substituted for a recollected heart and mind, nor should they become rote behaviors devoid of meaning and intention. Rather, like our posture and position, pious actions must move us toward our goal to pray, if they are to be useful at all.

Initially, we may use pious actions to help us become recollected, to aid us in our concentration, or to signal a shift from the business of the day to the business of the soul. However, as our prayer life grows and matures, spontaneous actions that flow from the soul's union with God often replace these conscious ones. Quite without thought, the head bows, the arms extend, and the lips "speak" a response to God's initiative. Even the pattern of our breathing may change.

This is as it should be. As we pray, our focus is no longer on our actions or on ourselves; instead, our focus is riveted on God, and our gaze is fixed totally upon Him. In a sense, as the Holy Spirit guides the soul in its quest for God, the body responds to the inspirations stirring within the soul, mirroring what is taking place interiorly.

The quiet solitude of our setting, the postures and positions we adopt in our prayer time, and the pious actions in which we engage help us to become recollected — to leave behind, for the time of our prayer, the hustle and bustle of the day with its demands and pressures, its duties and obligations, its worries and concerns — and to prepare ourselves to enter into conversation with God. It is a conversation that is certain to help us meet our daily activities with renewed strength and greater spiritual insight, and a conversation that is certain to lead us along the continuum of transformation.

AT THE WELL OF PRAYER

The Samaritan woman's time at the well with Jesus was a life-changing event. Through their conversation, she gained new understanding, let go of her sinful ways, experienced the living waters of eternal life, and became a conduit of grace in the lives of others. She was informed, reformed, transformed, and conformed to the will of God. That very day she became a new woman in Christ Jesus, a daughter of the New Covenant.

Our time of prayer is our well, our place to meet with Jesus. And because we meet Jesus during our prayer time, it, too, is to have the same effect upon us. It is meant to be an intimate time with our Lord and Savior, a time that illumines our heart and mind with truth, a time that convicts us of our sins and failings, a time that brings us grace and new life, a time that causes us to reflect the image of God. Through our time of prayer, we, too, are to taste the living water that gushes forth from the spring of everlasting life, and we, too, are to be made new. How, then, do we enter into conversation with Jesus?

This is a good question and must be answered if we are to make progress in a life of prayer. While great men and women of the spiritual life have already blazed the trail of prayer for us, leaving us clear guidance and instruction on how to progress along its holy path, each individual person's experience in prayer will be unique and singular. God, our Creator, knows each one of us intimately, and as a result, He knows the best way to communicate with us and how best to lead each of us into relationship with Him.

However, there are certain markers that indicate we are going in the right direction. In most cases, these signposts become clearer and more evident as we make progress on our journey and as we gain wisdom and understanding along the way. It is most helpful if we have an "older" brother or sister of prayer, one whose experience of the spiritual life is deeper than ours, who can assist us and

A Tip for Spiritual
S.U.C.C.E.S.S.

Surrender

The word "surrender" holds a negative connotation. No one wants to lose — but more importantly, no one wants to give up. While "losing" and "giving up" may be secular understandings of "surrender," it holds quite a different meaning in the spiritual life. In our relationship with God, "surrender" means success. It means opening ourselves to receive the fullness of God. And it means offering back to Him the gift of ourselves. Far from being a passive, defeated resignation of spirit, surrender to God is an active, life-giving movement of soul. And it is only through surrender that we come to experience grace in abundance. How, then, do we surrender?

The Blessed Virgin Mary shows us the way. So surrendered was she to the will of God that God himself was conceived within her womb by the power of the Holy Spirit. Three characteristics mark Our Lady's gift of surrender: receptivity, trust, and docility. Mary is "receptive" to the will of God. Rather than disbelieve the word that Gabriel comes to bring her, she accepts it as the truth, and is willing to embrace the reality. From this attitude of heart, she is ready to "trust." Though Mary doesn't understand how she can become the mother of the Messiah, she trusts that God will make it so. Through receptivity and trust, Mary is "docile." She gives her "yes" to God, surrenders completely to Him, and is overshadowed by the

continued on next page . . .

. . . continued from page 47

Holy Spirit. And through her surrender and overshadowing, Salvation himself comes into the world.

In the spiritual life:

Receptivity + Trust + Docility = Surrender

help us, advise us and counsel us, as our own life of prayer grows and develops. A spiritual director or companion who is committed to the teachings of the Catholic Church can make a significant contribution to our spiritual life.

The writings of the saints and the teachings of the Church are also helpful in this regard. The *Catechism of the Catholic Church,* for example, has a wonderful section on prayer that gives good, practical advice and insight. In addition, many current books on prayer are also available.

However, a word of caution is necessary here. The marketplace is flooded today with many works that offer a false spirituality, one that is not rooted in Jesus Christ. Real discernment is needed when selecting from contemporary books that are located in the "Religion" section of the bookstore or library. Because of the climate of the times, it is prudent to select publishers that are known for orthodoxy and faithfulness to the Magisterium.

The life of prayer, generally, follows a distinct path that is comprised of three distinguishable types of prayer, though there are subcategories under each: vocal prayer, meditation/mental prayer, and contemplation. Through the centuries, hundreds, indeed thousands, of books have been written on each of these ways of praying and the abundant benefits they provide to the soul. It is not within the purview of this chapter, nor of this book, to offer an in-depth perspective of vocal prayer, meditation/mental prayer, and contemplation. However, a brief discussion might prove beneficial.

In my book, *Full of Grace: Women and the Abundant Life*, I make this statement about the life of prayer:

> There are three main categories of prayer — vocal prayer, meditation, and contemplation. All three are important to every stage of the spiritual life. But, as we progress in the way of prayer, we will experience them at differing levels. Just as a hiker ascends a mountain and sees the landscape he has left behind from a new vantage point, perhaps noticing nuances that eluded him below, or appreciating the scene more fully having achieved a broader perspective, so too will one who is faithful to prayer appreciate an ever-expanding experience of the categories of prayer. Good meditation will produce more fervent vocal prayer; the fruit of contemplation will lead to a richer time of meditation; and fervent vocal prayer and rich meditation make good preparation for a more intimate and deeper contemplation.

This paragraph points out some key insights concerning the three types of prayer:

- One category of prayer is not more necessary than another. Each has its place in a life of prayer.
- No category of prayer is ever outgrown. All three are part of every stage of spiritual development.
- As a soul grows and matures, each of these categories of prayer deepens and develops.
- Each category of prayer lends support to the other categories of prayer. Each type enriches, enables, and encourages the other two.

This understanding of how the types of prayer interact with one another at every stage of spiritual development is important, for each type helps lead the soul to spiritual maturity.

Vocal Prayer

Vocal prayer is prayer that uses words. Whether these words are spoken aloud or in the inner recesses of the heart, this type of prayer uses words to express our sentiments to God. Vocal prayer is an "incarnational" form of prayer in that it uses the body to express the interiority of the soul. For this reason, the words we speak — whether silently or vocally — must be words that engage the heart: "This people draw near me with their mouth, and with their lips glorify me, but their heart is far from me," says the Lord to the prophet Isaiah (29:13; Douay-Rheims Version). If the heart is not engaged, our words are merely "noisy gongs" and "clanging cymbals" (1 Corinthians 13:1). If our words are to be prayer, they must originate in the soul, even if their ultimate expression is spoken with the voice. Father Moschner, in *Christian Prayer*, beautifully describes it this way:

> The word of the soul, empowered by the love of the Holy Ghost, wings its way into the Word, and in that most holy Word ours, too, stands before the Father, is with Him, and partakes of His divine life.

Our vocal prayer can use words that spontaneously arise from the depths of our being, in our own words, or it can use the words of others that have been formulated into prayer for us. The Our Father, Hail Mary, and Glory Be are all examples of formulated prayers. So are the psalms, the various litanies and novenas, and the prayers of saints that form a part of the Catholic prayer tradition.

The challenge with formulated prayers is to make them our own. Certainly, they are filled with the fervor and the ardent love for God of the person who first spoke them, but can that prayer express our own fervor and love for God? In other words, can a formulated prayer, especially one that we have prayed many times and know so well, honestly express the sentiments of our own heart and soul? The answer is "yes," but we must somehow work to make that happen. We must engage the mind and the heart if this is to take place, and we must exercise discipline in the way we say the prayers themselves.

One way to make formulated vocal prayer our own is to pray the prayer slowly and thoughtfully. Perhaps the biggest danger with formula prayers is that we know them so well. For many, these are the very prayers we were taught as children. Depending on our age, we may well have spoken each of them thousands upon thousands of times since we first learned them. Our familiarity with them becomes a trap and a real impediment to *praying* the prayers instead of merely *saying* the prayers. The words slip from our tongue in speedy fashion, making us sound much more like auctioneers than people engaged in conversation with God. Occasionally, someone will even brag that he can finish the Rosary in ten minutes. Finish it, yes; pray it, no. To overcome this tendency, we must S-L-O-W D-O-W-N. We must say the words, aloud or in our heart, clearly, distinctly, and prayerfully.

But we must also say the words with thoughtful intention if our use of formula prayers is to be advantageous to our spiritual life. In addition to slowing down our recitation of the prayer, it is helpful to pause after each phrase and consider what we are saying: How do these particular words resonate within my soul? What does this phrase mean to me? Do these words or does this phrase express my love of God? Is God saying something to me in this phrase or through these words? By using this method of praying formula prayers, many great saints were lifted to the heights of contemplation, some spending hours and even days on a single recitation of the Our Father. Their example gives us much to consider as we pray these prayers we know so well.

As our prayer life continues to deepen, we will notice that, almost unconsciously, our pace will slow, and we will linger longer over the words and phrases of the formula prayers we pray. We will have learned that these prayers contain hidden treasures not readily seen that can only be discovered by the thought and care we put into praying them.

Spontaneous vocal prayer, or free vocal prayer, often marks a deepening of the spiritual life. So in love with God is the soul now that it seeks its own words and phrases to declare its devotion. So touched is the soul by some movement of the Holy Spirit within it that it cries out in response to the consolation. So comfortable has the soul become in God's presence that it pours out its cares and concerns in full confidence that He hears and will make haste to help. The soul, growing more sensitive to the Spirit of God within it, desires to spend more time conversing with God, and spontaneous vocal prayer moves the soul toward that goal. St. John Vianney expresses this beautifully when he states:

> The more we pray, the more we wish to pray. Like a fish which at first swims on the surface of the water, and afterwards plunges down, and is always going deeper; the soul plunges, dives, and loses itself in the sweetness of conversing with God.

Meditation

Already we have spoken of meditation in our discussion on formulated vocal prayer when we talked about the need to pause and consider the phrases and words of the prayer. This is a good example of the way in which all three categories of prayer intertwine, one with the other, forming a strong cord, which binds together the whole of our life of prayer.

Meditation is the first rung on the ladder of mental prayer. Mental prayer refers to all of those subcategories of prayer leading to contemplation. Predominant in this form of prayer are pious affections or acts of the will. Meditation leads us in the direction of mental prayer — and when used effectively, meditation itself becomes a category of mental prayer.

Meditation, to be truly Christian, has Sacred Scripture as its source and engages the faculties of the mind to facilitate conversation with God. In its essence, meditation is a reflection on some truth of the faith, some aspect of our life in God, or some particular teaching or scene from Sacred Scripture. This reflection encourages the soul to consider the need for virtuous living, to evaluate its own situation in light of this need, to beseech God's help and assistance, and to resolve to make the necessary adjustments to live a Christian life.

Consideration, self-examination, petition, and resolution are the four elements of Christian meditation. The *Catechism of the Catholic Church* sums it up neatly by stating that meditation is a spiritual quest in which the mind desires to understand the Christian life so as to conform and respond to what the Lord is asking (no. 2705).

Writing in his spiritual classic, *The Spiritual Life*, Father Adolphe Tanquerey, says that meditation is "the most effective means of assuring one's salvation." St. Teresa of Ávila would have agreed. She says, "Meditation is the basis for acquiring all the virtues, and to undertake it is a matter of life and death for all Christians." Among meditation's many benefits, Father Tanquerey lists these: detachment from sin and its causes (the world, false pleasures, pride, and sensuality), strengthening of one's will, helping one to practice the Christian virtues, and initiating one's union with God.

Four faculties of the human person are involved in Christian meditation: his capacity to think, his imagination, his emotion, and his desire (CCC, no. 2708). Throughout the centuries, the saints have given us many methods of meditation that involve these attributes of the human person, but the one that is most ancient in form and also most basic to all other forms of meditation is *lectio divina* ("holy reading"). The following six steps help us to enter into *lectio divina* and to formulate a worthwhile time of meditation:

1. **Prepare to meet with God.** Come to your time of prayer with expectant faith, knowing that this prayerful meditation on the Word of God will yield fruit in your life even if it is not immediately apparent. Before beginning, rid yourself as much as possible of distractions.
2. **Select a Scripture passage.** There is no right or wrong way to select a passage. Use the readings of the day, the Office of Readings, a Scripture study guide, or just open the Bible and begin where your eyes fall. The passage need

not be lengthy, for the goal is not to make progress reading the Bible, but to make progress in your relationship with God.

3. **Ask the Holy Spirit to guide you.** Ask the Holy Spirit to remove any interior obstacles or blocks that might prevent you from hearing the Word of God.

4. **Read the passage of Scripture slowly.** Make yourself present to the Word through an act of faith. Consider the context of the passage, what is being said in the passage, and what the specific application might be for you in your life.

5. **Listen in the "bottom of your heart" for God's voice.** What is God saying to you through this passage? Is He teaching you a lesson, explaining a great truth, or shedding light on a circumstance in your life? Listen, listen, listen.

6. **Voice a response back to God.** St. Teresa of Ávila says, "All that should be sought for in the exercise of prayer is conformity of our will with the divine will, in which consists the highest perfection." With that in mind, and with the new insight gained in this time of prayer, what resolutions, decisions, or changes do you wish to make in your relationship with God, within yourself, or with others?

Spending time with Sacred Scripture — meditating upon its precepts and considering the importance of its life-giving words within the context of our own hearts and souls — prepares our hearts for contemplative prayer, which will lead us ever more deeply into the Trinitarian life.

Contemplation

As we progress in meditation, we will notice that sentiments of the heart begin to rise within us during our times of reflection. Seeing the goodness of God, recognizing His love for us through the insights He gives, and experiencing His mercy and forgiveness all lead our heart to respond with praise, contrition, and gratitude. When our time of meditation grows increasingly affective (motivated by intimations of the heart), our prayer is moving our soul toward contemplation. "Prayer is called meditation until it has produced the honey of devotion; after that it changes into contemplation," says St. Frances de Sales.

Father Moschner beautifully writes about the difference between contemplation and meditation in his classic work, *Christian Prayer*:

> [In meditation] the soul itself is active; God lovingly renders assistance because He Himself wants this activity. In meditation the soul works like a skilled craftsman, experienced, well-versed and adroit, whose hands fashion many beautiful things in conformity with the requests or designs of his customers, to everyone's delight, not least his own.
>
> But when we turn to contemplative prayer, the accent noticeably shifts to receiving, to keeping still. One is tempted to say that meditation is masculine in its essential characteristics, but contemplation is feminine. Life proceeding from God is received and here most inwardly absorbed. The soul is not merely guided by God, and held by His hand, but now follows Him step by step. It no longer pursues ways or notions of its own, but keeps most carefully in His wake, anxious almost not to make any movements at all unless they be in accord with His.

While the purpose of vocal prayer and meditation/mental prayer is to move us along the continuum of prayer toward union with God, contemplation is the realization of the goal: Contemplative prayer *is* union with God.

At first, contemplation quietly peeks through our moments of meditation and vocal prayer, hinting that there is something more to experience, some greater depth in which to plunge. So subtle is its initial entrance that the intellect may not even sense its presence.

Not so the soul, however. Having been tantalized by contemplation's brief appearance, the soul is no longer at peace with its previous modes of prayer. It is restless, desirous for more.

Vocal prayer sounds hollow, meditation is futile, and affective prayer becomes cumbersome. Like a butterfly bursting forth from a cocoon that has grown far too snug and confining, the soul needs to spread its wings and fly to the heights.

Slowly, in response to the grace operating within it, the soul yields. Prayer becomes more simplified, reflections less involved, the intellect quieter and more docile. Only a loving gaze directed toward God will do. Only a heart opened wide to receive Him will suffice. Only a soul surrendered to His Holy Spirit is worthwhile. As a bird rides the current of the wind, lifted and directed by its breezes and gusts, so too does the soul in contemplation ride the breath of the Holy Spirit. No longer active on its own, the soul has surrendered, willing to be carried along by the current of grace, which moves it. This is infused contemplation, and it is pure gift.

There is much more to be said about contemplative prayer and the movements of grace that lead to it. Books have been written about the prayer of simplicity, acquired contemplation, infused contemplation, and the manifestations of each. This same statement can be made about each of the presentations on the categories of prayers contained within this chapter. What is offered here is merely a glance at the vast richness the life of prayer contains. Perhaps, however, it will spark a desire to begin to pray. Leave the rest to God. He will carry you along if you are sincere.

HELPS FOR A FRUITFUL PRAYER TIME

An old maxim says that anything worthwhile is worth the effort. This presupposes that most things that are worthwhile require effort. We have already seen that effort is part of prayer. While God gives us the grace to pray, we must cooperate with it, and this cooperation is not always easy. Therefore, any discussion of prayer is incomplete if it does not speak to the difficulties that arise in the midst of our time of prayer. Though there is little we can do to prevent these prayer-time difficulties altogether, there is much we can do on a daily basis to minimize their effects on our time of prayer. Two strategies we can employ are, first, taking custody of the senses and, second, leading a recollected life.

Custody of the Senses

Custody of the senses refers to an ascetical practice that is a classic part of the spiritual life. Unfortunately, this spiritual habit is rarely talked about today. Essentially, it means we guard our five senses from taking in anything that could lead us to sin. Taking custody of the eyes, for example, would mean that we avoid movies, television programs, photographs, literature, or anything that would tempt us to sins of lust and impurity. Custody of the eyes also helps us make progress against sins of jealousy, consumerism, and vanity. It encourages us to use our eyes to take in that which brings glory and honor to God and lifts our mind and heart to Him. Spiritual reading, sacred art, and the beauty of nature all direct our gaze heavenward and do much to aid us in our time of prayer.

Custody of the ears prevents us from listening to coarse jokes, questionable music, gossip, and idle conversation. It encourages us to exercise temperance and prudence in what we hear, for what we hear often becomes fuel for the imagination and leads us in directions we ought not to go. In addition, what we hear frequently becomes a main source of distraction during our time of prayer. It creates a cacophony of noise that fills the mind and heart with questions, doubts, emotions, and memories that prevent the soul from hearing the gentle whisper of God's voice.

Custody of the tongue demands that we use our gift of speech to build up the body of Christ rather than to tear it down. Unkind words, obscene language, calumny, detraction, and slander are all sins that use the tongue to cause strife, rancor, suspicion, and division. St. James warns us that the tongue is a "restless evil, full of deadly poison" (James 3:8). How carefully we must guard it so that it does not become a source of sin for us! Rather than infecting the world with poisonous venom, we should use our gift of speech to bring praise and glory to God, and truth and hope to His people.

We also need to take custody of our sense of smell and our sense of taste. How often these two senses cooperate in leading us to the sin of gluttony and the sin of intemperance. We eat more than we should, and we drink more than we should. For the alcoholic, guarding his sense of smell against the scent of beer, wine, or liquor can be a healthy step in maintaining sobriety. And the same applies for the compulsive eater or overeater — avoiding locations where food is cooking or desserts are baking can be the biggest help in conquering the temptation to eat to excess.

In addition, psychologists tell us there is a powerful link between the sense of smell and sexuality, and between the sense of smell and memories. Taking custody of our sense of smell can help us remain chaste, as well as encourage us to leave the past in the past. Sometimes the best defense is a good offense.

All in all, taking custody of the senses protects us from sin and the temptation to sin, and helps us keep close watch over those areas of weakness where we are most prone. Given our contemporary culture, this is a big job and requires no small measure of virtue and diligence. One might even say it requires heroic virtue, the stuff of saints. But this is precisely what we are called to.

A Recollected Life

One spiritual writer reminds us that the way we live is the way we pray, and that the way we pray is the way we live. If our time of prayer is to be recollected in the Lord, then our style of living must also be recollected in the Lord. A temperate, simplified approach to activities, duties, and responsibilities; a careful monitoring of our material wants and desires; and a surrendered approach to our aspirations, goals, and ambitions all help to remind us that God is the Lord of our life. Cultivating a contemplative outlook is one strategy that helps us keep this in mind.

The spiritual habit of contemplative outlook has us cast a backward glance over the events of the day, seeking to see the hand of God in the midst of all that has transpired and to fit those events into the greater context of our life in Him. It requires that we ask the Holy Spirit to show us what God may be saying to us through the situations we confront, the trials we face, the joys we experience, and the challenges we meet. A contemplative outlook reminds us that God is intimately involved in the ebb and flow of our daily lives, and therefore it helps to encourage a life recollected in Him. As St. Francis de Sales says, "Our Lord pays continuous attention to the steps taken by his children." A contemplative outlook helps to remind us of just that.

Living a recollected life has a profound effect upon our life of prayer. Because we have reminded ourselves of God's presence throughout our day, we have been "with Him" in the inner recesses of our heart through the minutes and hours. Perhaps we have turned to Him and asked for His help as we worked on a project. Perhaps we have asked for His mercy following a weak moment. Perhaps we have sought His consolation when we experienced a disappointment. Perhaps we have invited His guidance as we made a decision.

By day's end, we will discover that we have turned our heart and mind to God many times, recollecting ourselves in Him and experiencing His presence in us. This interior recollection through the course of our day prepares the way for our time of prayer by doing much of the "work" already. We will focus on God more quickly, hear the intimations of the Holy Spirit more clearly, and enter more deeply into our conversation with God.

THE THREE DIFFICULTIES OF PRAYER: DISTRACTIONS, DISCOURAGEMENT, DRYNESS

Taking custody of the senses and living a recollected life are immeasurable helps to our prayer life. They smooth the way for a personal and intimate time with God. However, all who seriously commit to prayer will ultimately face periods of trial and testing as they pray. While there are many struggles that present themselves in our time of prayer, the ones most typically confronted are distractions, discouragement, and dryness (or aridity). Let's take a look at each in turn and discover the nature of these problems, some of the strategies we can employ to overcome them, and how God uses them to lead us along the continuum of transformation.

Distractions

Perhaps the most common and most persistent of difficulties in prayer are distractions. Distractions fall into two main categories: voluntary and involuntary. Only voluntary distractions nullify and weaken our prayer. Distraction during prayer arises for a number of reasons: the human condition, not enough preparation, and the tactics of the evil one.

Our human condition looms as one of the biggest distractions in prayer. We mentioned previously that prayer engages four faculties of the human person: the ability to think, the imagination, the emotions, and desire. All of these play an important part in leading us into conversation with God. However, these same faculties can also play havoc with our time of prayer, especially when we are beginners.

It is not uncommon to have the mind bombarded by any number of thoughts as soon as we sit down to pray. The day's agenda and chores suddenly come to mind. A forgotten appointment or an errand that we need to run persistently returns to our thoughts. An old memory from the past flits in and decides to stay. The grocery list, guest list, telephone list, or "to-do" list presses itself upon us. A dog barks, a baby cries, a horn honks, a plane flies by, and our mind travels thousands of miles away. We grow frustrated, weary, discouraged, and angry. A half-hour goes by and we think we are no better off than when we began. We feel defeated and depressed, and we give up. What can we do?

Some common-sense tips and aids can handle many of these kinds of distractions. Keeping a pad and pencil handy to jot down anything we fear we might forget can free us up to concentrate more effectively. Taking the telephone off the receiver or letting our voice-mail answer calls can eliminate unwanted intrusions. Scheduling our prayer at a more convenient time may take care of annoying interruptions. Selecting a quiet place can give us needed solitude. Turning off the television set, stereo, or radio can do away with distracting noise. Controlling our emotions can help us maintain a peaceful equilibrium. Within a few minutes, we will often find ourselves in deep conversation with God.

However, there are times when distractions are not so easily dismissed. In all cases, we must not engage them. Instead, we must repel them promptly as soon as we are aware of them. This should be done in an unaffected and unemotional way. The more upset we become — the more agitated we are — the more difficult it will be to regain our composure. Simply picking up the thread of our meditation where it was first dropped, praying the next Hail Mary or Our Father with more recollection, or calmly returning our gaze to God is generally enough to put our prayer time back on track.

Should we find that distractions persist throughout the whole of our prayer time, we need not be dismayed. This falls into the category of trial rather than fault, and it is a meritorious act to stay through our whole time of prayer even when it seems to be yielding no fruit. The reality is, God often permits these distractions as a means of strengthening our will and building our spiritual muscle. Sometimes prayer such as this becomes a real stepping-stone to a deeper, more committed spiritual life.

Another reason why distractions may persist in our time of prayer is lack of recollection or lack of preparation on our part. We have already discussed the value of leading a recollected life and taking custody of the senses, but we must also enter into our prayer time prepared to meet with Jesus. Therefore, our demeanor should be unhurried. This is our time to spend with Jesus. Our mind and heart should be filled with the Word of God. This provides our soul with fertile soil in which to sow seeds of love. Our intention should be serious. We are meeting with the Lord of lords and King of kings. Our heart should be open and receptive. The Holy Spirit longs to enter and lead us into union with God.

Finally, distractions are sometimes the temptations and tactics of the evil one. Anytime we are serious about our relationship with God, we can be certain that Satan will try to dissuade us in every way possible. He will taunt us, tempt us, and try us in an effort to make us give up and give in. Scripture tells us "Resist the devil and he will flee from you" (James 4:7). Remaining faithful to our time of prayer, regardless of distractions, will eventually yield great spiritual benefit.

Discouragement

Discouragement is another difficulty that can disturb our time of prayer. Like distractions, discouragement can also come from a variety of sources, including distractions themselves. Hopefully, the discussion and suggestions just mentioned will help eliminate any discouragement that comes from this source.

Discouragement can also come from sensing that our prayer life is moving more slowly than it should be. We must always remember that our prayer is a response to God's initiative in our life. Therefore, we are not in charge; He is. Whether we ever make the progress we think we should make is entirely beside the point. Our only desire should be receptivity to the will of God and the grace to cooperate with that will once He makes it known. Such an attitude of heart requires real humility, and such humility is an indication that we have already made great progress. It is encouraging to know that the great mystics considered themselves to be at the beginning stages of prayer. God protects His saints from pride and vainglory by concealing from them the depths they have attained.

One way to safeguard against this type of discouragement is to resist an unhealthy curiosity regarding our spiritual progress. Reading books about the spiritual life and trying to "buttonhole" ourselves into the descriptions, comparing spiritual experiences or aspects of our prayer life to that of others, and feigning spiritual consolations for the sake of feeling better are all to be avoided, lest we fall into the sin of pride. Instead, we should come to God as a little child, placing our confidence entirely in Him, knowing that He guides our prayer time precisely in the way best suited to bring us in union with Him. A spiritual director or companion can be especially helpful if discouragement in our time of prayer persists.

Dryness (Aridity)

One great suffering of our prayer life is also one great signpost that indicates a growing maturity in our spiritual walk. Dryness — or aridity, as it is called in classic spirituality — occurs when God withdraws His consolations from the soul. In the interior life, God lures a soul to himself much as a lover woos his bride. It is His desire to enter into the soul and inhabit the soul in a profound spiritual union. For this reason, God initially sends the soul many consolations. Like a young man who sends flowers to the girl he is

courting, God sends "spiritual flowers" in the form of sensible pleasures that the soul can experience. Infatuated and delighted with
the sweetness it feels, the soul approaches prayer with relish and
desire, and every prayer time seems to be filled with joy and bliss.

However, the soul at this stage is still self-centered. Like a
young woman who looks forward to her suitor's coming only for
the flowers he will bring, the soul looks forward to its time of prayer
more for the consolation it will receive rather than for the One
who brings them. But God's ultimate interest is to be in union
with the soul. And so, to test the love of the soul, God gradually
withdraws His consolations. If the soul turns away from Him because the consolations are gone, it proves itself not ready, at least
for the moment, to be drawn into deeper relationship. The soul
must come to discover that it loves the God of consolation rather
than the consolations of God.

Gradually, the soul recognizes that it has become accustomed
to God's presence, to the movement of His Spirit within it, and it
searches beyond the gift to behold the Giver. Now, one spiritual
rose means more than a whole bouquet — and if no spiritual rose
is given, what does that matter? The soul is at rest in the arms of
its lover. Finally, the soul is reaching maturity. It has discovered
the true bliss that comes from union with God alone. And it has
come to realize that its greatest growth has taken place in the cov-
ers of darkness and deprivation.

But dryness does not always come from God. Sometimes it
comes from a carelessness in our spiritual life or some physical or
emotional malady. When aridity in prayer presents itself, we must
look at its potential causes. Is it a result of God's movement in the
soul, or is it because the soul has moved away from God for some
reason? Are we physically sick? Are we suffering from some recent
trial or tribulation in our personal or professional life? Are we leading a converted life? Are we being faithful to our time of prayer?
Are we making use of the sacraments? Are we in serious sin?

If the answer is "yes" to any of these questions, our problem is
likely not "aridity" in the classic sense of the word. The resolution
here is professional help, the Sacrament of Penance, or an amended

will. However, if we are in the state of grace and maintaining a consistent life of prayer, the dryness we are experiencing has to do with God's action within us, and we must praise God for the great work that is transpiring, even though we have yet to behold it.

A Sacrifice of Prayer

As we have already come to see, one purpose of prayer is to lead us in the process of purification and sanctification. This means we need to confront our personal sins, our weaknesses and failings, and the unhealed areas of our heart.

Such interior honesty is rarely pleasant. Recall the Samaritan woman's response to Jesus when she began to see her situation through the light of truth — she tried to change the subject! We may wish to do the same. But there is no progress in the spiritual life without self-knowledge, and if we are going to move along the continuum of transformation, these difficult moments in prayer will surely come. In the midst of them, however, God will affirm His love for us. He will show us His mercy and kindness. He will prove that He is trustworthy and that He has springs of living water from which we can drink. If we remain faithful, if we persevere in truth and confidence, we will ultimately reap the abundant fruit that only comes from a life of prayer, and we will begin to experience grace in abundance.

WORKING THE STRATEGY

Engage in Prayer

1. The Samaritan woman came to see the truth about herself when she encountered Jesus. Is there a truth about yourself that Jesus would have you see? What is it and why would He want you to recognize it?
2. Do you have a regular and consistent time of prayer? How does it reflect the suggestions given in this chapter regarding

solitude, posture, and pious actions? Are there ways you can improve your prayer time in these areas?

3. To what extent do you live a recollected life, and to what extent do you take custody of your senses? What are some actions you can take to accomplish these goals?

4. Does your prayer time include vocal prayer? Meditation/mental prayer? Some quiet moments of contemplation? For the next two weeks, use the steps given for meditation. In a journal, note any insights, guidance, or wisdom you have gained. Also, note any nuances that might indicate a deepening of your prayer experience. Seek to include meditation/mental prayer in your daily time of prayer in the future. If this practice proves beneficial, make it a regular part of your time of prayer.

5. What difficulties in prayer are most typical for you? How has the discussion in this chapter helped you understand them better? What steps can you take to overcome these difficulties?

STRATEGY THREE

Make Use of the Sacraments

෴

In the last chapter, we saw how important prayer is to the spiritual life. Prayer forms the backbone of our relationship with God, and it leads us in the way of holiness. Prayer informs us, reforms us, and transforms us. It purifies us and strengthens us. It sanctifies us and draws us close to God. Through prayer, we experience freedom and liberation. We experience hope and new life. We experience comfort and consolation. All of this is necessary if we are to attain eternal life.

But as we have seen, the work of prayer goes deeper still. Prayer illumines the hidden secrets of our heart; it reveals our weaknesses and frailties, our sins and frustrations. It points out our deficiencies and disorders, our motivations and intentions. Prayer removes the blinders from our eyes. It strips away our pretence. It dismantles our false sense of self. It causes us to see that we are in great need of a Savior.

And so, in humility and repentance, we turn to the One who is Messiah and Redeemer, who is Savior and Lord. We turn to Jesus Christ, to His mercy, to His compassion. He is "the way, and the truth, and the life" (John 14:6). As we have seen, only in Christ do we discover who we truly are, the ultimate purpose of our existence, and the grand mission to which we have been called. Only in Jesus Christ do we come to the marvelous truth that God has created us in love, to know His love, and to be His love in the world.

In the interior of our hearts, made open through the action of the Holy Spirit, we formulate a response to this truth and all that God intends for us through it. We surrender ourselves to the Father, asking Him to let His Son be "All in all of us." This is what it means to be "Christian," to be "another Christ." St. Paul's words to the Galatians sum up the goal completely: "And I live, now not I: but Christ liveth in me" (Galatians 2:20; Douay-Rheims Version). These are to be our words as well.

But can prayer alone take us to this ultimate goal, or is something else necessary besides — something that immerses us in the life of Christ even as Christ himself comes to dwell in us? The answer, of course, is "yes," there is "something else necessary besides." What is "necessary besides" is the sacramental life of our Catholic faith. Through the sacraments, we are incorporated into the life of Christ and immersed into His Mystical Body. Through the sacraments, Christ comes to live in us.

THE SACRAMENTS:
GATEWAY TO LIFE IN CHRIST

What is a sacrament? St. Thomas Aquinas, the great Dominican theologian, describes the sacraments as "God's eternal secrets finally revealed in Christ." For him, they are "visible signs of invisible things whereby man is made holy."

Echoing this definition, the Baltimore Catechism states that a sacrament is "an outward sign, instituted by Christ to give us grace." Father Adolphe Tanquerey, in his book *The Spiritual Life*, tells us that the sacraments are "sensible signs instituted by our Lord Jesus Christ [that] *symbolize* and *confer* grace." More recently, the *Catechism of the Catholic Church* says, "The sacraments are efficacious signs of grace, instituted by Christ and entrusted to the Church, by which divine life is dispensed to us" (no. 1131). All of these definitions communicate the essential facts regarding the sacraments: They are signs; they are instituted by Christ; and they confer grace — divine life — upon the recipient. Let's look at each of these in turn.

AN OUTWARD SIGN

Each of the definitions for a sacrament uses the word "sign." What is a sign? Webster's New World College Dictionary (third edition, 1997) defines the word as "1) something that indicates a fact, quality, etc.; 2) a gesture or motion that conveys information, gives a command, etc.; 3) a mark or symbol having an accepted and specific meaning."

These definitions are helpful because they tell us several things about a sign.

First, a sign is perceptible — it is experienced by the senses. We see it. We hear it. We may even taste it or smell it.

Second, a sign represents something else — it *indicates* a fact, or it *conveys* information, or its very appearance *specifies* a concept or an idea.

Third, the sign's value is in the message it communicates. The sign itself is transcended by the object or idea it represents or signifies.

Signs are a common part of everyday life. Dark clouds gathering in the sky indicate that rain is on the way. The smell of smoke tells us a fire is nearby. A telephone ringing lets us know someone wants to speak with us. A wave of the hand conveys, "Good-bye." The index finger held to the lips communicates, "Be quiet." A handshake says that an agreement has been reached. A curb painted yellow means "No parking." A red light means "Stop." An image of a cigarette in a circle with a diagonal line drawn through it means "No smoking." A wedding band circling the third finger of the left hand signifies the person wearing it is married.

Words themselves are signs. They are simply sound patterns that indicate something greater than the sound pattern itself. For example, in English-speaking countries, the sound pattern "f-l-o-w-e-r" stands for an object that emits a fragrant odor and is comprised of petals, a stamen, a pistil, and sepals. When someone utters the sound pattern "f-l-o-w-e-r," others who hear it think of or picture a *flower*. Now, the combination of sounds that comprise the word "flower" is not the flower itself. The sound pattern simply *represents* the fragrant object with petals, a stamen, a pistil, and sepals.

Some sound patterns become words that are known universally — the sounds associated with "m-a-m-a" are an example of a universal word. Most words, however, are only understood once someone has been initiated into their meaning, formally or informally, through education. This is the case with all signs. We must come to know what they mean if we are to understand the greater realities that they signify.

Sacraments, too, use signs, and the signs they use are much like the ones we have discussed. The sacraments use sensible objects, gestures or actions, and words to convey a message. Water and wine, bread and oil, extended hands, a cross traced on a forehead or drawn in the air, words, phrases, and sentences are perceptible signs used to communicate spiritual realities. In the language of the Church, these signs comprise the *matter* (objects and actions) and *form* (words) of the sacraments.

But there is something fundamentally different about the "signs" of the sacraments and the everyday signs with which we are familiar. The signs of daily life have no power to *effect*, or cause to happen, that which they represent. They simply are indicators. For a red light to effect that which it represents, for example, it would have to climb down from the pole on which it hangs, enter oncoming traffic, and physically stop the cars in their tracks by its own power. While this is the stuff of cartoons, it is not the stuff of ordinary experience.

Sacraments on the other hand are *efficacious*, as the definition from the *Catechism of the Catholic Church* (no. 1127) tells us. This means that not only do they *indicate* a spiritual reality, but they also *make that spiritual reality happen*. They have the power to *effect* what they signify and indicate. St. Thomas Aquinas explains this by saying that the sacraments not only signify, but they *cause*; and *it is by signifying that they cause*.

For this reason, very clear rules known as "rubrics" govern how the sacraments are administered. The *Catechism* states, "No sacramental rite may be modified or manipulated at the will of the minister or the community. Even the supreme authority in the Church may not change the liturgy arbitrarily, but only in the obedience of faith and with religious respect for the mystery of the liturgy" (no. 1125).

Rubrics make the signs of the sacraments universal. Thus, the sacramental signs speak a language, both through matter and form, which can be understood by all Catholics throughout the world. We have only to be educated about their meaning.

INSTITUTED BY CHRIST

Because the sacraments are signs that cause what they signify, the Church describes their action by the Latin phrase *ex opere operato*, which is literally translated "from the work wrought." This term indicates that the grace received from a validly administered sacrament is conferred by virtue of the *sign* itself. The sacrament's grace is not dependent upon the minister's virtue or merit, nor is it dependent upon the one who receives the sacrament. The grace is given "by the very fact of the action's being performed" (CCC, no. 1128).

This stands in marked contrast to the way in which grace is conferred through meritorious acts such as prayer and good works. The Church describes their action of grace by the Latin phrase *ex opere operantis,* which means "from the work of the worker." As the phrase suggests, with these spiritual activities the effect has some connection to the sanctity of the human agents involved and their merits and spiritual condition. Selfish motives and unrepented sin can thwart the efficacy of prayer and good works, while purity of heart and sanctity of soul greatly increase their merit. This is why the intercession of the saints is so effective: They have been purified and perfected, and are in complete conformity to the will of God.

Now, let's consider what we have just discussed. If, then, the grace conferred by God through meritorious acts comes by way of the sanctity and dispositions of the individuals involved, through whom do the *signs* of the sacraments derive their efficacy and power? St. Thomas Aquinas answers this question clearly: The power of the sacraments flows from Christ himself, from His very life, and most specifically from His passion and death — the Paschal Mystery. While the grace of meritorious acts must flow through the weaknesses and frailties of human agents, the grace of the sacraments flows from the Spotless Lamb, the Second Person of the Blessed Trinity, who is present in a mystical way in the ministers of His Church. The sacraments, then, are *instituted* — *founded upon* and *initiated by* — Jesus Christ. They are revealed to us through the events of His life, and they are made available to us by His passion and death.

The *Catechism* states it succinctly:

> Jesus' words and actions during his hidden life and pub-
> lic ministry were already salvific, for they anticipated the
> power of his Paschal mystery. They announced and prepared
> what he was going to give the Church when all was accom-
> plished. The mysteries of Christ's life are the foundations
> of what he would henceforth dispense in the sacraments,
> through the ministers of his Church, for "what was visible
> in our Savior has passed over into his mysteries."
>
> — CCC, NO. 1115, QUOTING ST. LEO THE GREAT

But that is not all. Because the sacraments are imbued with
the very life of Christ himself, they become portals of grace through
which we are *incorporated* into His life — we immersed in Him,
He living in us. Thus, the events of our lives become forever imbued by the events of His, a mystical reflection forever marked by
Christ's journey of passion, death, and resurrection. This is what it
means to be a member of the Mystical Body of Jesus Christ, and
this is what it means to be a Christian.

In his work *Summa Theologiae: A Concise Translation*, Timothy McDermott writes this about St. Thomas Aquinas's perspective of the sacraments:

> [St. Thomas Aquinas] thinks of the sacraments as so many
> re-enactments of the mystery of Christ's passion and death
> and resurrection, that journey from death to life . . . the tool
> of God's salvaging of creation. The re-enactments are not
> meant to repeat the journey, nor merely to recall it, but they
> are meant, as he says, to *apply* it to the participants, to draw
> the participants into the journey, or (in a striking phrase that
> Thomas uses more than once) to pass on to them the effects
> of that journey *as if they themselves had been the ones who suffered
> and died.* . . . Through the sacraments of the Church the mys-
> teries of Christ's life put their mark on ours; Christ continues
> his work of salvage with our cooperation in our lives.

Father M. Eugene Boylan, O.Cist.R., in his classic work, *This Tremendous Lover*, expresses this life-giving application of the sacraments in words that stir the heart and ignite the spirit. He writes:

> In every sacrament the principal minister is Christ, the secondary and human minister only acts in His name. Christ still lives in His Church — He has promised to be with her all days even to the end of the world — and nowhere is His living Power more evident than in the administration of the sacraments, nowhere can He be found in such an effective way as by approaching them. There He speaks to us, there He forgives us, there He strengthens us, there He sanctifies us, there He gives us the kiss of reconciliation and of friendship, there He gives us His own merits and His own power, there He gives us Himself. . . . For the sacraments seize upon us, digest us and make us part of Christ.

TO GIVE US GRACE

Now we come to the truth of the sacraments. Now we come to their power and their efficacy. Now we come to their value and worth. Each sacrament we receive, and each time we receive a sacrament, we are immersed into the life of Jesus Christ, and He in ours. Neither boundary of time nor boundary of space can limit the supernatural reality of this incorporation. Each sacrament plunges us into the sacred mysteries of Christ's life, His passion, His death, and His resurrection. In a wholly mysterious way, we are made part of His salvific work, and He becomes part of our life's events, situations, and circumstances. Through Him, the very stuff of our lives takes on redemptive value.

Christ, His life and His Paschal Mystery, is the Fountainhead of grace for each and every sacrament. And this Fountainhead of grace, given to us in the sacraments, has everything to do with our lives, both temporally and eternally. That is why, quoting the Council of Trent, "the Church affirms that for believers the sacraments of the New Covenant are *necessary for salvation*." She teaches:

"Sacramental grace" is the grace of the Holy Spirit, given by Christ and proper to each sacrament. The Spirit heals and transforms those who receive him by conforming them to the Son of God. The fruit of the sacramental life is that the Spirit of adoption makes the faithful partakers in the divine nature by uniting them in a living union with the only Son, the Savior. — CCC, NO. 1129

Thus, the sacraments are indispensable for ultimate transformation and union with God to take place.

THE TRANSFORMING AND CONFORMING POWER OF THE SACRAMENTS

How is it that the sacraments transform us and conform us to the Son of God? How does each sacrament make us partakers in the divine nature by uniting us in a living union with the only Son, the Savior? A brief look at each sacrament will give us the answer as it discloses the "sacramental grace" specific to each. Using the *Catechism of the Catholic Church* as our guide, we will look at the sacraments according to three categories: the sacraments of initiation, the sacraments of healing, and the sacraments at the service of communion.

The Sacraments of Christian Initiation: Baptism, Confirmation, and the Eucharist

The *Catechism of the Catholic Church* tells us that Baptism, Confirmation, and the Eucharist are called the "sacraments of Christian initiation" because they lay the foundations of the Christian life (no. 1212).

Of the three, Baptism and Confirmation can be received only once. In Baptism and Confirmation, the subject receives an indelible *character*, or *seal*, upon his soul. This seal signifies that a special call or mission is being conferred upon him along with the supernatural power to carry it out. Only one other sacrament places an indelible character on the soul: the Sacrament of Holy Orders. The *Catechism* tells us that this indelible seal "remains for ever in the Christian as a positive disposition for grace, a promise and guarantee of divine protection, and as a vocation to divine worship and to the service of the Church" (no. 1121).

The importance of these three sacraments cannot be overestimated. They form the essential means by which the faithful are initiated into the divine life. Quoting Pope Paul VI in *Divinae Consortium Naturae*, the *Catechism* reminds us that the supernatural life bears some similarity to the natural life: It has an origin; it must strengthen and develop; and it requires nourishment to survive. The sacraments of Christian initiation are the means by which this takes place: "The faithful are born anew by Baptism, strengthened by the sacrament of Confirmation, and receive in the Eucharist the food of eternal life" (no. 1212). Baptism, Confirmation, and Eucharist bring us spiritual life and are, therefore, the initial portals of divine union.

Baptism: The Sacrament of Spiritual Rebirth

Baptism is often called the "sacrament of regeneration" because through its waters we are reborn as the sons and daughters of God; we are freed from original sin; we are incorporated into the Mystical Body of Jesus Christ, the Church; and we become sharers in her mission. It is the sacramental grace of Baptism that makes this so. As the *Catechism* tells us, "Holy Baptism is the basis of the whole Christian life, the gateway to life in the Spirit . . . and the door which gives access to the other sacraments" (no. 1213).

Furthermore, Baptism identifies us with the cross of Christ and with His death. St. Paul reminds us, "Do you not know that all of us who have been baptized into Christ Jesus were baptized into his death?" (Romans 6:3). Our immersion into the baptismal waters is a sign of that death, and our rising from it a sign of the new life — the eternal life — that Christ's passion and death gained for us.

The passage from Romans continues: "We were buried therefore with him by baptism into death, so that as Christ was raised from the dead by the glory of the Father, we too might walk in newness of life" (6:4). Each struggle and trial we face can be met with the sacramental graces of our baptism, forever flowing from

Calvary's hill into our lives. Each struggle and trial can be transformed by baptismal grace as we consciously unite it to the passion and death of Jesus Christ. Each struggle and trial in our lives can then be said to be a redemptive moment, issuing forth in us and through us the grace of salvation that ultimately leads to final resurrection in Christ Jesus.

Everything about the baptismal rite indicates the sacramental grace specific to Baptism. The child or adult is signed with the cross, an imprint of Christ, which both reminds him of the cost of his redemption and indicates to whom he now belongs. The proclamation of the Word of God instructs all present with the truths of the faith and encourages a faithful response to those truths. The exorcisms pronounced over the candidate free him from sin and from the wiles of the evil one. The baptismal water is consecrated by a prayer invoking the Holy Spirit to come upon the waters so that the one who is about to be immersed may be "born of water and the Spirit" (John 3:5).

The essential rite of the sacrament — the triple immersion into the water (or the water poured over the head three times) — brings death to sin and entry into the Trinitarian life by configuring the candidate to the Paschal Mystery. The anointing with sacred chrism signifies the gift of the Holy Spirit to the newly baptized. The white garment symbolizes that the newly baptized has "put on Christ" (Galatians 3:27), and the lighted candle lets all know that this person is now enlightened by Christ and called to be "the light of the world" (Matthew 5:14; also see Philippians 2:15).

Confirmation: The Sacrament of Spiritual Maturation

"Reception of the sacrament of Confirmation is necessary for the completion of baptismal grace," says the *Catechism of the Catholic Church* (no. 1285). It "completes" baptismal grace in that Confirmation is the sacrament that brings about the spiritual "coming of age" of the baptized person. As such, it is a sacrament of spiritual maturation. Through Confirmation, the baptized person receives the strengthening of the Holy Spirit so that he may fulfill his call to be a witness to Christ and to defend the faith by word and deed when circumstances demand it. So unified are Baptism and Confirmation that the Eastern Church administers Confirmation at the time of Baptism.

The Sacrament of Confirmation is profoundly related to Our Lord's own baptism in the Jordan River by St. John the Baptist. It was thus Jesus began His public ministry and it was thus His mission was confirmed by the presence of the Holy Spirit in the form of a dove, and by the voice of the Father proclaiming, "This is my beloved Son, with whom I am well pleased" (Matthew 3:16-17). So, too, each of us is confirmed by the Father through the Son as we are anointed in the power of the Holy Spirit to carry out the work and mission to which God has called us by virtue of our baptism. And that mission is to proclaim Jesus Christ to the world and to defend His Church. The *Catechism of the Catholic Church* puts it this way:

> By Confirmation Christians, that is, those who are anointed, share more completely in the mission of Jesus Christ and the fullness of the Holy Spirit with which he is filled, so that their lives may give off "the aroma of Christ."
> — CCC, no. 1294

The matter and form of Confirmation indicates the sacramental grace inherent to it. The confirmand is anointed with sacred chrism, a mixture of balsam and oil that emits a pleasant fragrance indicative of the "aroma of Christ." The anointing signifies the infilling of the Holy Spirit and the diffusion of grace. The anointing also indicates that the candidate has received the "mark" or "seal" of the Holy Spirit.

The idea of a seal stems back to Old Testament days and enjoys a long tradition within Church history. In ancient times, soldiers were marked with the seal of their leader, and slaves were marked with the seal of their owner. The seal served two purposes: It identified the soldier or the slave as belonging to this leader or that owner, and it ensured that the soldier's or slave's needs would be met by the one to whom they professed allegiance.

In the Sacrament of Confirmation, the seal, signified by anointing, indicates something of the same. The confirmand is now identified as a "soldier for Christ." He is "slave-like" in that he now belongs totally to Christ and promises to be in Christ's service forever. His promise is a response to God's own promise that the confirmand will be afforded divine protection through the power of the Holy Spirit who has been given to him. This protection comes by way of the gifts of the Holy Spirit conferred on him to aid him in his mission in the world. The gifts of the Holy Spirit proper to Confirmation are wisdom, understanding, counsel, knowledge, fortitude, piety, and fear of the Lord (Isaiah 11:2-3).

The rite of Confirmation shows its close connection to Baptism. The liturgy begins with a renewal of the baptismal promises and the profession of faith. The bishop extends his hands over the entire group of confirmands and prays for the outpouring of the Holy Spirit. In the Latin Church, the essential rite of the sacrament is conferred through the anointing of the forehead with chrism, which is done by the laying on of hands, with the pronouncement of the words "Be sealed with the Gift of the Holy Spirit." In the Eastern rites, the forehead, eyes, nose, ears, lips, chest, back, hands, and feet are anointed, accompanied by the words "the seal of the gift of the Holy Spirit" (CCC, no. 1300).

According to the *Catechism of the Catholic Church* (no. 1303), Confirmation brings an increase and deepening of baptismal grace by:

- Rooting us more deeply in the divine filiation.
- Uniting us more firmly to Christ.
- Increasing the gifts of the Holy Spirit in us.
- Rendering our bond with the Church more perfect.
- Giving us the special strength of the Holy Spirit to spread and defend the faith by word and action as true witnesses of Christ, to confess the name of Christ more boldly, and never to be ashamed of the cross.

Eucharist: The Sacrament of Spiritual Nourishment

Christian initiation is completed by the Holy Eucharist. The *Catechism of the Catholic Church* tells us, "Those who have been raised to the dignity of the royal priesthood by Baptism and configured more deeply to Christ by Confirmation participate with the whole community in the Lord's own sacrifice by means of the Eucharist" (no. 1322). Because the Eucharist is "the Lord's own sacrifice" and we have been called to participate in it, the Eucharist is the "source and summit of the Christian life" (no. 1324).

In the Eucharist, the Paschal Mystery is made present to us — Jesus' passion, death, and resurrection. He is the Spotless Lamb offered to the Father in atonement for the sins of the world — the perfect sacrifice, the final sacrifice, the eternal sacrifice prophesied of old and now fulfilled.

The *Catechism* tells us that there are many names for this sacrament. Each one brings with it a deeper understanding and appreciation of its inexhaustible richness while at the same time evoking its various aspects (no. 1328). It is called:

- *Eucharist* because it is an action of thanksgiving to God.
- *Breaking of the Bread* because Jesus used this same rite when He blessed and distributed the bread at the Last Supper.
- *Eucharistic assembly* because it is celebrated amid the faithful.
- *Memorial* of the Lord's passion and resurrection.
- *Holy Sacrifice* and *Holy Sacrifice of the Mass* because it makes present the one sacrifice of Christ the Savior.
- *Holy and Divine Liturgy* and *Sacred Mysteries* because the Church's whole liturgy centers around this sacrament.
- *Most Blessed Sacrament* because it is the Sacrament of the sacraments.
- *Holy Communion* because through this sacrament we are united to Jesus Christ, who makes us sharers in His Body and Blood (also called *the holy things, the bread of angels, bread from heaven, medicine of immortality,* and *viaticum* for a similar reason).

- *Holy Mass* because the liturgy sends forth (*missio*) the faithful to fulfill God's will in their daily lives.

Central to the Eucharistic celebration are the matter of bread and wine and the form (or words) of consecration. Following the proper rubrics and through the invocation of the Holy Spirit and the pronouncement of Jesus' words at the Last Supper, the bread and wine become "in a way surpassing understanding" (no. 1333), the Body and Blood, Soul and Divinity, of our Lord and Savior, Jesus Christ.

The *Catechism of the Catholic Church* quotes the Council of Trent and Pope Paul VI (*Mysterium Fidei*, no. 39) in proclaiming:

> In the most blessed sacrament of the Eucharist "the body and blood, together with the soul and divinity, of our Lord Jesus Christ and, therefore, *the whole Christ is truly, really, and substantially* contained." "This presence is called 'real' — by which is not intended to exclude the other types of presence as if they could not be 'real' too, but because it is presence in the fullest sense: that is to say, it is a *substantial* presence by which Christ, God and man, makes himself wholly and entirely present." — CCC, NO. 1374

A Crisis of Faith

Though these words succinctly state Church teaching, contemporary polls suggest that less than half of the church-going Catholics in the United States believe that Jesus is truly, really, and substantially present in the Eucharist. They form a cross-section of the Catholic population — from those in the pew to those who hold positions of authority within the institutional Church.

While this is lamentable, it is understandable. Sadly, authentic catechesis on the Eucharist was absent from many religion classes, homilies, and spiritual-formation programs for more than thirty years. This unfortunate fact has had its results. Many people have never attended any form of Eucharistic adoration. Often, a general "thoughtlessness," marked by a lack of decorum or reverence, is displayed in church before and after Mass begins and during the reception of Holy Communion. Even architecture has been affected, with many sanctuaries more closely resembling community halls than temples that house God himself.

However, lack of belief in the Real Presence is not a new crisis in the Church. It was, in fact, the first cause of division among the followers of Jesus. This sad day is chronicled in Chapter 6 of St. John's Gospel. It is here that Jesus referred to himself as the "bread of life." The disciples found this a hard teaching to believe and asked themselves, "How can this man give us his flesh to eat?" Soon, their words and murmurings turned angry, and they broke into open quarrelling.

But Jesus did not recant what He had said. In fact, He repeated His teaching:

"Truly, truly, I say to you, unless you eat the flesh of the Son of man and drink his blood, you have no life in you. . . . For my flesh is food indeed, and my blood is drink indeed. He who eats my flesh and drinks my blood abides in me, and I in him." — JOHN 6:53, 55-56

To emphasize that He meant exactly what He had said, Jesus repeated the phrase "Truly, truly, I say to you" over and over again (John 6:26, 32, 47, 53).

Still, some could not accept what they heard, and "many of his disciples drew back and no longer went about with him" (John 6:66). Even in the face of this, however, never once did Jesus modify His language or take back what He had said. He stuck to His teaching and so has His Church.

A Consistent Teaching

From St. Paul (1 Corinthians 11:23-30; c. A.D. 50), to St. Ignatius of Antioch (d. c. 107), to St. Justin Martyr (150), to St. Irenaeus of Lyons (end of the second century), to St. Athanasius of Alexandria (373), to St. Cyril of Jerusalem (approximately 450), to St. Thomas Aquinas (thirteenth century), to the Council of Trent (1545-1563), through all of the intervening pontiffs and councils, up to the present Holy Father and the current *Catechism of the Catholic Church* — the *catena* ("chain") of Church teaching has universally held and proclaimed that at the moment of consecration, ordinary bread and wine become the Body and Blood, the Soul and Divinity of the Second Person of the Blessed Trinity, our Lord and Savior, Jesus Christ. Consider these words of St. Paul, for example:

> Whoever, therefore, eats the bread or drinks the cup of the Lord in an unworthy manner will be guilty of profaning the body and blood of the Lord. Let a man examine himself, and so eat of the bread and drink of the cup. For any one who eats and drinks without discerning the body eats and drinks judgment upon himself. — 1 CORINTHIANS 11:27-29

And these words of St. Ignatius of Antioch:

> They abstain from the Eucharist and from prayer, because they do not confess that the Eucharist is the flesh of our Savior Jesus Christ, flesh which suffered for our sins and which the Father, in his goodness, raised up again.

And these words of St. Justin Martyr:

> The food that has been made the Eucharist by the prayer of His Word, and which nourishes our flesh and blood by assimilation, is both the Flesh and Blood of that Jesus who was made flesh.

And this said by St. Cyril of Jerusalem:

> Do not, therefore, regard the Bread and Wine as simply that; for they are, according to the Master's declaration, the Body and Blood of Christ. . . . Let your faith make you firm.

And this expressed by St. John of Damascus:

> If I am asked how bread is changed into the Body of Christ, I answer: "The Holy Ghost overshadows the priest and operates in the same manner in the elements which He effected in the womb of the Virgin Mary."

And these words said by St. Basil the Great:

> It is good and beneficial to take Communion every day, and to partake of the Holy Body and Blood of Christ. For He distinctly says, "He who eats my flesh and drinks my blood has eternal life" (John 6:54). And who doubts that to share frequently in life is the same thing as to have abundant life?

And these words taken from the great hymn of St. Thomas Aquinas, *Adoro Te Devote,* a beautiful theology of the Eucharist:

> Godhead here in hiding, whom I do adore
> Masked by these bare shadows, shape and nothing more,
> See, Lord, at thy service low lies here a heart
> Lost, all lost in wonder at the God thou art.
>
> Seeing, touching, tasting are in thee deceived;
> How says trusty hearing? That shall be believed:
> What God's Son has told me, take for truth I do;
> Truth himself speaks truly or there's nothing true.

These words all attest to the words that Jesus himself has given us:

> "I am the living bread which came down from heaven; if any one eats of this bread, he will live for ever; and the bread which I shall give for the life of the world is my flesh."
> — JOHN 6:51

The Spiritual Effects of Holy Communion

The *Catechism of the Catholic Church* tells us that the Eucharist is our spiritual nourishment through which we are led into intimate union with Jesus Christ:

> What material food produces in our bodily life, Holy Communion wonderfully achieves in our spiritual life. Communion . . . preserves, increases, and renews the life of grace received at Baptism. This growth in Christian life needs the nourishment of Eucharistic Communion, the bread for our pilgrimage until the moment of death, when it will be given to us as viaticum." — CCC, NO. 1392

St. Peter Julian Eymard writes:

> The soul, physically speaking, has received from God a life which cannot die; it is immortal. But the life of grace — received at Baptism, recovered and restored by the Sacrament of Penance — the life of holiness, a thousand times more noble than the natural life, is not sustained without nourishment; and its principal food is Jesus in the Eucharist. The life found anew in Penance will be perfected by the Eucharist, in a way, or which will purify us of our attachment to sin, will blot out our daily faults, will give us strength to remain faithful to our good resolutions, and will drive away from us occasions of sin.

The *Catechism* tells us that the spiritual nourishment received through the Eucharist strengthens our charity, wipes away our venial sins, preserves us from future mortal sins, unites us to the Mystical Body of Christ, commits us to the poor, and encourages us to seek unity among all Christians (nos. 1394-1398).

Simply stated, the Body and Blood of Jesus Christ, active within us, becomes a transforming agent for ourselves and for others. Thus, if we are to make progress in the spiritual life and become a catalyst of Christ's love in the world, we must do it by the means Jesus has given us: through reception of His Eucharistic presence. In his work *The Three Ages of the Interior Life*, Dominican Father Reginald Garrigou-Lagrange writes, "We, who are always inclined to pride, to lack of consideration, to forgetfulness of the greatest truths, to spiritual folly, need to be illumined by contact with the sovereignly luminous intellect of the Savior, who is 'the way, the truth, and the life.'"

Ways to Enhance Your Experience of the Eucharist

While the Eucharist is replete with spiritual blessings, its effectiveness in our lives depends upon the disposition or holy desire we bring to the Sacrament. Though all of Jesus is received in the Eucharist, a weak desire or shallow fervency in us greatly prohibits the effect our Communion will have in our spirit. Only by coming to the Sacrament with desire and expectant faith do we experience the full measure of grace offered to us through the Body and Blood of Jesus Christ.

According to Father Garrigou-Lagrange, a great Thomistic scholar, a fervent Communion is marked by four characteristics: humility, respect for the Eucharist, a living faith, and an ardent desire to receive Jesus.

1. **The Virtue of Humility.** Though acquiring the virtue of humility is often the work of a lifetime, it can be encouraged by a prayerful consideration of who Jesus Christ is and who we are. By cords of love, Our Lord draws us to himself. It is His mercy, not our worthiness, which gives us the great privilege of receiving Him in the Eucharist.

2. **Respect for the Eucharist.** Respect for the Eucharist is the second characteristic of a fervent Communion. Our physical demeanor in the presence of the Lord reveals the attitude of our hearts. Our body language, style of dress, and tone of voice all help, or hinder, the spiritual benefits we receive in Holy Communion. We must seek to develop an abiding respect for the Eucharistic presence of Jesus Christ, and everything about us must reflect it. Genuflect-

ing, kneeling with erect posture, and bowing before receiving the Eucharist all help us to remain focused on the One who gives himself to us.

3. **A Living Faith.** A living faith keeps the fire of our desire burning for Jesus. This type of faith is engendered through a consistent prayer life, a temperate lifestyle, charitable actions, and an attitude of gratitude for the blessings God bestows on us each day. Another way to practice a living faith, especially in reference to the Eucharist, is by making a proper thanksgiving after receiving Our Lord. As true appreciation for God's gracious generosity wells up within us, so does a holy desire to remain united to Him.

4. **Ardent Desire.** The final characteristic of a fervent Communion is ardent desire. This desire is demonstrated by a consistent longing to be united to Jesus *all of the time*. A conscious anticipation for the Eucharist, accompanied by a frequent turning of the heart and mind to God, becomes the daily rhythm of the soul imbued with ardent desire. This holy response to the Eucharistic presence is the pre-eminent grace of the Sacrament. And it is a defining feature of all the great saints throughout the ages.

Though no contact with Jesus is greater than receiving Him in the Eucharist, adoration of the Blessed Sacrament is another way in which we can be spiritually nourished by the Eucharistic presence. Whether the Sacred Species is exposed in the monstrance or reposed in the tabernacle, coming before Our Lord is efficacious and spiritually beneficial.

Pope John Paul II, a man of deep prayer and Eucharistic adoration, has encouraged Catholics everywhere to seek the rich spiritual benefits available through Eucharistic worship. He writes:

> Indeed, since the Eucharistic Mystery was instituted out of love, and makes Christ sacramentally present, it is worthy of thanksgiving and worship. . . . The Church and the world have a great need of eucharistic worship. Jesus waits for us in

TEST YOUR FERVENCY

Is your reception of the Holy Eucharist characterized by fervency and expectant faith? Answer each question *honestly*, score 1 point for each "yes" answer, and add them up.

___ 1. I see Holy Communion as a privilege rather than an entitlement.

___ 2. My preparation to receive Jesus starts before Mass begins.

___ 3. I consider it important to show acts of piety toward the Eucharist — kneeling, genuflecting, dressing appropriately, etc.

___ 4. My lifestyle, daily habits, and attitudes of heart reflect Jesus alive in me.

___ 5. I strive to keep a consistent time for prayer.

___ 6. I frequently find my heart and mind turning to God through the course of the day.

___ 7. My thanksgiving after Holy Communion is heartfelt rather than routine and perfunctory.

___ 8. Adoration of the Blessed Sacrament is an important aspect of my spiritual life.

___ 9. I seek ways to respond to the physical and spiritual needs of others.

___10. Each day I consciously thank God for the blessings I have received.

9-10   Ready for canonization.

7-8   On the road to holiness.

5-6   The fire of desire is getting lukewarm.

2-4   Time for renewal.

0-1   A serious examination of conscience is in order.

this sacrament of love. Let us be generous with our time in going to meet Him in adoration and in contemplation that is full of faith and ready to make reparation for the great faults and crimes of the world. May our adoration never cease.

—DOMINICAE CENAE, NO. 3

The same four characteristics of humility, respect, living faith, and ardent desire should mark our time of Eucharistic adoration as well. Let us come to each encounter of the Eucharistic presence of Our Lord with hearts opened wide, ready to receive every spiritual blessing in the heavens (Ephesians 1:3). And, vivified by Him who brings us spiritual life, may we become lights in the world who point the way to Jesus Christ.

The Sacraments of Healing: Penance and the Anointing of the Sick

Though the sacraments of Christian initiation make us partakers of the divine nature and lead us in the way of spiritual rebirth, maturity, and nourishment, we remain creatures, nonetheless. Suffering, illness, death, spiritual weakness, and frailty define our existence. But the vicissitudes of life do not affect only our body. So, too, is our soul battered and beleaguered by the onslaught of temptation and sin. For this reason, Christ instituted two sacraments of healing: Penance and the Anointing of the Sick. Each of these sacraments has the restorative power of grace to aid us physically and spiritually. Of the two, however, spiritual healing is of primary importance, "For what doth it profit a man, if he gain the whole world and suffer the loss of his own soul?" (Matthew 16:26; Douay-Rheims Version).

Penance: The Sacrament of Reconciliation

Any discussion of the Sacrament of Penance must include a discussion on sin. Sin is not a very popular topic these days. In fact, some contemporary circles, including some churches, would consider the very word taboo. This "silence on sin" has done us a great disservice. It has led many to believe that sin no longer exists. Nothing could be further from the truth. All of us have sinned and fallen short of the glory of God (Romans 3:23). And it is precisely because of this reality that Christ instituted the sacrament.

Jesus instituted the Sacrament of Penance on the evening of His glorious resurrection from the dead. In John 20:19-23, Scripture tells us that even though the disciples had locked the doors of the place where they were staying for fear of the Jews, Jesus came and stood before them. "Peace be with you," He said to them. After showing them His wounds so that they would know it was truly He, Jesus repeated again, "Peace be with you. As the Father has sent me, even so I send you." With that, the Lord breathed on them and said, "Receive the Holy Spirit. If you forgive the sins of any, they are forgiven; if you retain the sins of any, they are retained."

These verses reveal much to us about the sacrament. First, the Sacrament of Penance brings us peace. Remember the discussion in the first chapter ("Strategy One: Believe the Truth About Yourself") regarding the triple harmony that was shattered by original sin. All sin destroys. It dis-integrates. It destroys man's relationship with God, his relationship with others, and his own interior unity or integrity. Peace cannot be found in dis-integration. It can only be found in wholeness. The Sacrament of Penance *reconciles* us to God, to one another, and to ourselves. Thus, peace is restored. The fact that Jesus' first words confer peace and that He offers peace to the disciples twice is indicative of its importance and its association with the sacrament He is about to institute.

Secondly, Jesus transfers His mission to His disciples. "As the Father has sent me, even so I send you," He tells them. The word "sent" is significant. It informs the disciples that they are to carry on the mission of salvation entrusted to Jesus Christ. And what was that mission? Christ's mission was to save man from the consequences of sin and, in so doing, to give him everlasting life. Here, Jesus entrusts to His disciples His mission of reconciling sinful man to God.

This transference of mission is accomplished through the power of the Holy Spirit. Jesus "breathes" on them — indicating the coming of the Holy Spirit. Scripture scholars tell us that this breathing on the disciples was not symbolic. Rather, it conferred upon them the Spirit of the Living God. Then, Jesus says to the disciples,

"Receive the Holy Spirit. If you forgive the sins of any, they are forgiven; if you retain the sins of any, they are retained." With these words, Jesus invests in His disciples, and in all who will follow after them in their priestly mission, the power to forgive sin or to retain sin.

The use of the word "retain" is interesting. The dictionary defines the word as meaning (1) to hold or keep in possession or (2) to keep in a fixed state or condition. This tells us that if our sins are not forgiven, they are held or kept in possession against us. It also suggests that if the sin is retained, we, in some way, are held bound by the sin itself. This communicates to us something about the nature of sin. It keeps us in bondage by holding us captive "in a fixed state or condition." Sin has a paralyzing effect — an effect that stultifies our relationship with God and stunts our spiritual growth.

Thus, sin has power over us. Like binding chains, sin holds man in a vice-like grip preventing him from experiencing the grace in abundance that God longs to give him. The Sacrament of Penance is God's antidote to the debilitating consequence of our personal sin.

Two Types of Sin: Mortal and Venial

The Church has always distinguished between mortal sin and venial sin. Mortal sin is "deadly" sin, in that it deals a mortal blow to our relationship with God and our hopes of everlasting life. Through mortal sin, we separate ourselves from divine love by attaching ourselves in an inordinate manner to some created good, as Father Adolphe Tanquerey explains in *The Spiritual Life*. Thus, we place the created good and our affection for it above God and His love. Mortal sin is indeed a grave matter.

The *Catechism of the Catholic Church* (nos. 1857-1859) tells us there are three conditions necessary to constitute a mortal sin:

1. The act must be something serious, *a grave matter* specified by the Ten Commandments.
2. Mortal sin requires *full knowledge*. One must know the sinful character of the act and of its opposition to God.

3. Mortal sin requires *full consent*. The act must be a free-will decision, done deliberately. Pretending to be ignorant of the true nature of the sin or persisting in hardness of heart (a condition caused by repeated offenses against God) does not lessen the severity of the voluntary act but instead increases it.

Father Tanquerey lists the effects of mortal sin: It expels God from our soul; we lose sanctifying grace (that grace whereby our soul lives in communion with the Trinity), as well as the virtues and gifts that go with it; we lose all past merits gained through prayer and good works; and we forfeit the opportunity to acquire any more while we remain in the state of mortal sin. Finally, if the sinner remains unrepentant until the end, he loses all chance for salvation and goes to hell. Because of these serious effects of mortal sin, it "necessitates a new initiative of God's mercy and a conversion of heart" (CCC, no. 1856), which is most normally accomplished within the Sacrament of Penance.

Venial sin, on the other hand, while still an offense against the love of God, does not separate man from God. Rather, it weakens his relationship with Him. The *Catechism* tells us that even though it offends and wounds, venial sin allows charity to subsist (no. 1855). According to the *Catechism*, "One commits *venial sin* when, in a less serious matter, he does not observe the standard prescribed by the moral law, or when he disobeys the moral law in a grave matter, but without full knowledge or without complete consent" (no. 1862).

However, this does not mean that venial sin should be winked at and taken lightly. It, too, has effects that damage our spiritual life. Venial sin weakens charity, manifests a disordered affection for created goods, impedes the soul's progress in practicing the virtues and the moral good, merits temporal punishment, and disposes us to mortal sin (CCC, no. 1863).

Sin is no small matter. All of the saints agree that, with regard to sin, the best defense is a good offense. St. Dorotheus, for example, advised:

When you are tormented by any passion or evil inclination, if you be so weak as to yield to it, and let it lead you, take it for a certain truth, then it will take deeper root, wage a more violent war against you. But if you resist it courageously at first, it will daily diminish. Every day it will have less strength to act upon you, till at length, it will come to have none at all.

This is advice well worth taking.

Reaping the Benefits of the Sacrament: How to Make a Good Confession

Mother Teresa of Calcutta says:

The first lesson of the heart of Jesus is our examination of conscience: Know thyself. The examination of conscience consists of facing ourselves with Jesus. We should not waste time looking at our misery, but we are rather to look into His light.

These words give us good counsel and direction, and they impart to us the first step to reaping the benefits of the Sacrament of Penance: an examination of conscience.

It is rarely easy to look at the truth of our condition. But, as Mother Teresa suggests, knowing ourselves is the first lesson in spiritual growth. As she suggests, looking into the light of Jesus Christ, His love for us, and the great gift of reconciliation that He offers us through the sacrament can free us from the fear of seeing ourselves as we truly are and encourage us to seek the grace that awaits us.

Any examination of conscience should begin with a prayer asking the Holy Spirit to illumine our heart, our memory, and our motives. Then, we should evaluate our thoughts and deeds according to the Ten Commandments, the Beatitudes, and the teachings of the Holy Catholic Church. We should also look for sins of omission — opportunities not taken by us to exercise charity and practice virtue. Many valuable aids are available to help us in our examination, and we should avail ourselves of them. They can help us see our sins more clearly, especially if our sensitivity to wrongdoing has been compromised.

Once we see our sins, a good confession requires that we be truly sorry. St. Thomas Aquinas tells us that such sorrow is already a sign of God at work in us, for He is the One who turns our hearts to Him. But we must cooperate with this movement through an act of faith. These are the requirements for a good confession: sincerity and humility of heart; true contrition for our sins; a firm purpose of amendment — to sin no more and to avoid the occasions of sin; the confession of our sins to a priest; and satisfaction for our sins through penance. As the *Catechism* states, "Only priests who have received the faculty of absolving from the authority of the Church can forgive sins in the name of Christ" (no. 1495).

Effects of the Sacrament

Pope Pius XII lists the following benefits of making use of the Sacrament of Penance on a regular and consistent basis: "Genuine self-knowledge is increased, Christian humility grows, bad habits are corrected, spiritual neglect and tepidity are resisted, the conscience is purified, the will strengthened, a salutary self-control is attained, and grace is increased in virtue of the sacrament itself."

The *Catechism of the Catholic Church* (no. 1496) lists the benefits to be:

- Reconciliation with God by which the penitent recovers grace.
- Reconciliation with the Church.
- Remission of the eternal punishment incurred by mortal sins.
- Remission, at least in part, of temporal punishments resulting from sin.
- Peace and serenity of conscience, and spiritual consolation.
- An increase of spiritual strength for the Christian battle.

In closing this discussion on the Sacrament of Penance, the words of St. Isidore of Seville seem particularly fitting. He said:

> Confession heals, confession justifies, confession grants pardon of sin. All hope consists in confession. In confession, there is a chance for mercy. Believe it firmly. Do not doubt, do not hesitate, never despair of the mercy of God. Hope and have confidence in confession.

The Sacrament of the Anointing of the Sick

Suffering, illness, and death are part of the human condition. All of us will have opportunities in life to experience suffering and illness, sometimes in small ways and sometimes in great ways. And unless Jesus comes again during our lifetime, each of us will experience death, the logical conclusion to our life on earth. The question we should ask, then, is "What will I do when I suffer?" The answer to that question impacts greatly on our spiritual life and ultimately makes all the difference regarding the trials and tribulations of life.

Bitterness, resentment, anguish, self-absorption, despair, and rebellion against God can make our time of suffering perilous not only for the effects such a psychology has on our physical and emotional life, but more seriously the effect it wields on our spiritual life. On the other hand, uniting our sufferings to the cross of Christ, discerning what is of essential importance in life, offering our pain to God in solidarity with others who are suffering, and turning our heart to Our Lord at every turn can bring us to great spiritual maturity. The Sacrament of the Anointing of the Sick helps us to unearth the pearl of great price that lies hidden in the depths of every great trial.

A God of Compassion

Suffering and death are consequences of original sin. However, our God is a God of compassion. We see this compassion revealed throughout the pages of Sacred Scripture from the Old Testament to the New. Time after time, God relented of His wrath toward the Israelites, delivering them from self-imposed misery and leading them to freedom and hope.

In the New Testament, Jesus heals the physically and mentally ill, lovingly identifying himself with their suffering through His passion and death ("He took on our infirmities and bore our diseases" [Matthew 8:17; also see Isaiah 53:4]) and extending to them spiritual healing by forgiving their sins. After His ascension into heaven, Jesus continued His ministry of healing through the apostles and through His Church (Acts 9:34; 14:3; James 5:14-15), where it continues to the present day.

The *Catechism* tells us, "The Church believes and confesses that among the seven sacraments there is one especially intended to strengthen those who are being tried by illness, the Anointing of the Sick" (no. 1511). Quoting the Council of Trent, it continues: "This sacred anointing of the sick was instituted by Christ our Lord as a true and proper sacrament of the New Testament. It is alluded to indeed by Mark, but it is recommended to the faithful and promulgated by James the apostle and brother of the Lord."

A priest or bishop administers the Sacrament of the Anointing of the Sick in a group setting or to an individual. It can be celebrated as part of a parish liturgy, in a family home, in a hospital, or on the side of a road. In wartime, the sacrament is celebrated on battlefields and in trenches by chaplains committed to bringing Christ to His people no matter the circumstance. Whenever possible, the Eucharist should always be part of the Anointing of the Sick as *viaticum* — "food for the journey" of passing on to eternal life. The rite of the sacrament consists of an act of repentance followed by the Liturgy of the Word and specific prayers.

The elements of the Sacrament of the Anointing of the Sick includes the priest, the laying on of hands, the epiclesis or prayers proper to the sacrament, and the anointing with the oil blessed by the bishop.

Effects of the Sacrament
The *Catechism* (nos. 1520-1525) outlines the following as the effects of the sacrament:

- A *particular gift of the Holy Spirit* to strengthen the sick person and give him peace and courage. This gift renews faith and trust in God and combats discouragement and anguish. This action of the Holy Spirit is meant to bring healing of soul to the sick person and leave open the possibility of physical healing if it be God's will. This particular gift also includes the forgiveness of sins.
- *Union with the passion of Christ* through which the person's suffering acquires a new meaning and a redemptive value.
- *Ecclesial grace* constituted through the communion of saints, who intercede for the sick person, while the sick person offers his sufferings for the sanctification of the Church and the good of all men.
- *Preparation for the final journey*, which fortifies the end of our earthly life like a solid rampart for the final struggles before entering the Father's house.
- *Viaticum*, reception of the Holy Eucharist, which prepares the sick for their passing from this world to the Father.

The *Catechism* beautifully states that "just as the sacraments of Baptism, Confirmation, and the Eucharist form a unity called 'the sacraments of Christian initiation,' so too it can be said that Penance, the Anointing of the Sick and the Eucharist as viaticum constitute as the end of the Christian life 'the sacraments that prepare for our heavenly homeland' or the sacraments that complete the earthly pilgrimage" (no. 1525).

The Sacraments at the Service of Communion

All seven sacraments of the Church impart grace in specific and unique ways intended for specific and unique purposes. We have already seen how Baptism, Confirmation, and the Eucharist are the sacraments of Christian initiation and lead us in the way of union with God. Penance and the Anointing of the Sick are the sacraments of healing whose grace and purpose are to heal us spiritually and, if it be God's will, physically, as we strive to make progress in our spiritual journey.

The final two sacraments seek the salvation of others as their goal and give us grace to be of service to the people of God. Through this service, we are also purified and made holy. They confer a special mission in the Church and are intended to build up the body of Christ. These sacraments are Holy Orders and Matrimony.

Holy Orders: The Sacrament of Priesthood

Earlier in the chapter, we discussed that the grace of the sacraments flows from Christ himself. He is the source of the ministry in His Church. But in our discussion on the Sacrament of Penance, we saw that Jesus transferred His mission to His apostles on the night of His resurrection. They were now "sent" by Christ to continue the work He had begun. He breathed upon them, and they received the power of the Holy Spirit to accomplish the mission He was entrusting to them.

In a wholly singular way, the apostles became Christ's representatives. They did not speak or act under their own authority, "but by Christ's authority; not as a member of the community, but speaking to it in the name of Christ" (no. 875). The apostles, and subsequently all who succeed them in the mission of the Church as priest, act under the power and authority of Jesus Christ bestowed upon them through the Holy Spirit. Therefore, they speak and act *in persona Christi Capitis* ("in the person of Christ the Head").

The *Catechism* explains the character of service of the priesthood: "Entirely dependent on Christ who gives mission and authority, ministers are truly 'slaves of Christ,' in the image of him who freely took 'the form of a slave' for us" (no. 876).

The ministerial priesthood was first recognized in the Old Testament. Out of the twelve tribes of Israel, the tribe of Levi was set aside by God to provide the ministers of the liturgical service. To signify this special mission, a special rite was used to consecrate them. Their function was to represent the Israelites to God, to act on their behalf by offering gifts and sacrifices for sins (Hebrews 5:1; also see Exodus 29 1-30; Leviticus 8). Though this priesthood had no power to bring about salvation, the Church sees in it a prefiguring of the ordained priesthood, established by Jesus Christ in the New Covenant.

Like the priests of the Old Testament, a special rite conse-crates the man to the service of God. The *Catechism* tells us that the Sacrament of Holy Orders "communicates a 'sacred power' which is none other than that of Christ. The exercise of this au-thority must therefore be measured against the model of Christ, who by love made himself the least and the servant of all" (no. 1551).

There are three degrees of the Sacrament of Holy Orders: the episcopacy, the presbyterate, and the diaconate. Both the episco-pacy and the presbyterate participate in the ministerial priesthood of Christ, while the diaconate is intended to help serve them.

The Rite of the Sacrament

Only a bishop in the line of succession to the apostles can ordain a man to the diaconate or the ministerial priesthood. Be-cause ordination is essential to the life of the Church, the celebra-tion calls for as many of the lay faithful as possible to take part, and it finds its proper place in the Eucharistic liturgy.

The essential rite of the Sacrament of Holy Orders consists in the imposition of the hands by the bishop on the head of the ordinand. The bishop prays to God and asks for the outpouring of the Holy Spirit and the gifts proper to the ministry to which the candidate is being ordained.

The various liturgical traditions in the Church have additional rites that surround the celebration that are common to them. In the Latin Church, for example, the initial rites include the presentation and election of the ordinand, instruction by the bishop, examina-tion of the candidate, and the Litany of the Saints. These attest that the selection of the candidate has been made according to the prac-tice of the Church. The initial rite also prepares for the solemn act of consecration, after which several other rites symbolically express and complete the mystery that has been accomplished. These in-clude anointing with chrism, signifying the special anointing of the Holy Spirit, who makes the ministry fruitful (bishop and priest); giving the Book of Gospels (bishop and deacon, with the former also receiving the ring, the miter, and the crosier); and the presentation of the paten and chalice, "the offering of the holy people," which he (the priest) is called to present to God.

Many prayers accompany the elements of the rite of ordination, many of which show the pastoral office of the bishop — as one who instructs and one who protects. The following two prayers of instruction are beautiful examples of the bishop in his role of shepherd. Upon presenting the Book of Gospels to the newly ordained deacon, the bishop prays:

> Receive the Gospel of Christ, whose herald you now are. Believe what you read. Teach what you believe. Practice what you teach.

And after presenting the newly ordained priest with chalice and paten, as well as the bread and wine to be consecrated, the new priest kneels before the bishop while he prays these words:

> Accept from the holy people of God the gifts to be offered to him. Know what you are doing, and imitate the mystery you celebrate: model your life on the mystery of the Lord's cross.

The Effects of the Sacrament

Like Baptism and Confirmation, Holy Orders places an indelible character on the soul of the priest. This spiritual mark is permanent. (The *Catechism of the Catholic Church* states, "It is true that someone validly ordained can, for grave reasons, be discharged from the obligations and functions linked to ordination, or can be forbidden to exercise them; but he cannot become a layman again in the strict sense, because the character imprinted by ordination is for ever" [no. 1583].)

Because the priest operates *in persona Christi Capitis*, his unworthiness or personal situation does not prevent Christ from acting. St. Augustine states it well:

> As for the proud minister, he is to be ranked with the devil. Christ's gift is not thereby profaned: what flows

through him keeps its purity, and what passes through him remains clear and reaches the fertile earth. . . . The spiritual power of the sacrament is indeed comparable to light: those to be enlightened receive it in its purity, and if it should pass through defiled beings, it is not itself defiled.
— CCC, NO. 1584, QUOTING ST. AUGUSTINE

However, as is the case with all the people of God, the call to the ministerial priesthood is holiness and sanctity of life. The grace of the Sacrament of Holy Orders is to configure the man to Christ "as Priest, Teacher, and Pastor" (CCC, no. 1585). He is called to proclaim the Gospel message, to love with the heart of Jesus Christ, to model the way of sanctification, and to identify himself in the Eucharist with Christ the Priest and Victim.

As the *Catechism* reminds us, the Doctors of the Church felt an urgent and ongoing call to conversion so as to conform their whole lives to Christ Jesus. St. Gregory of Nazianzus, proclaimed:

We must begin by purifying ourselves before purifying others; we must be instructed to be able to instruct, become light to illuminate, draw close to God to bring him close to others, be sanctified to sanctify, lead by the hand and counsel prudently. — CCC, NO. 1589

Without the ministerial priesthood, the Catholic Church is nothing. No priesthood, no Eucharist. No Eucharist, no Church. That is why the priesthood is the top target of the evil one. The devil despises the sacred reality that takes place at the moment of consecration. And he despises the man through whom this sacred reality is made manifest. Therefore, the priesthood needs the continuous and holy prayers of the lay faithful, and the man ordained to Holy Orders needs the prayerful support and encouragement of good friends and good Christians. The following, from Our Sunday Visitor's *Manual of Prayers*, is one prayer that can beg God for the protection necessary for this holy and essential vocation:

Prayer for Priests

Lord Jesus, you have chosen your priests from among us and sent them out to proclaim your word and to act in your name. For so great a gift to your Church, we give you praise and thanksgiving. We ask you to fill them with the fire of your love, that their ministry may reveal your presence in the Church. Since they are earthen vessels, we pray that your power shine through their weakness. In their afflictions, let them never be crushed; in their doubts, never despair; in temptation, never be destroyed; in persecution, never abandoned. Inspire them through prayer to live each day the mystery of your dying and rising. In times of weakness send them your Spirit, and help them to praise your heavenly Father and to pray for poor sinners. By the same Holy Spirit, put your word on their lips and your love in their hearts, to bring good news to the poor and healing to the brokenhearted. And may the gift of Mary, your Mother, to the Disciple whom you loved, be your gift to every priest. Grant that she, who formed you in her human image, may form them in your divine image, by the power of your Spirit, to the glory of God the Father. Amen.

The Sacrament of Matrimony: 'And the Two Shall Become One'

Tuxedos and gowns. Veils and bouquets. Streamers and smiles. Cakes, kisses, waltzes, wishes — all a happy prelude to the days and weeks, months and years, that a husband and wife will spend together. Indeed, the festivities are all part of the wedding celebration. But it is the covenanted union of a man and woman promised before God that provides the real substance for a lifetime together. That is why marriage is a sacrament. In the Latin rite, the celebration of marriage between two Catholic faithful usually takes place during the Holy Mass. The *Catechism of the Catholic Church* explains:

In the Eucharist the memorial of the New Covenant is realized, the New Covenant in which Christ has united himself for ever to the Church, his beloved bride for whom he gave himself up. It is therefore fitting that the spouses should seal their consent to give themselves to each other through the offering of their own lives by uniting it to the offering of Christ for his Church made present in the Eucharistic sacrifice, and by receiving the Eucharist so that, communicating in the same Body and the same Blood of Christ, they may form but "one body" in Christ. — CCC, NO. 1621

'And the Two Shall Become One Flesh'

The closing words of the quote from the *Catechism* give us the spiritual reality of the sacrament. In the Sacrament of Matrimony, a man and a woman are joined together and become one body, one flesh. Speaking to this reality, one commentator, Severus Cataline, has cautioned that "getting married means giving half your soul to your spouse and receiving in return the other's half. If both halves complement each other, what heaven it shall be! But if they do not, what hell shall be suffered! For whereas before we had two complete lives, now we have two broken and shattered halves. Let those in love, therefore, take careful stock of the soul they surrender as well as of the soul surrendered to them."

These words of advice are good ones, indeed. They underscore the spiritual and temporal reality of the marital union, a union that requires surrender and sacrifice, a union intended to bring holiness and purification. For such surrender and sacrifice to occur, a special and unique grace is needed. Such is the sacramental grace specific to Matrimony.

The grace "proper to the sacrament of Matrimony is intended to perfect the couple's love and to strengthen their indissoluble unity" (CCC, no. 1641). Through this grace, they "help each other to attain to holiness in their married life and in the rearing and education of their children" (*Lumen Gentium*, no. 11). It is the grace of Matrimony that strengthens a couple to endure the hardships of life and solidifies the sacredness of their union in pain and suffering. And it is sacramental grace that encourages spouses to share forgiveness, tenderness, patience, and gentility. This should come as no surprise since Christ himself is the source of this grace and dwells with them in their sacrament.

Conjugal Love

The way in which the married couple celebrates the covenant of their matrimony is through their physical union in the marriage bed. This love "involves a totality, in which all the elements of the person enter — appeal of the body and instinct, power of feeling and affectivity, aspiration of the spirit and of will" (CCC, no. 1643). By its very nature, conjugal love requires fidelity, loyalty, faithfulness, and indissolubility. It is a deeply personal union intended to bring about not only unity in flesh, but unity in mind and heart as well. The physical union of husband and wife, edifying in its own right, is but a symbol of the spiritual reality of the marital covenant — "and the two shall become one flesh." It is for this reason that the only proper domain for conjugal love is within the Sacrament of Matrimony. St. Josemaría Escrivá de Balaguer puts it rightly when he states, "Marriage is a sacrament that makes one flesh of two bodies."

Pope John Paul II talks about the spiritual reality of marriage when he compares it to the life of the Trinity. He tells us that the fundamental and innate vocation of every human being is love. In the first chapter ("Strategy One: Believe the Truth About Yourself"), we saw that God is love. And love is an act of total self-donation. This gift of self-donation is perfectly present in the Holy Trinity. Each of the Divine Persons gives himself completely to the others while maintaining His own unique and distinctive Person. In so doing, a complete union or, as our Holy Father so often puts it, a *communion of persons*, is established.

In like fashion, when man and woman come together in marital union, it must be an act of total self-donation — neither party withholding anything from the other — a surrender of body to body — soul to soul — a communion of persons.

This giving of self to the other, springing from a free-will decision, is pure gift. It is through the body that our love for the other is expressed and given, and it is through the body of the other that our love is received and cherished. Thus, the coming together of husband and wife becomes a sign and an image of the love of the Divine Persons of the Trinity.

Openness to Life

As we began to see in the first chapter, the conjugal union of man and wife images the Trinitarian life in yet another way as well. The life of the Trinity is a creative reality. In Genesis, we read that the "love experience" of the divine communion of Persons leads God to create man: "Let us make man in our image, after our likeness" (Genesis 1:26). Scripture then tells us that "in the image of God he created him; male and female he created them" (Genesis 1:27).

The love of the Divine Persons is boundless and is therefore manifested in the creation of man in God's own image and likeness. Though God did not need to create man and woman, He did so to show forth His glory, His love, and His goodness (CCC, nos. 293 and 295).

Notice the very next verse. God then invites the "created" to do likewise: "And God blessed them, and God said to them, 'Be fruitful and multiply, and fill the earth and subdue it' " (Genesis 1:28). God invites man and woman to participate in His most sublime role of Creator, and He calls them to recognize this invitation as "blessing."

Thus, just as the life of the Trinity is a creative reality that births mankind, so, too, is the marital gift of conjugal love a creative action intended by God to bring new life into the world. Marriage is ordered to the procreation of children, and when a couple is so blessed, their offspring are the crowning glory of their marital union:

> Hence, while not making the other purposes of matrimony of less account, the true practice of conjugal love, and the whole meaning of the family life which results from it, have this aim: that the couple be ready with stout hearts to cooperate with the love of the Creator and the Savior, who through them will enlarge and enrich His own family day by day. — GAUDIUM ET SPES, NO. 50

This is the supernatural reality of marriage. And this is why God has elevated it to a sacrament.

The Vocation of Matrimony
However, for people to live the beautiful and supernatural reality of covenanted union is no small task. As our culture becomes more and more pagan in its worldview, more and more egocentric and narcissistic, to live the Sacrament of Matrimony requires heroic virtue. That is why Holy Mother Church calls marriage a vocation.

What is a vocation? A vocation is a loving design of God conceived for every human being from all eternity. It is a path chosen for us by God that leads to sanctity and holiness of life. Writing in his apostolic exhortation on the laity, *Christifideles Laici*, Pope John Paul II tells us that the *prime and fundamental vocation* for the Christian faithful is the vocation to holiness.

With this statement, the Holy Father echoes the words of St. Paul. Recall Ephesians 1:4, which tells us that God chose us in him before the world began to be holy and blameless in his sight, to be full of love. Holiness, blamelessness, love-fullness — these three define the ultimate purpose for every human person. "The call to holiness," the Holy Father continues, "is *rooted in Baptism* and proposed anew in the other Sacraments. . . . [The lay faithful] therefore have the ability to manifest this holiness and the responsibility to bear witness to it in all that they do" (no. 16).

These words of the Holy Father suggest that the call to holiness has both an "interior" and an "exterior" mission. Holiness of life assures our personal sanctification — the interior mission — and this sanctification effects a change in the world around us — its exterior mission. For married couples, the way in which this fundamental vocation is lived out and experienced is through their matrimony. Their life together as man and wife is the path chosen for them by God to lead to sanctity and holiness of life, and the path by which they will effect a change for good in the temporal order.

As such, Matrimony is a vocation. The *Catechism of the Catholic Church* (no. 1601) tells us that the two-pronged mission of the vocation of Matrimony is the procreation and education of children when so blessed (its exterior mission), and the personal enrichment and perfecting of the couple (its interior mission). The Sacrament of Matrimony, rightly lived, becomes a sign of contradiction that challenges the materialism of today's culture and elevates the hearts and minds of pagan society to the things of God.

But, as mentioned before, the Sacrament of Matrimony requires heroic virtue. It requires a persevering attitude of heart that constantly calls husband and wife to the gift of total self-donation, a profound dying to self that places the will of God and the needs of the other above selfish considerations and desires. It requires the melding together of two divergent personalities into a "complementarity" that images the perfect harmony of the Trinitarian life. It requires the hope-filled anticipation of the eternal rather than the consumerist emotionalism of the temporal. It requires a steadfast discipline of body, mind, and spirit that tames unbridled desire for passion, pleasure, and ease. It requires sacrificial love — a decision to love — in spite of poor health, in spite of ill temper, in spite of setbacks, reversals, or problems. It requires openness to life in every coming together in the marital bed. In short, the vocation of Matrimony is not for the fainthearted! For some, the call is too great.

Living the Sacrament of Matrimony

Self-help books abound on bookstore shelves spooning secular wisdom and offering the conventional advice on how to make a marriage sound and healthy. However, only when marriage is perceived through the eyes of God can the couple attain the fullness of life that God desires for them through their covenanted union.

How, then, can married couples cooperate with God's loving design for them? Bishop Fabian Bruskewitz gives husbands and wives five guidelines to encourage them in their vocation. In his book *A Shepherd Speaks*, Bishop Bruskewitz says that these guidelines are the "keys" in marriage that unlock the doors of temporal and eternal happiness:

Key 1: Make a commitment to prayer as a married couple.
Bishop Bruskewitz tells us, "Pastors, who get to see marriages in every state of growth, development, and decay, can attest to the fact that marriages without a strong prayer component are almost certainly doomed to fail."

Some marriages begin on the sure footing of a solid prayer life. Others do not. If your marriage has not, begin a prayer life where you can — with yourself. And then, gradually introduce prayer into the activities of your family life — mealtime always provides a good starting point. Eventually, suggest prayer to your spouse at opportune moments — in thanksgiving for a blessing received; as you face decisions, difficulties, or doubts; or when serious issues arise with the children.

This "daily expression" of prayer should be in addition to regular attendance at Mass and reception of the sacraments. If your spouse does not practice the faith, be sure to invite him/her to join you and the children for Sunday Mass. Many a soul has been led back to God in just this way.

Key 2: Practice "togetherness." Too many couples today live their lives as "married singles." Separate interests, separate activities, and separate vacations ultimately lead to lives separated by unhappiness and divorce. The bishop reminds couples that marriage needs the "presence" of partners.

Search for activities and pursuits that you can enjoy together. Try to develop interest in a spouse's hobby or career. Take time alone as husband and wife — for a "date," a quiet walk, lunch or dinner, or a cup of coffee after the children are in bed. Make Sundays a day set aside for family "togetherness."

Key 3: Rule out hyper-possessiveness. There is a chasm between "togetherness" and "hyper-possessiveness." The former breathes life into a relationship; the latter deals destruction. Bishop Bruskewitz writes, "It is a flawed marriage that smothers every vestige of the 'inner person' or that is hyper-possessive because of a lack of trust or because of a false love that disguises possession, ownership, or manipulation."

He says that couples can validly enjoy varied and divergent interests so long as they are not excessive and do not take priority over the "togetherness" aspect of marriage. Leave room for some privacy while at the same time being ready to give and sacrifice for the other. Many a marriage has failed because of an exclusive or overriding interest in career, sporting activities, social pursuits, friends, or relatives. Likewise, many a marriage has failed because of a neurotic possessiveness rooted in insecurity.

Key 4: Share thoughts and feelings. It is true that women are more communicative than men. Statisticians say that on average women speak 25,000 words a day while men speak a scant 10,000. Even with this disparity, however, healthy marriages develop good communication. Sharing thoughts and feelings is essential to a vibrant marriage.

Conversations and moments of quiet sharing should not only concern the day-to-day activities of running a household but should also include those elements necessary for the building up of the "domestic church" which is the true nature of family life.

Given the "interior" mission of marriage — the personal enrichment and perfecting of the couple — husbands and wives can do much to aid each other in spiritual growth. A kind word, a helpful and loving suggestion, or a charitable admonition can do much to assist sanctity and holiness of life.

Key 5: Respect each other and each other's conscience. Nothing does more to tear at the delicate fiber of marriage than harsh words, bitterness, and lack of forgiveness. Spouses must recognize that God has brought them together to help each other attain salvation. The best means to accomplish this goal is through respect for the person of the other.

Respect is shown in thoughts, words, and deeds. But the battle for it is fought in the heart. Take up arms against holding grudges or plotting paybacks. When difficult words must be spoken, wait until heated emotion has subsided, and then choose to speak with gentleness and love. Performing small acts of charity and being a helpmate whether it is convenient or not are deeds that show respect and communicate love. Spouses must treat each other in a Christlike way, for they are to be Christ to each other.

When husbands and wives follow these five guidelines, not only do they attain temporal and eternal happiness, but they also model for their children the essence of Matrimony, and witness to the world at large what it means to establish a marriage on the firm rock of Christ and His Church.

A Survival Kit for Marriage

Someone once shared a letter with me that suggested accumulating the following items: a toothpick, a rubber band, a Band-Aid, a pencil, an eraser, a stick of chewing gum, and a candy kiss. They are to serve as reminders of what it takes to form good relationships. I see them as "tools" in a "survival kit" for marriage. Perhaps their accompanying Scripture passages might serve as a study guide for the married life:

- **Toothpick** — to remind you to pick out the good qualities in your spouse (Matthew 7:1).
- **Rubber band** — to remind you to be flexible. God will work things out (Romans 8:28).
- **Band-Aid** — to remind you to heal your hurt feelings or your spouse's (Colossians 3:12-14).
- **Pencil** — to remind you to list every day the blessings your spouse brings to you (Ephesians 1:3).
- **Eraser** — to remind you that everyone makes mistakes — including you and your spouse (Genesis 50:15-21).
- **Chewing gum** — to remind you to stick with it (Philippians 4:13).
- **Candy kiss** — to remind you that your spouse needs a hug each day (1 John 4:7).

May all marriages be a reflection of God's love in the world today, as husband and wife seek the will of God in and through their sacrament.

WORKING THE STRATEGY

Make Use of the Sacraments

1. In what specific ways can you use the grace of your confirmation to be a soldier for Jesus Christ in the everyday circumstances of your life? List these ways. In what specific ways can you utilize Confirmation grace to be a soldier for Jesus Christ in the public square? List these ways. Is there anything that would prevent you from following through on these actions? How can you overcome it?

2. To what extent has your own belief in the Real Presence been compromised? What practical steps can you take to re-form your belief?

3. Develop a plan to put the "Ways to Enhance Your Experience of the Eucharist" into effect. What steps can you take immediately?

4. When was the last time you made use of the Sacrament of Penance? Strive to make use of the sacrament on a monthly basis.

5. For the next two weeks, do a daily examination of conscience. Which sin do you repeat most often? How can you begin to overcome that sin through the grace of the sacrament?

6. If you are a priest, in what ways can you cooperate more effectively with the grace you received at your ordination? To answer, consider the following: Does your preaching reflect the whole Gospel and the teachings of the Church? Does it tackle the tough issues — contraception, abortion, promiscuity, false spiritualities, etc? Do you minister according to the spiritual and corporal works of mercy? Which one work of mercy do you most need to work on? To what extent do you prepare yourself before the celebration of the Eucharist? Are you willing to correct and admonish with charity and love?

7. If you are a married person, in what ways can you cooperate more effectively with the grace you received at your matrimony? To answer, consider the following questions: Is your

physical union open to the possibility of new life? Do you place the needs of your spouse and your family above your own wants and desires? In what practical ways do you safeguard your marital covenant through the words you speak, the activities you choose, and the friendships you maintain? What three things can you do to make your marriage a better reflection of Christ's love for His Church? Which of Bishop Bruskewitz's five keys do you most need to implement? Which of the tools in your "survival kit" do you most need to keep on hand?

STRATEGY FOUR

Embrace the Cross

❧

When I was thirteen years old, President John F. Kennedy was assassinated. I remember the day well. Sister Mary Gabriel, my elementary school principal, wheeled a television set into the classroom. We children sat in stunned silence as a reporter's voice told us that the president of the United States had been shot dead by a sniper's bullet.

The events of September 11, 2001, were somewhat like that. They will be forever impressed upon my memory. I was driving on a major highway in our area to an appointment. It was about 8:30 in the morning, and traffic was piled up in front of me. I decided to pray a Hail Mary to ease the tension. I completed my prayer. And then I prayed another Hail Mary, and another one, and another one. I prayed a litany of Hail Marys, thinking it odd that I was praying so many of them for the sake of relieving tension in traffic. The prayers seemed to come of their own accord, one after the other. Deliberate, measured, intense.

And then, I noticed something peculiar. With each Hail Mary, my attention was riveted to the words ". . . pray for us sinners now and at the hour of our death. Amen." Hail Mary after Hail Mary focused my attention on this specific part of the prayer. The words resonated within me. I arrived at my appointment, completed my business, and headed to the offices of Living His Life Abundantly ® International, Inc. It was then I heard the news that a plane had struck the World Trade Center. Shortly thereafter, a second plane struck the second tower. After that, a plane hit the Pentagon. And then another plane crashed in rural Pennsylvania. Only in my time of prayer that evening did I realize that my Hail Marys were being offered as the terrorist attacks were unfolding.

In the Mystical Body, we are one in Christ Jesus. We are no longer Jew or Greek, slave or free, we are one body (1 Corinthians 12:13). And as members of that one body, in some spiritual and mystical way, we are affected by others' joys and sorrows, triumphs and failures, strengths and weaknesses. This unity in the Mystical Body of Christ is no more keenly witnessed than in moments of trial, tribulation, and devastation. In these moments, we sense the needs of the other and enter into his travail. "If one member suffers, all suffer together" (1 Corinthians 12:26). Even when it is not consciously experienced, suffering — the common denominator of the human condition — unites us with an unbreakable bond.

But suffering itself begs us to ask questions: Why do we suffer? Why does God permit suffering to exist? What is suffering's purpose?

SUFFERING'S GRAND ENTRANCE

As universal as suffering is to all men in all generations, so too is the question of why suffering exists and why it is part of the human condition.

Man's introduction to suffering occurs early in his history. In fact, it happens very soon after his creation. The story is found in the third chapter of the Book of Genesis. Here we learn about the origin of suffering, the various sufferings mankind experiences, and the ultimate consequence of suffering — death.

But before looking at this chapter in some detail, it is important to see what man's state was prior to the events of Genesis 3. In Chapters 1 and 2 of Genesis, we discover that man, in the person of Adam, existed in a state of interior and exterior harmony. In the first chapter of this book ("Strategy One: Believe the Truth About Yourself"), we identified this as the "triple harmony." His relationship with God was one of union and trust (Genesis 1:26; 2:18-22); his relationship with creation was one of ease and provision (Genesis 1:29-30); and his relationship with another human being was one of honesty and love (Genesis 2:23; 2:25). Because of man's relationship with God, all aspects of his life were well ordered; and, because all aspects of his life were well ordered, man was at peace within himself.

This harmony of life, however, was interrupted and forever altered in Chapter 3 of Genesis. Here, as you remember, evil entered the world through seduction, deception, temptation, and disobedience. The serpent tempted Eve to eat the fruit from the tree of the knowledge of good and evil, the only tree in the garden from which God had forbidden Adam and Eve to eat. The serpent was cunning in his temptation. First, he broke Eve's trust in God (3:4); then he appealed to her pride (3:5); and, finally, he beguiled her through her senses (3:1-6). Once she had given in to the temptation, Eve gave the fruit to her husband.

Adam's disobedience exacted a heavy price, and a serious penalty was incurred by each of the transgressors. God told the serpent he would be cursed among all creatures, that he would crawl on his belly for all time, and that, in the end, he would know defeat (3: 14-15). Thus, the ultimate consequence for his sin struck at the very heart of his pride.

Next, God addressed Eve. To her He said:

> "I will greatly multiply your pain in childbearing; in pain you shall bring forth children, yet your desire shall be for your husband, and he shall rule over you." — GENESIS 3:16

God's words to Eve are significant. This is the first verse in the Bible to speak of pain. The consequence of Eve's sin introduces the reality of suffering into the life of man. And not only will this suffering be physical, but emotional and spiritual as well. Speaking to this the *Navarre Bible Commentary* states:

> The pain of childbirth also points to the presence of physical pain in mankind, a consequence of sin. Sin is also the cause of disorder in family life, especially between husband and wife: the text expressly instances a husband's despotic behaviour toward his wife. Discrimination against women is here seen as the outcome of sin; it is something, therefore, that the Bible regards as evil. Sin is also the reason why people fail to appreciate the dignity of marriage and the

family — a widespread failing denounced by the Second Vatican Council: "the dignity of these partnerships is not reflected everywhere, but is overshadowed by polygamy, the plague of divorce, so-called free love, and similar blemishes; furthermore, married love is too often dishonoured by self-ishness, hedonism, and unlawful contraceptive practices. Besides, the economic, social, psychological, and civil climate of today has a severely disturbing effect on family life" (*Gaudium et Spes*, 47).

Thus, the effects of Eve's sin strike at the very heart of the feminine vocation — wife and mother — and they thwart her innate desire — to give love and to receive love, to bear children, and to give herself completely for the well-being of her family and husband.

Finally, God spoke to Adam:

"Because you have listened to the voice of your wife, and have eaten of the tree of which I commanded you, 'You shall not eat of it,' cursed is the ground because of you; in toil you shall eat of it all the days of your life; thorns and thistles it shall bring forth to you; and you shall eat the plants of the field. In the sweat of your face you shall eat bread till you return to the ground, for out of it you were taken; you are dust, and to dust you shall return." — Genesis 3:17-19

From these words, Adam discovers that the harmony he has experienced with nature has come to an end. Now, he will labor to make the ground produce the food he needs. He will toil and sweat with no promise of yield. His work will be hard and his efforts burdensome. The ease of provision God intended for man through the goods of the earth has been perverted through Adam's sin.

While this is devastating news for man, God's closing words reveal the ultimate consequence of sin: Man will die. He will return to the ground out of which he has come — "you are dust, and to dust you shall return," says God. Adam discovers that the wages of sin is death (Romans 6:23).

Pain, suffering, disintegration, turmoil, tribulation, trial, the inevitability of death — all are brought about by man's disobedience to God. The happiness for which he was created is destroyed. Man's relationship with God, his union with woman, his experience of creation, his interior peace — all are corrupted. Man's sin, in and of itself, creates evil in all its forms.

This first sin, original sin, has a devastating effect on all mankind. "Revelation gives us the certainty of faith that the whole of human history is marked by the original fault committed by our first parents" (CCC, no. 390, quoting the Council of Trent). St. Paul tells us, "By one man's disobedience many [that is, all men] were made sinners . . . sin came into the world through one man and death through sin, and so death spread to all men because all men sinned" (Romans 5:12, 19).

This reality is soon borne out in Scripture. By the end of Genesis 4, murder and polygamy enter the world. By Genesis 6, evil and wickedness are so rampant that God limits man's lifespan, and determines to destroy the earth with a flood. The depravity of man, caused by sin, brings misery, pain, suffering, and death.

And so, it has been through all time. Man's sin brings war, famine, disease, disorder, family unrest, injury, and malice. Through the annals of history, sin brings damage and destruction, evil and wickedness, devastation and distress. Down to the present day, down to the events that rocked the world on September 11, 2001, sin brings shock and horror.

A COMMUNION OF SIN

Each person who sins cooperates in bringing suffering to the world. Though some sins are more heinous than others, every sin drags down the moral order and contributes to the debasement of all society. Speaking to this, the *Catechism of the Catholic Church* teaches:

> Sin makes men accomplices of one another and causes concupiscence, violence, and injustice to reign among them. Sins give rise to social situations and institutions that are

contrary to the divine goodness. "Structures of sin" are the expression and effect of personal sins. They lead their victims to do evil in their turn. In an analogous sense, they constitute a "social sin." — CCC, NO. 1869

Commenting on this, Pope John Paul II stated in 1984:

> One can speak of a communion of sin, whereby a soul that lowers itself through sin drags down with itself the church and, in some way, the whole world. In other words, there is no sin, not even the most intimate and secret one, the most strictly individual one, that exclusively concerns the person committing it. With greater or lesser violence, with greater or lesser harm, every sin has repercussions on the entire ecclesial body and the whole human family. According to this first meaning of the term, every sin can undoubtedly be considered as social sin. — RECONCILIATIO ET PAENITENTIA, NO. 16

Though sin is a personal act, it reaps a corporate effect. And the corporate effect reaps an evil of greater or lesser degree. Like our mother Eve, every human being is tempted to distrust God, to prideful reliance on self, and to inordinate desire for the things of the world. To the extent that we give in to temptation and sin, it is to that extent we cooperate in the evil one's plans to bring damnation to man.

"So," one might ask, "is man doomed to evil displays, heinous crimes, and fouled-up relationships?" Left to his own devices, yes. But recall the words of John 3:16: "For God so loved the world that he gave his only Son, that whoever believes in him should not perish but have eternal life." God has a solution. God has a plan. It involves His Son, Jesus Christ. And it involves you and me.

WHOSE FAULT IS IT, ANYWAY?

With brutal force, evil explodes into our lives, strips us of a sense of well-being, and leaves us trembling in the wake of its destruction. Shaken, confused, and conflicted, we pick our way through the rubble of shattered dreams, lost ideals, and dashed hopes. Our frayed sensibilities send us groping for an explanation, and our broken hearts cry out for solace.

Such is the universal experience of evil. It robs us of a good that ought to be ours and leaves us suffering in the privation. Whether we experience the loss of good health through illness or disease, the loss of companionship through the death of a loved one, or the loss of security through the terrorist actions of a fundamentalist sect, evil steals what should be ours and gives us anguish instead.

Why does God permit suffering to exist, and what is suffering's purpose? Why does God cause such horrible things to happen? These are the questions people ask when tragedy strikes. They are the questions that batter the mind and wring the heart. They reveal a soul deeply struggling to find meaning and purpose in the midst of pain and travail. How do we respond? The answer, though not simplistic, is emphatic: God does not *cause* evil. This would be opposed to His very nature. He is, as St. John tells us, love. Love, by its very definition, wills only the good. Because evil is the absence of a good, God cannot will it.

The events of September 11, 2001, illustrate the point. Evil deprives us of something that *ought* to be ours. In the case of our national tragedy, the people in the World Trade Centers *ought* to have been safe, and we as a nation *ought* to have been secure. The families who lost a loved one *ought* to have that person to love, and the citizens of every country *ought* to be free from the fear of terrorism. Safety, security, love, and freedom rightly belong to the human person. These are goods that God wills. On September 11, 2001, these goods were wrested from us. What should have been no longer was. Therein lies the evil. And the absence of these goods is the cause of our suffering.

St. Augustine puts it this way: "The only cause of any good that we enjoy is the goodness of God, and . . . the only cause of evil is the falling away from the unchangeable good of a being made good but changeable, first in the case of an angel, and afterward in the case of man."

If God doesn't cause evil to happen, then who does? St. Augustine's quote gives us a hint. The answer to this question is implicit in one of the very goods that God has willed for us — freedom. God has endowed the human person with the gift of free will. This gift, a good in and of itself, can be used rightly or it can be used wrongly. Rightly used, this gift frees man to love God with all his strength and to love his neighbor as himself. Wrongly used, this same gift gives man the ability to commit great atrocities and dastardly deeds. What God intends for good, man can use for evil. As Russell Shaw states in his book *Does Suffering Make Sense*, "The source of evil, in other words, is not God's will but mine — my will and that of my fellow creatures." Evil, and the suffering it perpetrates, is caused by man's abuse of freedom.

Does this mean that man's fate is to experience evil and the subsequent suffering it brings? Or does God have another solution, one that does not violate man's free will but at the same time restores the good that evil steals and mitigates the suffering that man experiences? The answer, of course, is "yes." God does have a solution, and that solution has a name. His name is Jesus Christ.

MAN'S SALVATION

Recall that even as original sin was being committed, God, in His goodness, was making provision for man. In Genesis 3:15, though pained by the transgression committed against His divine love, God promises a solution to the misery of man's condition. He says that the seed of the woman will smite the head of the serpent, thereby bringing salvation and redemption.

The woman to whom God refers is the Blessed Virgin Mary. The seed is Mary's son, Jesus Christ, whose very name reveals His mission and His work. *Christ* means anointed, sacred, consecrated. *Jesus* means Savior. As Dom Columba Marmion, O.S.B. writes in *Christ in His Mysteries*: "The two names therefore complete each other and are henceforward inseparable. 'Christ Jesus' is the Son of God . . . Who, by His sacrifice, is the Saviour of all humanity." Out of the evil and suffering caused by sin, God ordains to bring good. Thus, St. Paul tells the Romans, "We know that in everything God works for good with those who love him, who are called according to his purpose" (8:28). Sin's debris will be the instrument for man's greatest hope.

"How can God 'work together for the good' with the likes of evil and suffering?" we might ask. As Marmion's statement tells us, He will send His Son, Jesus Christ, "Who, by His sacrifice," will save humanity. What stunning evidence of love! God makes ready to rescue man from the consequences of his own sin and disorder through the ultimate display of love — the sacrifice of His own Son! What stunning paradox! God will use the most profound consequence of original sin — suffering and death — as the very means through which man attains eternal life! The Son of God who knew no sin will become sin so that in Him man might become the very holiness of God (2 Corinthians 5:21).

Stunning though it may be, such love and such logic are completely within the perfect goodness of God. The Second Vatican Council tells us this:

> God, who through the Word creates all things (see John 1:3) and keeps them in existence, gives men an enduring witness to Himself in created realities (see Rom. 1:19-20). Planning to make known the way of heavenly salvation, He went further and from the start manifested Himself to our first parents. Then after their fall His promise of redemption aroused in them the hope of being saved (see Gen. 3:15) and from that time on He ceaselessly kept the human race in His care, to give eternal life to those who perseveringly do good in search of salvation (see Rom. 2:6-7). — DEI VERBUM, NO. 3

A SERVANT SENT TO SUFFER

Throughout the Old Testament, God's provision for man through the sacrifice of His own Son is prefigured in numerous places. Abraham's intended sacrifice of his son, Isaac; the tribulations and trials suffered by the good man Job; the exquisite portrayal of the man of sorrows in Isaiah 53 — all point to the coming Messiah, who will bring redemption and salvation to mankind. In each of these illustrations, God uses suffering as an instrument to work great good.

Hidden in them, too, are the manifest ways man suffers. Physical and mental agony, alienation from God and others, desolation and near despair, and sadness and deep sorrow are all depicted in these prefigurements of Christ. An excerpt from Isaiah 53 proves the point well:

> He had no form or comeliness that we should look at him,
>   and no beauty that we should desire him.
> He was despised and rejected by men,
>   a man of sorrows, and acquainted with grief;
> and as one from whom men hide their faces
>   he was despised, and we esteemed him not.
>
> Surely he has borne our griefs and carried our sorrows;
> yet we esteemed him stricken, smitten by God, and afflicted.
> But he was wounded for our transgressions,
>   he was bruised for our iniquities;
> upon him was the chastisement that made us whole,
>   and with his stripes we are healed.
> All we like sheep have gone astray;
>   we have turned every one to his own way
> and the Lord has laid on him the iniquity of us all. . . .
>
> He shall see the fruit of the travail of his soul and be satisfied;
> by his knowledge shall the righteous one, my servant,
>   make many to be accounted righteous. — ISAIAH 53:2-6, 11

Here, the man of sorrows becomes the suffering servant. He takes upon himself the iniquities of all mankind so that we might be made righteous. He bears within his own tortured flesh the punishment we should all endure. His suffering is both substitutive and redemptive — "upon him was the chastisement that made us whole, and with his stripes we are healed," says the prophet.

The suffering servant of Isaiah 53, the man of sorrows whose passion redeems, is Jesus Christ. In His agony, He bore the cross of our predilection. In His suffering, He bore the infirmity of our sin. And, in His dying, He bore the consequence of our transgressions. Ridiculed, mocked, tortured, beaten. Stripped, spat upon, and scourged. Betrayed, pierced, abandoned, forsaken. He bore it all for love of us.

And, through this passion, Jesus assigns a new value to suffering. With His own precious blood, He ennobles it, and invests into it a dignity capable of leading to eternal life. In Him, suffering becomes a holy occupation, a most righteous vocation. Sin, death, alienation, disintegration — all that was lost in the garden is won back. "Death is swallowed up in victory. O death, where is thy victory? O death, where is thy sting. . . . But thanks be to God, who gives us the victory through our Lord Jesus Christ" (1 Corinthians 15:54-56). All evil, all darkness is overcome by the passion and death of Jesus, by His consummate act of love, by His gift of total self-donation.

"Suffering must be borne if it is to be overcome," says Jürgen Moltmann, and overcome it is. Love wins the day, and suffering is the means that expresses it. By investing divine life into the void of evil, God makes suffering a suitable instrument out of which He can work the greatest good — the salvation of mankind. This is suffering's new purpose.

A SHARED REALITY

The passion and death of Jesus Christ show us something else as well. As the words from Isaiah remind us, Jesus bore "*our* griefs and carried *our* sorrows" (53:4; emphasis added). Thus, He suffers with us in the midst of our suffering, travails with us in the midst of our travail, cries with us in the midst of our sorrows. Jesus is Emmanuel — "God with us" — and no evil or suffering is exclusively ours. It belongs to Him as well. He suffers in us and with us, and thus ennobles our suffering, investing it with divine life and making it capable of bringing salvation.

What does this say, then, to you and me? What does it mean for each circumstance that imprints the pain of loss upon our hearts?

How can the suffering we experience be a source of life for others? Let us see what the saints of the Church tell us.

SUFFERING'S NEW VALUE

About suffering, St. Thérèse of Lisieux says:

Yes, I desire them, those heart-thrusts, those pin-pricks that give so much pain. . . . Sacrifice I prefer to all ecstasies: therein lies happiness for me.

And Dom Columba Marmion, O.S.B., writes:

Happy are those souls whom God calls to live only in the nudity of the cross. It becomes for them an inexhaustible source of precious graces.

Mother Teresa of Calcutta says:

Suffering — pain, humiliation, sickness, and failure — is but a kiss of Jesus.

And St. Francis Borgia exclaims:

Those who have not altogether lost their fervor for the spiritual life can find true happiness nowhere but in the cross of Christ. All the pleasures of the world seem to them heavy and wearisome when once they have experienced the sweetness of the Savior's yoke.

St. Sebastian Valfré sums it all up succinctly by saying:

Life without a cross is the heaviest cross of all.

What did these holy men and women know? What secret had been revealed to them about suffering? What possible purpose can pain, travail, trial, and distress have in our lives?

In and of itself, suffering has no value, no meaning, no purpose. To this day, suffering remains the bitter fruit of man's rebellion against God and the constant reminder of his need for a Savior. But as we have discussed, it was through the passion and death of His Son, Jesus Christ, that God redeemed the world. And it was through the passion and death of Jesus Christ that suffering itself was "redeemed." Eternal life flowed through Christ's mortal wounds.

But Christ's passion and death did something more as well. It established a new relationship between God and man. And this new relationship has everything to do with the value of our suffering and pain, our misery and travail. What is this new relationship, and what does it mean? To answer, let us see what St. Paul said to the Galatians. He writes them, "When the time had fully come, God sent forth his Son, born of woman, born under the law, to redeem those who were under the law, *so that we might receive adoption as sons*" (Galatians 4:4-5; emphasis added).

This passage is significant. It tells us that the nature of this new relationship between God and man is one of *sonship*. The passion and death of Jesus Christ forged a relationship of divine "filiation" between God the Father and mankind. We became the "adopted sons" of God, joint heirs with Christ (Romans 8:17), partakers of the divine nature. With Jesus, man could now cry out, "Abba! Father!" (Romans 8:15)! He could receive "every spiritual blessing in the heavenly places" (Ephesians 1:3)! A way had opened up for man, and all man had to do was open his heart and receive this new way, this new relationship, this new grace. Christ himself is, was, and forever will be the "Way," and the means to the "Way" is the Sacrament of Baptism.

A MYSTICAL UNION

In our third chapter ("Strategy Three: Make Use of the Sacraments"), we discovered that the *Catechism of the Catholic Church* tells us that the Sacrament of Baptism is the basis of the Christian life, the gateway to life in the Spirit, and the door that gives access to the other sacraments. But it tells us more as well. It tells us that

Baptism frees us from sin and gives us new birth as "sons of God" (no. 1213). What exactly does this mean?

As we have seen, through Baptism "we become members of Christ." We are "incorporated" into Him and made sharers in His mission. The Holy Spirit, whom we receive in the sacrament, communicates this grace of participation to the believer; and as long as the believer remains in a state of grace, the Holy Spirit dwells within him. Every other sacrament is built upon this foundation and works to this end.

Participation in the divine life through the indwelling presence of the Holy Spirit unites the Christian to Christ in a mysterious union, a "mystical union." "By communicating His Spirit, Christ made His brothers, called together from all nations, mystically the components of His own Body" (*Lumen Gentium*, no. 7). These brothers form His Church, and Jesus, together with them, form a Mystical Body wherein He is the Head. St. Augustine refers to this union of Christ with His members as "the Whole Christ." He writes:

> What is the Church? She is the body of Christ. Join to it the Head, and you have one man: the head and the body make up one man. Who is the Head? He who was born of the Virgin Mary. . . . And what is the body? It is His Spouse, that is, the Church . . . [and] the Father willed that these two, the God Christ and the Church, should be one man.
>
> All men are one man in Christ, and the unity of Christians constitutes but one man.
>
> Let us rejoice and give thanks. Not only are we become Christians, but we are become Christ. My brothers, do you understand the grace of God that is given us? Wonder, rejoice, for we are Christ! If He is the Head, and we are the members, then together we are *the whole man*.
>
> When the Head and the members are despised, then the *Whole Christ* is despised, for the *Whole Christ*, Head and body, is that just man against whom deceitful lips speak.

As St. Augustine states, all baptized believers become members of Christ's Mystical Body, and in so doing they enter into a mystical union with Christ, who takes up residence in them and they in Him. In addition, this union in Christ binds the believers to one another as well. Caryll Houselander, in *This War is the Passion*, writes, "The whole meaning of our Catholic faith is union, union with Christ, and through Him, union with one another. . . . [I]t is not a unity such as one finds in a society or group. . . . It is oneness like the oneness of the various parts of the body."

This has always been the understanding of the Church. From its earliest days, this divine union between Christ and His members, and among His members, has been expressed, proclaimed, and heralded.

Jesus says:

"Abide in me, and I in you. . . . I am the vine, you are the branches. He who abides in me, and I in him, he it is that bears much fruit, for apart from me you can do nothing. If you abide in me, and my words abide in you, ask whatever you will, and it shall be done for you." — JOHN 15:4, 5, 7

And again, when praying to His Father for all believers, He says:

"The glory which thou hast given me I have given to them, that they may be one even as we are one, I in them and thou in me, that they may become perfectly one."

— JOHN 17: 22-23

St. Paul says:

For just as the body is one and has many members, and all the members of the body, though many, are one body, so it is with Christ. For by one Spirit we were all baptized into one body . . . and all were made to drink of one Spirit.

— 1 CORINTHIANS 12:12-13

And again, the apostle teaches:

> We are afflicted in every way, but not crushed . . . always carrying in the body the death of Jesus, so that the life of Jesus may also be manifested in our bodies. — 2 CORINTHIANS 4:8, 10

And finally, Paul exclaims:

> It is no longer I who live, but Christ who lives in me.
> — GALATIANS 2:20

This mystical reality of our union with Christ is not something symbolic, nor is it something vague or uncertain. Rather, it is the rock upon which our faith is built. It is not a truth to be experienced only by saints and scholars but rather a truth to be actualized in the life of every believer. All are called to plumb the depths of true union with Christ. What, then, can we expect to discover?

THE PASCHAL MYSTERY

Our baptism in Christ has profound significance in our lives. Every action we perform, when directed by the Spirit of God and given over to the will of the Father, becomes a conduit of grace. A simple act of kindness becomes an act of charity; a word of consolation becomes a source of hope; a tender look becomes a builder of faith. Such was the case for Jesus; and as members of His body, such is the case for us. Referencing Galatians 3:27, the *Catechism* tells us, "The baptized have 'put on Christ' " (no. 1227). Therefore, it is Christ we are called to radiate — not in an eccentric, exaggerated fashion, but in an authentic, reasoned expression of our mystical union with Him.

But what of the moments of tribulation? What of the moments of trial and the moments of misunderstanding, harsh judgment, rejection, and betrayal? What of the sufferings of life, the tenuous times, trauma, and strife? What are we to make of those moments? Jesus says this to His disciples:

"If any man would come after me, let him deny himself and take up his cross and follow me. For whoever would save his life will lose it, and whoever loses his life for my sake will find it." — MATTHEW 16:24-25

With these words, Our Lord prepares His disciples for a great reality — and in preparing them, He prepares us as well. Our baptism in Christ is also our baptism into the Paschal Mystery. Our baptism is an entry into Christ's passion, Christ's death, and Christ's resurrection. The contradictions of life, the difficulties, the daily stresses, the ordinary and persistent duties, the painful occurrences, the horrors and the injustices — all of these are gateways to the Passion. Jesus tells His disciples:

"If the world hates you, know that it has hated me before it hated you. . . . Remember the word that I said to you, 'A servant is not greater than his master.' If they persecuted me, they will persecute you; if they kept my word, they will keep yours also." — JOHN 15:18, 20

"I have said all this to you to keep you from falling away."
— JOHN 16:1

"I have said this to you, that in me you may have peace. In the world you have tribulation; but be of good cheer, I have overcome the world." — JOHN 16:33

Grasping hold of this reality, St. Paul exclaims to the Philippians:

I want to know Christ and the power of his resurrection and the sharing of his sufferings by becoming like him in his death, if somehow I may attain the resurrection from the dead. — PHILIPPIANS 3:10-11; NRSV

What Paul expresses here is the certain reality that incorporation in Christ leads us into the way of the cross; but when we offer our sufferings to the Father in union with Christ's sufferings, they achieve redemptive value and become the occasion of new life — for ourselves and for others. Russell Shaw states in his book *Does Suffering Make Sense*:

> As members of the Mystical Body, we live with Christ, we suffer with him. . . . Had there been no Jesus, we would still suffer, but our suffering would be as many people still continue to experience it: sterile and meaningless. As it is, Jesus has transformed our lives and, specifically, our suffering by giving us a role with him in the work of redemption.

Every suffering in our lives can become an opportunity to participate in the Paschal Mystery. And, therefore, every suffering holds the promise of transformation in Christ. By offering our suffering in union with Christ's suffering, we participate in His act of redemption. Thus, we become co-redeemers with Christ. Pope John Paul II explains in his apostolic letter on the Christian meaning of human suffering:

> Christ achieved the Redemption completely and to the very limits but at the same time he did not bring it to a close. . . . [I]t seems to be part *of the very essence of Christ's redemptive suffering* that this suffering requires to be unceasingly completed. — *Salvifici Doloris*, no. 24

And this is a cause for great joy. St. Paul writes to the Colossians:

> Now I rejoice in my sufferings for your sake, and in my flesh I complete what is lacking in Christ's afflictions for the sake of his body, that is, the church. — Colossians 1:24

And herein lies the secret that all the great saints knew, a secret revealed to them in the depths of their own sufferings, pains, torments, and trials: that in the midst of the greatest difficulty, we do not suffer alone, but rather Christ suffers with us. And when we unite our suffering to His passion, He suffers in us, and our suffering becomes redemptive. In a mysterious way, as members of His Mystical Body, we participate in the redemptive work, filling up what is "lacking in Christ's afflictions for the sake of his body, that is, the church." And we become a channel of redeeming grace in the world. We, with Him, bring new life to souls.

Caryll Houselander states this reality beautifully in her book *The Risen Christ*:

> [Jesus], in his sacred humanity, could suffer no more; he could not be wounded or die any more; his life had become peace, joy, the absolute power of consummated love; and now by a supreme expression of that love, which completely passes our understanding and our realization, he gives us that life of joy. He gives that joy and peace to be at the very heart of our suffering, to make suffering and joy, for us as it was for him, not two things incompatible with each other, but just one thing, love — and he gives us his own power of consummated love to use for one another, to comfort and heal and restore one another; even, in a mysterious sense that those who have really known sin and sorrow and love will understand, to raise one another from the dead.

Now do we understand a Thérèse of Lisieux, a Dom Columba Marmion, a Mother Teresa of Calcutta, a Francis Borgia, and a Sebastian Valfré. Now do we see the great gift given to us in every contradiction and trial. Now do we see the pearl of great price hidden in the horrid and ugly. Now do we see the shimmering grace veiled by the ordinary and mundane. Writing in his exemplary apostolic letter on suffering, John Paul II states:

> Those who share in Christ's sufferings have before their eyes the Paschal Mystery of the Cross and Resurrection, in which Christ descends, in a first phase, to the ultimate limits of human weakness and impotence: indeed, He dies nailed

to the cross. But if at the same time in this *weakness* there is accomplished His *lifting up*, confirmed by the power of the Resurrection, then this means that the weaknesses of all human sufferings are capable of being infused with the same power of God manifested in Christ's cross. In such a concept, *to suffer* means to become particularly *susceptible*, particularly *open to the workings of the salvific powers of God*, offered to humanity in Christ. . . . For, *whoever suffers in union with Christ* . . . not only receives from Christ that strength already referred to but also "completes" by his suffering "what is lacking in Christ's afflictions." . . . In so far as man becomes a sharer in Christ's sufferings — in any part of the world and at any time in history — to that extent *he in his own way completes* the suffering through which Christ accomplished the Redemption of the world. — *Salvifici Doloris*, nos. 23-24

Now, will we lay hold of this great truth and, like St. Paul and all the other great saints through the ages, embrace the cross with joy, knowing that by so doing we, in Christ, are bringing salvation to others?

UNITING OUR SUFFERINGS TO CHRIST

How then can we unite our sufferings to Christ in practical and everyday ways? The following are some suggestions that might prove beneficial.

Practice Self-Mastery

To participate in the sufferings of Christ through the trials and tribulations we encounter in our lives requires spiritual strength. Just as an athlete prepares for an event by spending weeks and months in a rigorous and disciplined training program, so too do we "train" for the challenges of life by strengthening ourselves spiritually. This requires self-mastery. Each day offers us many ways to grow stronger in our spiritual commitment and resolve. On page 132 are some ways to flex our spiritual muscles in the area of personal discipline:

A Tip for Spiritual
S.U.C.C.E.S.S.

Uniformity to God's Will

*A*s the Blessed Virgin Mary so perfectly demonstrates, great things happen when we surrender to the will of God. But short of sending us an angel, how does God communicate His will for us? God's will is manifested in two ways: through His "signified will" and His "will of good pleasure."

God's signified will tells us what we must and must not do. It is made known to us through Sacred Scripture, the Ten Commandments, the teachings of the Catholic Church, and the inspirations of grace we receive. We "do" God's will when we work with grace to bring our will into uniformity with the moral norms God prescribes. A daily examination of conscience according to the laws of God and His Church helps us gauge how nearly we conform to His signified will.

While God's signified will is made known to us explicitly, God's will of good pleasure is manifested to us implicitly through the providential events of our lives. Because God is all-knowing, nothing occurs without His knowledge. Because God is all-powerful, nothing occurs without His permission. Because God is all-loving, nothing occurs that is not intended for our ultimate good. Therefore, even the most difficult moment is permitted by God for our sanctification and eternal benefit.

This can be hard to accept in the midst of a trial. But through trust and hope in God, even the worst event can be

continued on next page . . .

... continued from page 131

a source of grace. Our goal should be to use God's grace to "submit" to His will of good pleasure in all things. Perhaps the trial we are experiencing today will be our greatest blessing tomorrow. Isn't this what Our Lady knew as she stood at the foot of the cross?

- Make use of the sacraments and wage a holy war against personal sin and weakness.
- Strive to overcome bad habits with which we have grown comfortable — tardiness, poor health habits, complacency toward obligations, complaining, idle conversation, inattention to necessary details, etc.
- Attend to duties and responsibilities with greater diligence and consideration.
- Give up licit pleasures for a period of time. Examples would include television, favorite foods, desserts, and alcoholic beverages.
- Practice mortifications in conformity with your state in life. Rise an hour earlier, do another family member's chores for a day, take a cold shower instead of a hot one, or eat a food that you don't like for dinner.

Visit the Sick

Many people avoid this corporal work of mercy. It often strikes too much at the heart of our own mortality. We find ourselves uncomfortable, ill at ease, and troubled by the experience. However, hospital chaplains attest that such an act of mercy not only brings comfort to the one who is suffering, but it brings them abundant blessings as well. As John Paul II reminds us in *Salvifici Doloris*:

> *In suffering there is concealed a particular power that draws a person interiorly close to Christ*, a special grace. . . . When this body is gravely ill, totally incapacitated, and the person is almost incapable of living and acting, all the more do interior *maturity and spiritual greatness* become evident, constituting a touching lesson to those who are healthy and normal.
> — SALVIFICI DOLORIS, NO. 26

It is often in suffering that deep interior conversion takes place, and this conversion becomes both a source of divine life for the suffering one as well as for the others who witness it.

Yet another reason to visit the sick is to place ourselves in solidarity with them. As we have learned, through Christ Jesus we are one body (1 Corinthians 12:12). When one member suffers, all suffer with him (1 Corinthians 12:26). Visiting an ill person can do much to relieve his sorrow and his travail, his misery and suffering. Just being present to him can bring comfort and solace, hope, and consolation. The parable of the Good Samaritan gives us insight. Pope John Paul II tells us:

> A Good Samaritan is *one who brings help in suffering*, whatever its nature may be. . . . He puts his whole heart into it, nor does he spare material means. We can say that he gives himself, his very "I," opening this "I" to the other person. Here we touch upon one of the keypoints of all Christian anthropology. Man cannot "fully find himself except through a sincere gift of himself" (*Gaudium et Spes*, 24). A Good Samaritan is *the person capable of* exactly *such a gift of self*. — SALVIFICI DOLORIS, NO. 28

Visiting the sick, with the heart of a "Samaritan," encourages us to see suffering through the lens of our Catholic faith.

'Reframe' Our Notion of Suffering

Hopefully, this chapter is helping you to do that. We must look at suffering as a grace-filled opportunity for ourselves and for others when we offer it in conjunction with the passion of Jesus Christ. It is a door through which new graces can be added to our lives and the lives of others. This can be difficult to remember when pain consumes our body or when swords pierce our heart. However, in those moments we can remember the great value our suffering can have when we surrender it to God. Offering up a particular sorrow in union with Christ for the needs of a specific person or for the needs of the whole world can become a source of transforming grace and peace.

Meditate on the Passion of Christ

Prayerful meditation on the sufferings of Christ is one of the greatest spiritual exercises. Through it, we come to a deeper appreciation of the cost of our redemption and to a deeper and more consistent love of the Person whose blood bought it for us. This love becomes a fire of desire that fills us with zeal to unite all of our sufferings to the cross of Jesus Christ so that they can become a conduit of redemptive grace in the lives of others.

The rich tradition of our Catholic Church gives us many ways to meditate on the passion and death of Our Lord. The Stations of the Cross, the Sorrowful Mysteries of the Rosary, the stained-glass windows in our churches, the crucifix, and the Gospel accounts in Sacred Scripture all help us to nail our trials, tribulations, sufferings, and contradictions to the life-giving cross of Jesus.

Praise God in the Midst of Our Adversities

When we praise God in the midst of our sufferings — even thanking Him for giving them to us so that we might join ourselves to the sufferings of His Son, Jesus Christ — great spiritual strength and graces are given to us. In my book *Full of Grace: Women and the Abundant Life*, I outline four reasons to praise God in the midst of our adversities.

First, Psalm 22:3 tells us that God inhabits the praises of His people. Through praise, God comes to us and through His Holy Spirit, He brings us the comfort we need. We find that, indeed, His grace is sufficient for us (2 Corinthians12:9), and that nothing can separate us from the love of God — not tribulation, not distress, not persecution nor famine, not nakedness, not peril, not even the sword. In all these things "we are more than conquerors" through the love of Him who saved us (Romans 8:35, 37).

Second, praise takes our attention off our trials and focuses it on the love and mercy of God. We find that through His presence in us, we can face the next minute, hour, day, or week. The enormity of His love encompasses us and gives us the certitude that He will never abandon us or forsake us. Our problem becomes a portal through which we can experience grace in abundance.

Third, as St. Augustine reminds us:

> Our pilgrimage on earth cannot be exempt from trial. We progress by means of trial. No one knows himself except through trial or receives a crown except after the victory, or strives except against an enemy or temptation.

Our suffering becomes an opportunity for great spiritual progress when accepted and united to the cross of Christ.

Fourth, suffering forces us to look at ourselves as we truly are. Faults, weaknesses, frailties, and sinful ways all stand out starkly against the tableau of suffering. A sacrifice of praise in thanksgiving for seeing the truth of ourselves is an appropriate response. Can we praise God for the insights we have received? Can we ask Him for the courage to practice virtue instead of vice? Can we beg Him to give us the strength we need to turn this suffering or trial into a springboard of growth and development? Can we seek His wisdom to provide us with greater trust and love?

In closing this chapter on embracing the cross, perhaps the best words are the words of Pope John Paul II:

> Suffering is certainly part of the mystery of man. Perhaps suffering is not wrapped up as much as man is by this mystery, which is an especially impenetrable one. The Second Vatican Council expressed this truth that ". . . only in the mystery of the Incarnate Word does the mystery of man

take on light. In fact. . . , Christ, the final Adam, by the revelation of the mystery of the Father and his love, *fully reveals man to himself* and makes his supreme calling clear"(*Gaudium et Spes*, 22). If these words refer to everything that concerns the mystery of man, then they certainly refer in a very special way to human suffering. Precisely at this point the "revealing of man to himself and making his supreme vocation clear" is particularly *indispensable*. It also happens — as experience proves — that this can be particularly *dramatic*. But when it is completely accomplished and becomes the light of human life, it is particularly *blessed*. "Through Christ and in Christ, the riddles of sorrow and death grow meaningful" (Ibid.). — *SALVIFICI DOLORIS*, NO. 31

WORKING THE STRATEGY

Embrace the Cross

Our human condition guarantees that suffering will visit us throughout our life in many and varied ways. Meditating on the passion of Our Lord helps to prepare us for those times. Read St. Mark's account of the Passion (14:32-72; 15:1-41). Make a list of the words that describe Jesus' emotional, psychological, and physical suffering. Then answer the following:

1. What current trial or tribulation are you experiencing now? What is at the root of your concern? How do you see this same pain or suffering in the Gospel account?
2. What past personal suffering can you see reflected in the passion of Jesus? How did God bring you through that trial? What does this tell you about His concern for you in this present difficulty? Are you willing to trust Him yet again?
3. In Romans 8, St. Paul tells us that God works all things to the good. List three past sufferings. What good did God work

through them? If the good is difficult to see, ask for the illumination of the Holy Spirit to show you.

4. In light of the section "Uniting Our Sufferings to Christ," how can you attach your suffering to the passion of Jesus in practical ways? How can you use your suffering to be a conduit of grace in the lives of others? Are you willing to begin now? Why or why not?

STRATEGY FIVE

Hope in God

❧

Charles Dickens began his literary classic A *Tale of Two Cities* with the memorable line, "It was the best of times, it was the worst of times." How aptly this line applies to those moments of travail we experience in our lives. On the one hand, the difficulty of the moment or the pain of our situation holds us in a vice-like grip. With unrelenting fury, it rips at us and threatens to tear us asunder. However, at the same time, hidden within this terrible trial, we have received a "pearl of great price." Our suffering is laden with grace that can be released if we embrace this cross and unite our suffering to the passion of Christ.

Easy to say, but not so easy to do. When pain racks our body or grief fills our heart, all seems dark and gray. What do we do in such moments? How do we get through such difficult times? What enables us to mine the treasure of grace that awaits us? How do we keep from being overwhelmed by the moment?

HOPE: THE VIRTUE OF PERILOUS TIMES

A spiritual writer once wrote that there is no courage without fear. G. K. Chesterton, the great Catholic journalist and philosopher, made a similar remark about hope: There is no hope without uncertainty. He wrote:

> As long as matters are really hopeful, hope is a mere flattery or platitude; it is only when everything is hopeless that hope begins to be a strength at all. Like all the Christian virtues, it is as unreasonable as it is indispensable.

Perilous times, difficult circumstances, tenuous situations, and heartrending trials form the crucible in which hope is tested, refined, purified, and proven. When everything natural tells us to give up and give in, hope springs from the eternal and tells us to hang in and hang on.

What is the "stuff" of this hope? How can we attain it? From whence does it come? Chesterton gives us the answers as he points out the difference between the hope of "mere flattery or platitude" and Christian hope.

The hope of flattery and platitude is the hope of natural optimism. Such hope comes with a smile on the face and a wink of the eye. It is the hope expressed when victory is close at hand — like the hope of the football coach whose team is leading 37 to 3 at halftime, or the hope of the salesman who is making a presentation to his father-in-law. In these cases, hope is merely a veneer, for the desired result is almost certain and assured.

The hope that is Christian virtue, however, is quite another matter. It is forged in the face of almost certain defeat, and it runs long and deep in the Christian soul. This hope fills us with strength in our weakest moment, steels our nerves in the direst strait, and tempers our fear in the face of death. This hope buoys up a drooping spirit, inflates a flagging heart, and lifts up an overwhelmed soul.

Christian hope finds its source not in our abilities or capacities, nor in our gifts or talents. It is not reliant on the likelihood of success, nor does it depend on "best-case scenarios." Rather, Christian hope is a grace that emanates from our baptism and the life of God dwelling within us. It strengthens our will to withstand the tempests of life and to see in them the will and purposes of God. It gives us the confident assurance of God's presence and inspires us to wait for "things not seen" (Hebrews 11:1). Ultimately, Christian hope leads us to God, for it springs from Him and has Him as its end. That is why, in all of our lives, God will permit many opportunities to practice Christian hope. It is the "stuff" of saints.

GROWING IN HOPE

Spiritual writers define "virtue" as a good habit. This definition implies that, though the seeds of virtue are sown in the Christian soul through Baptism, they must be acted upon in order to come to full maturity. Growing in virtue, then, is not passive. If the virtue is to become a permanent disposition of the soul, it requires an active, engaged response whenever the opportunity presents itself. A comment made to me years ago by a Protestant friend illustrates the point. "Never pray for patience," she told me, "God will give you tribulation." Her point was well taken. How can we learn patience unless we have many situations in which to practice it?

St. Paul tells the Romans something similar about hope. It is acquired by enduring affliction with faith and confidence in God:

> We rejoice in our sufferings, knowing that suffering produces endurance, and endurance produces character, and character produces hope, and hope does not disappoint us, because God's love has been poured into our hearts through the Holy Spirit which has been given to us. — ROMANS 5:3-5

It was Christian hope, for example, that fortified and strengthened the early Christians to preach Jesus Christ in the face of persecution and martyrdom. It was Christian hope that inspired early missionaries to travel uncharted seas and terrain with evangelistic zeal. It is Christian hope that has fueled compassionate hearts to tend the world's sick, to feed the world's poor, and to minister to the world's imprisoned. It is Christian hope that has compelled holy men and women to console the brokenhearted, to counsel the distressed, and to advise the confused.

It is Christian hope that inspired Mother Teresa to lift the diseased and dying out of gutters, Mother Angelica to found an international television and radio apostolate, and Pope John Paul II to stand firm in Catholic teaching despite opposition from within and without the Church. And it is Christian hope that keeps us anchored in the heart of God when the winds of doubt, disappointment, hurt, and shame whirl about us, threatening to knock us off course.

DESPAIR: HOPE'S GREAT ENEMY

In Dante's *Inferno*, the entrance to hell is inscribed with the words, "All hope abandon, ye who enter here." These words are chilling. Hell is a hope-less place, a place of ultimate and eternal despair.

The *Catechism of the Catholic Church* says this about despair:

> By *despair*, man ceases to hope for his personal salvation from God, for help in attaining it or for the forgiveness of his sins. Despair is contrary to God's goodness, to his justice — for the Lord is faithful to his promises — and to his mercy.
> — CCC, NO. 2091

Scripture gives us the classic example of despair. After Jesus is condemned to death, Judas attempts to right his wrong. He goes to the chief priests and tries to return the thirty pieces of silver they gave him for handing Jesus over to them. But the chief priests would not take the money back. Judas throws the money into the Temple and goes off and hangs himself.

Judas lost hope. He despaired. Had he but asked for mercy, had he but repented of his sin, he would have found hope and healing and new life. However, he may well have found hell instead.

In the midst of life's sufferings, in moments of trauma and pain, in the heart of confusion and doubt, despair seeks to rob us of hope. It seeks to convince us that God has abandoned us; that our sin is too great; that nothing could ever change; and that the problems we face personally or corporately can never be solved. It is precisely then that we must exercise Christian hope. It is then that we must lean into the struggle and find God's provision hidden there. It is then that we must hang in and hang on, for God is faithful to His promises, and He will rescue us. St. Paul tells the Corinthians:

> No testing has overtaken you that is not common to everyone. God is faithful, and he will not let you be tested beyond your strength, but with the testing he will also provide the way out so that you may be able to endure it.
> — 1 CORINTHIANS 10:13

Our faith, our confidence, and our hope must be placed in God. How, then, do we practically apply this in the face of challenge? "Hope" itself provides us with an acronym that reveals the answer.

H.O.P.E. FOR THE JOURNEY

HOLD on to the Truths of the Faith

If we are going to make it through the difficulties of life with Christian hope, we must know the faith we have received. Paul writes to the Romans, "For whatever was written in former days was written for our instruction, that by steadfastness and by the encouragement of the scriptures we might have hope" (Romans 15:4); and he exhorts Timothy, "Follow the pattern of the sound words which you have heard from me, in the faith and love which are in Christ Jesus; guard the truth that has been entrusted to you by the Holy Spirit who dwells within us" (2 Timothy 1:13-14).

Our source for knowing the faith is Sacred Scripture and the teachings of the Catholic Church. The Bible and the *Catechism* should play a preeminent role in our time of study and prayer. Reciting Scripture passages, referencing the *Catechism* for clarification and insight, and standing on the promises of God all help us to hold on to hope in the face of uncertainty. In addition, reading biographies of the saints often gives us guidance and direction as we observe their response to the difficulties and trials they faced in their journey of faith. How often their witness inspires and encourages us!

OWN the Challenge

Escapists run from the challenges of life. Optimists paint them with a rosy hue. Pragmatists analyze them according to the cold calculations of cause and effect. And fatalists give in to discouragement and despair. For the Christian, however, challenges are not to be feared, denied, explained away, or given in to. For the Christian, challenges are to be faced with clear-sightedness and supernatural hope.

A Tip for Spiritual
S.U.**C**.C.E.S.S.

Constancy

Coming to know God's will as it is presented to us through His signified will and His will of good pleasure is one thing. Following His will, day in and day out, is quite another matter. But this is precisely what leads us to experience grace in abundance.

For this kind of "spiritual stamina," the virtue of constancy is needed. Father Adolphe Tanquerey, in his book *The Spiritual Life*, says that constancy "consists in struggling and suffering to the end, without yielding to weariness, discouragement, or indolence." How, then, do we grow in this virtue? Elisabeth Leseur tells us. Writing in her diary, she said:

> In barren times, when duty seems difficult and the daily task has no charm, when all spiritual consolation is refused us, and the beautiful light that gilds life is veiled, then humble prayer alone can uphold us and give us hour by hour and day by day the will to act "against our will."

Prayer is the answer. Prayer not only gets us through our time of spiritual travail, but it also helps us act in accordance with the will of God even when we are tempted to "throw in the towel." Prayer helps us to "hang in there," to trust that God is with us, and to place our confidence in

continued on next page ...

... continued from page 143

Him. Prayer is what the Blessed Virgin Mary did when she faced the contradictions of her life as mother of the Messiah. St. Luke tells us that she "kept all these things in her heart" (3:51). It was there that Our Lady found the grace and consolation she needed. In our "barren" times, we need to pray more, not less. Grace in abundance will be our reward.

In the Book of Sirach, we find good instruction on how to own the challenge:

> My son, if you come forward to serve the Lord,
> prepare yourself for temptation.
> Set your heart right and be steadfast,
>   and do not be hasty in time of calamity.
> Cleave to him and do not depart,
>   that you may be honored at the end of your life.
> Accept whatever is brought upon you,
>   and in changes that humble you be patient.
> For gold is tested in the fire,
>   and acceptable men in the furnace of humiliation.
> Trust in him, and he will help you;
>   make your ways straight, and hope in him. — SIRACH 2:1-6

And the psalmist tells us, "Be strong, and let your heart take courage, all you who wait for the LORD" (Psalm 31:24).

"Owning the challenge" means we admit it exists; we engage in the battle; we rely on God's strength rather than our own; we use all of the tools given to us to make wise and prudent decisions; and we move forward in faith and confidence that God is in charge.

PERSEVERE in Patience

Hope often comes easily at the beginning of a struggle, but when the difficulty persists we can grow weary and tired. Fatigued by the battle, our defenses weaken, and we leave ourselves open to discouragement and despair. We begin to think that God does not see our need, or that surely He has abandoned us. With such thoughts rattling our brain, our already depleted resources fade even more quickly. In these moments, it is more important than ever to invest ourselves in Christian hope.

St. Paul writes to the Hebrews, "We desire each one of you to show the same earnestness in realizing the full assurance of hope until the end, so that you may not be sluggish, but imitators of those who through faith and patience inherit the promises" (Hebrews 6: 11-12). And he tells the Romans, "Hope that is seen is not hope. For who hopes for what he sees? But if we hope for what we do not see, we wait for it with patience" (Romans 8:24-25). And to the Corinthians, "For this slight momentary affliction is preparing for us an eternal weight of glory beyond all comparison, because we look not to the things that are seen but to the things that are unseen; for the things that are seen are transient, but the things that are unseen are eternal" (2 Corinthians 4:17-18).

Passages such as these, especially when taken to prayer, can restore Christian hope to the beleaguered heart. And they remind us of something else as well: We are "pilgrims on the way." Our final destiny is not this life, but the life hereafter. Our trials and difficulties, when surrendered to God and confronted with Christian hope, can help us to attain the "eternal weight of glory." Knowing this truth can help us float atop the very waves that seek to overwhelm us.

EXPECT God to Intervene

In Jeremiah 29:11, we find a verse spectacular in its promise and in its hope: "For I know the plans I have for you, says the LORD, plans for welfare and not for evil, to give you a future and a hope."

Our God is not the God of the Deist, who created the universe, wound it up like a clock, and then left it to itself. No, the

Christian God, the God of the Bible, the God whose Son, Jesus Christ, founded the Catholic Church, is intimately involved in the history and destiny of the world.

But not only that, our God is intimately involved and lovingly concerned with each person who lives in that world, for He has made all men in His image and in His likeness — and His ultimate desire is that each one spends all eternity with Him in heaven. In this, we can place our hope, our faith, and our confidence.

St. Paul tells the Corinthians, "On him we have set our hope that he will deliver us again" (2 Corinthians 1:10b). God will intervene. He will come to our aid. He does have a plan. And His plan is devised for our welfare. This calls us to prayerfully consider each of the circumstances in our life. It calls us to prayerfully reflect on the challenges we are facing, the difficulties that are presenting themselves, the trials that are bearing down upon us, and to ask this question: Where is God in this situation, and what is He saying to us? We know that He is involved — Scripture has just told us that. So what are His will and His purpose in the midst of this event?

That is the question we need to contemplate. Whether the trial is a personal struggle, a challenge being faced by the institutional Church, or an event that is political in nature, this is the question we need to take to prayer. And when we do, not only can we expect God to intervene, but we will see that He has already begun His intervention! With H.O.P.E., we can experience grace in abundance no matter the trial or circumstance.

WORKING THE STRATEGY

Hope in God

1. St. John Chrysostom wrote, "Trees that grow in shady and sheltered places, while externally they develop with a healthy appearance, become soft and yielding, and they are easily dam-

aged by anything at all; whereas trees that grow on the tops of very high mountains, buffeted by strong winds and constantly exposed to all types of weather, agitated by storms and frequently covered by snow, become stronger than iron." What benefit of suffering does this passage reveal? How have you seen this to be true in your own life? How can it give you hope in your current struggle or trial?

2. List three past trials that you have endured. Next to each, write a sentence describing the most difficult part of each situation. How did God provide for that particular suffering? What does this suggest to you about a current problem you are facing? What does it tell you about all future situations?

3. How does Christian hope differ from optimism? How does it differ from escapism? Are you prone to confuse hope with either of these? Have you done so in the past? How can you correct your understanding?

4. How does keeping our final end in sight give us hope in the midst of life's sufferings? How does this perspective differ from fatalism?

5. In what practical ways can you be a source of hope to others who may be suffering? Make it a point to follow through with a strategy.

Part Two

OUR RELATIONSHIP WITH OTHERS

STRATEGY SIX

Live a Life of Justice

⌁

The first four chapters have given us insight into our relationship with God. We have discovered that our fundamental vocation is to be holy and blameless in His sight — to be full of love. We have seen that prayer and the sacraments are the essential means by which this transformation takes place. And we have seen how even the sufferings and contradictions of life are tools in the hand of God to lead us in the way of perfection and sanctity.

But our relationship with God and our incorporation into Christ is not meant for ourselves alone. We are called to be a reflection of God's love in the world, a reflection so filled with the presence of Christ that lives are changed, hearts are healed, souls are saved, and the culture is transformed. For this to take place, we have to become "authentically" Christian, "authentically" Catholic. A profound unity must exist between our spiritual life and our everyday life. Our relationships, decisions, political choices, thoughts, words, and deeds must reflect the presence of Christ in us.

Pope John Paul II has written about this unity of life in his apostolic exhortation on the laity, *Christifideles Laici*:

> In discovering and living their proper vocation and mission, the lay faithful must be formed according to the *union* which exists from their being *members of the Church and citizens of human society*. There cannot be two parallel lives in their existence: on the one hand, the so-called "spiritual" life, with its values and demands; and on the other, the so-called "secular" life, that is, life in a family, at work, in social relationships, in the responsibilities of public life and in culture. The branch, engrafted to the vine which is Christ, bears its fruit in every sphere of existence and activity. In fact, every

area of the lay faithful's lives, as different as they are, enters into the plan of God, who desires that these very areas be the "places in time" where the love of Christ is revealed and realized for both the glory of the Father and service of others. Every activity, every situation, every precise responsibility — as, for example, skill and solidarity in work, love and dedication in the family and the education of children, service to society and public life and the promotion of truth in the area of culture — are the occasions ordained by Providence for a "continuous exercise of faith, hope and charity" (*Apostolicam Actuositatem*, 4). — CHRISTIFIDELES LAICI, NO. 59

St. Josemaría Escrivá de Balaguer puts it simply when he says, "We Christians cannot resign ourselves to leading a double life — our life must be a strong and simple unity into which all our actions converge."

As Pope John Paul II instructs us and as St. Josemaría Escrivá reminds us, such authenticity of life, such unity, and such integration of the spiritual and the temporal are the call of every baptized Christian. We are to make a mark on the culture of the day through the witness of our very lives. For this to happen, we must look at the world and look at one another through the eyes of God. When we do, we will discover that the virtue of justice must be at the heart of every thought, every word, and every deed. In this chapter, we will look at this virtue, and hopefully grow in a deeper understanding of it even as we seek to live justice in the practical circumstances of our everyday lives.

WHAT IS JUSTICE?

To begin our discussion on justice, I'd like to share an excerpt from Peggy Eastman's book *Godly Glimpses: Discoveries of the Love that Heals*. It provides us with food for thought:

Please Don't Touch

Walking toward Capitol Hill from Union Station in the warming air of a sunny pre-springtime day, I stopped in a little park not far from two massive U.S. Senate buildings to notice the daffodils poking their heads up for some sunshine. I'll just pause awhile before the Senate hearing, I thought, heading for the park bench I saw just ahead. But — something was different about this park bench. I stood looking at it, my mouth open in astonishment.

The park bench was wooden and had black wrought-iron arms on both ends like others I'd seen, but this one also had two extra black wrought-iron arms on the central part of the bench itself, so that three people could sit there separated from one another by the partitions of the extra arms. Three people could sit there and look straight ahead, not at one another, and never touch elbows. I had never seen a park bench like this one before. There was something forbidding, and punitive about it. The signal this bench sent was unmistakable: Please don't touch. If I sit down next to you, look straight ahead, and pretend you don't see me; I'll do the same, and we can pretend we don't even know the other one is there.

Who had deemed such partitions necessary? What was their real message? That strangers must never, ever brush up against one another, not even so much as the cloth of their jacketed arms? That a homeless person who bathed infrequently might want to sit next to a freshly showered legislative staff person and thus had to be kept within the confines of his own seat? That human beings must have their own space to maintain their privacy, especially in public places?

Is it really possible to partition our lives, as someone had partitioned these park benches? Can we partition our affections, our concerns for others? Are some people more worthy of sitting next to than others? Isn't the Christian message about getting rid of partitions, wherever we find them? For, as Paul tells us, we are neither Jew nor Greek, but sisters and brothers in Christ. We do not need partitions on park benches, and we do not need them in our hearts. Jesus, the revolutionary for love, spent His short life breaking barriers down, barriers between the poor and the wealthy, the sinner and the scribe, the sick and the well. Shouldn't we try to do the same?

The author's walk in the park on a sunny spring day turned her thoughts from pretty daffodils to a deep truth — justice is a profoundly Christian affair. It is that moral and supernatural virtue that inclines the will to render unto God and unto neighbor that which is strictly their due (see Father Adolphe Tanquerey's *The Spiritual Life*, no. 1037; also see CCC, no. 1807). In its essence, justice belongs to a Christian worldview — one that admits God as the source of all goodness and righteousness. And one that admits that man, made in His image and likeness, is entrusted to act in accordance with that goodness and righteousness. When he does, beauty, truth, and life prevail. When he does not, horror, alienation, and death take over.

In the Christian scheme of things, man is the summit of creation. He is "the only creature on earth that God has willed for its own sake." From his conception, man is destined for eternal beatitude (CCC, no. 1703). He is not the product of a random act of nature, as materialists are wont to say, but rather the result of God's deliberate and freewill selection. His worth is not determined by class, or property, or fortune, as the consumerist mentality would seek to convince, but by the privilege of life given to him by a loving Creator. And his dignity is measured not by his size or appearance, his carriage or his bearing, or by his color, race, or creed, but by the divine image present within him. Made in the image and likeness of his Creator, man is called to participate in his Creator's divine nature and in his Creator's virtues and attributes. One attribute of his Creator is justice (Deuteronomy 32:4). And so, as God is just, man is called to be just, to be like Him.

HOW IS A VIRTUE ACQUIRED?

As the wrought-iron partitions on the bench in the park so poignantly illustrate, the way of man bends toward injustice, toward an exclusivity that makes selections and judgments based on external conditions rather than interior truths. This is the lingering effect of original sin and of the personal sin that follows in its wake. And, like the author's horror at its depiction, we are appalled by its consequences.

However, as alarming as injustice is, the virtue of justice does not come easily to man. It must be desired before it can be acquired. Justice must reside in the will before it can become infused in the soul. Such is the case with all moral virtue: The desire for the virtue, strengthened through intellectual assent, sparks the will or the resolve of the individual to bring all areas of his life into conformity with the virtue he hopes to acquire. And through subjugating his thoughts, words, deeds, and sufferings to that virtue, the virtue comes to inhabit the soul.

The virtue of patience provides us with a good example. Not only is it a virtue we all need to acquire for its own sake, but it is also a necessary companion to the virtue of justice. First, we must desire patience. Perhaps our last irritable moment, outburst, temper tantrum, or argument has convinced us that we are sorely in need of this holy virtue. Through the prism of the unhappy incident, we gain insight into a remarkable aspect of our fallen condition — that in certain situations we are an impatient boor. Clarity has come with regard to our weakness and failing, and we now *desire* to change — to become, with God's help, a patient, loving person.

This is good, but desire alone does not bring us the virtue. Now, we must give it our *intellectual assent*. We must *make a decision* to follow through with the desire. Since we have noticed that our impatient incidents are disruptive to all parties concerned — including us — and since we know that this same impatience is an affront to God, to our loved ones, and to our neighbor, we are motivated to move forward. We *decide* to change. With this decision, real progress is made: We have now set out on the path of "virtue acquisition."

But we are still only at the beginning. Our goal of patience still looms in the distance. Desire, intellectual assent, and decision

— necessary as they are — cannot take us where we ultimately want to go. They are but engines driving us forward to the next step: the actual *practice of the virtue*. We will never acquire patience or any other virtue unless we *practice* it.

Here is where real self-mastery and cooperation with God's grace come into play. Here is where real sanctity is forged. Here is where real heroic virtue begins to manifest itself. If we truly want to grow in a specific virtue, we must practice it in *all* areas of our life, whether it comes naturally or not, whether our emotions resonate with it or not, whether it suits our temperament or not, and whether we *feel* like it or not. As a famous advertising slogan encourages: *Just do it!* Addressing this as it regards the virtue of patience, Archbishop Fulton J. Sheen wrote:

> There are many who excuse themselves, saying that if they were in other circumstances they would be much more patient. This is a grave mistake, for it assumes that virtue is a matter of geography, and not of moral effort. It makes little difference where we are; it all depends on what we are thinking about.

If we are thinking *patience*, looking for *patience*, seeking *patience*, praying for *patience*, using sacramental grace to acquire *patience* (confessing impatience), we will recognize every opportunity to lose our patience as a privileged moment of grace to practice it instead. And one thing is for sure: When we determine to acquire a virtue, whether it be patience or any other virtue, God in His goodness will give us plenty of opportunities to do just that! They will greet us at every turn!

Through practice of the virtue we wish to acquire, we will discover in time that the virtue has taken up residence within us. Its opposite may still rub, may still aggravate, may still tempt, but we will have flexed enough spiritual muscle to be strong enough to overcome. The virtue will win the day, and our virtuous action will do much to communicate God's love to the world.

BUT WHAT ABOUT THE VIRTUE OF JUSTICE?

As we have noted, justice is a moral virtue. The two main categories of virtue are theological and moral. The theological virtues are received at Baptism. They are faith, hope, and charity. They are called "theological" because they "adapt man's faculties for participation in the divine nature" (CCC, no. 1812). The moral virtues, on the other hand, are acquired by our own effort. Prudence, justice, fortitude, and temperance are the four main moral virtues. They are called the "cardinal" virtues because every other virtue "hinges" on them.

Moral virtues are "good habits," which can be acquired through frequent repetition of good acts. Anyone who seeks to lead an upright life can become naturally "virtuous" by acting in conjunction with the moral virtues. However, the moral virtues can become "supernaturalized" by the life of God active within the human person. Reception of the sacraments, daily prayer, and meritorious acts all work to increase and supernaturalize the moral virtues within us. When the moral virtues are infused with grace, they are of a far higher perfection than their simply "natural" counterparts; and when they are performed for love of God, they yield an effect in the world quite beyond what the moral virtues can produce simply through man's efforts.

The life of God — that is, grace — within the human person helps to dispose the individual to practice the virtues; and when he cooperates with the grace and practices the virtues, with God's love as his motive, the moral virtues lead him into deeper union with God. However, even though aided by grace, as we have discussed, the individual's facility in practicing acts of virtue grows through frequent repetition of the acts themselves.

Four distinct areas of life become the school in which the virtue of justice is acquired, and every person, by the very fact of his existence, is called to enroll. These four areas of life correspond to the four forms of justice: *commutative justice*, which relates to our personal interactions with others; *distributive justice*, which corresponds to the obligations of authority to its subordinates; *legal justice*, which relates to our social and moral obligations to those in the world community; and finally *equity*, an intellectual and spiritual pursuit that seeks the *spirit* of the law rather than its dictums. Graduates from this school discover that when the will is put to the rigors of such serious intention, it becomes purified, strengthened, healed — and ultimately, the acquired virtue of justice yields to the infused virtue of charity.

THE HALLS OF JUSTICE

Commutative Justice

Justice can seem like such a lofty term to use to describe the common interactions of everyday life, and yet it is justice itself that causes those interactions to make life a reflection of God's love for one another. From a simple smile, to a helping hand, to a contract executed fairly, to a promise kept, justice is to be the girder that supports. Only when justice is missing from such daily activities does the true worth of it appear. Commutative justice governs the sphere of all such interactions, for at its heart is concern and respect for the person of the other.

Commutative justice causes us to examine ourselves and ask if we have shown the true face of God to our neighbor in words and deeds. It causes us to ask if we have violated him in any way: Have we been truthful, honest, aboveboard? Have we spoken well of him? Have our words been a cause of detraction, calumny, or slander? Do we tell the truth — regularly? To what extent have I ridiculed, mocked, or falsely accused? Have I judged rashly? In any way, have my words or my deeds sullied the reputation of another? Have I stolen from my neighbor, from my employer, from a family member? Have I been abusive in any way, or have I physically injured another with full intention?

The answers to these questions tell us much about our reflection of Christ in the world. And when we find that we come up short, when commutative justice has been violated, reparation becomes a duty. Stolen goods must be returned or paid for. Untruths must be corrected. Insults must be amended. And reputations must be restored. In short, reparation must be made to the fullest extent possible.

While we must guard against bringing sorrow through injustice, we must actively seek ways we can bring joy through justice. Given the many opportunities we have for acting with justice in our daily lives, we should examine our conscience each day to check our progress in this first hall of justice. "For justice," as Pope John Paul II has pointed out, "is the fundamental principle of life, and of men living together, of human communities, of societies and of peoples."

Distributive Justice

There is a temptation to see distributive justice only within the framework of the community's obligation to the citizen. Seen in this context, distributive justice can be diminished to a social program with little thought for the personal dignity of each person who presents himself. In reality, distributive justice is much more than this. Its scope is broad. It requires a just and fair wage; the respectful and proper treatment of employees; the respect for all persons as children of God, regardless of social class or distinction; and the search for the ways and means for each human person to be a productive and viable member of society.

In addition, distributive justice demands pastoral care. For example, care must be exercised to safeguard the truly capable person from a disproportionate share of duties and responsibilities simply because he can accomplish much. And, conversely, care needs to be taken to guard against giving a disproportionate share of work to those with whom one might have a problem or a personality clash. These can be temptations experienced in everyday life in a variety of settings, from classrooms to boardrooms, from families to religious communities, and from places of employment to volunteer organizations.

Finally, distributive justice demands that praise be given when praise is due; that encouragement be given to those who require it; that help be offered to the needy; and, when circumstances demand it, that correction be offered with fraternal charity. Again, a daily examination of conscience regarding our expression of distributive justice helps us to acquire it with greater facility.

Legal Justice

While distributive justice is concerned with society's due to its constituents, legal justice is concerned with the constituents' due to the community. In the political sphere, this requires a person's concern for observing the laws, ordinances, and constitutions of the society to which he belongs. But it also requires an active participation in the developing, instituting, and safeguarding of laws, ordinances, and constitutions by which he is governed. By conscience, each person is compelled to seek legislation that protects the dignity and respect of the human person, and he must work for it in ways available to him.

Further, legal justice requires an active participation in works of social justice — issues which affect the common good — and it requires a gift of self-donation regarding time, talent, and treasure to those activities that speak for the poor, weak, disenfranchised, or forgotten.

St. Josemaría Escrivá de Balaguer puts it this way:

> We have to uphold the right of all men to live, to own what is necessary to lead a dignified existence, to work and to rest, to choose a particular state in life, to form a home, to bring children into the world within marriage and to be allowed to educate them, to pass peacefully through times of sickness and old age, to have access to culture, to join with other citizens to achieve legitimate ends, and, above all, to enjoy the right to know and love God in perfect liberty.

Finally, legal justice applies to all societies in which an individual finds himself. While his world community is most obvious, the same zeal must be shown for his Church community, his family community, his work community, and any lay group or association with which he is affiliated.

A Tip for Spiritual
S.U.C.**C**.E.S.S.

Continuous Conversion

*T*he primary vocation of every Christian is holiness of life. Only through holiness can we experience grace in abundance. Therefore, our lives must be a journey of continuous conversion — working with God's grace to grow more like Him every day. Breaking with mortal sin and cooperating with grace to eliminate venial sin are obviously needed if we are to make spiritual progress. But what do we do about our weaknesses and frailties? How can we triumph over these?

St. Teresa of Ávila gives us the first step. She says there is no spiritual growth without self-knowledge. This means we must *know* our weaknesses before we can work on them. Our daily examination of conscience should reveal these to us. But if we are still blind to our deficiencies, a family member or a trusted friend will be happy to point them out, I'm sure! Pray for the humility to ask, and for the humility to hear.

All of the saints knew the spiritual key to the next step. Once we know our faults, we need to practice the virtues opposite them. For example, combat selfishness with generosity, gossip with custody of the tongue, and complaining with praise and thanksgiving. Through the guidance of the Holy Spirit, we should work on one weakness at a time —

continued on next page ...

...continued from page 161

in that way, more progress will be seen, and we will become less discouraged.

Finally, we should ask our Blessed Mother to intercede for us. She will obtain every grace we need to continue our journey of conversion and to win the victory over even our smallest defects.

Mary, help of all Christians, pray for us.

Much can be accomplished for the good of mankind when legal justice is sought and acquired. One way to gauge its significance is to become involved with a specific social action or issue. Changed lives and restored communities will do much to prove its worth.

Equity

Equity is considered the highest of the four forms of justice, for it is the one most closely associated with wisdom and charity. In this form of justice, concern is not so much for the letter of the law as for the spirit of the law — for the intent of the legislator. Gone is the desire to split hairs over a preposition or conjunction; rather, the intention is for the ultimate benefit of the one to whom the law pertains. Its ultimate goal is directed to the dignity and respect due the human person in all his various circumstances of life. It is a Christlike view of the law rather than a pharisaic one. Equity never gives sway to a false or convenient interpretation of the law, but instead seeks the truth in love.

And thus, equity brings justice to the very threshold of charity. While still distinguished from the virtue of charity, equity calls us to regard others as our brothers and sisters in Christ, and it encourages us to seek their ultimate benefit even when that benefit is greater than a strict interpretation of justice would suggest.

This is the summit of justice. As Dominican Father Reginald Garrigou-Lagrange explains in *The Three Ages of the Interior Life*:

> In brief, as St. Thomas [Aquinas] well shows, justice considers our neighbor another person, in that he is a distinct person; charity considers him as another self. Justice respects the rights of another; charity gives over and above these rights for the love of God and of the child of God.

Equity, when practiced with love of God and love of neighbor, takes us to the greatest of all virtues — charity itself.

An examination of conscience regarding equity might help us discover how nearly our attitude toward justice conforms to that of Christ's, as opposed to that of the Pharisee. Should work need to be done in this area, a prayer to Our Lady Help of All Christians might bring good recourse and bountiful grace to help us in this regard.

MAKING A DIFFERENCE IN THE WORLD: JUSTICE AND THE LIFE ISSUES

One area of today's culture where justice is viciously under attack concerns the life issues. Life, both at its conception and at its end, has been maligned, threatened, and ended by attitudes, initiatives, and laws antithetical to a Catholic understanding of justice and the sanctity of the human person. In addition, new technologies serve as a means of further degradation of the human person. In vitro fertilization, the freezing of embryos, stem-cell research using aborted babies, and the whole macabre prospect of cloning all stand in stark contrast to the procreative gift of the marital union and the sanctity of life it is meant to protect.

Pope John Paul II has put it aptly in stating that we now live in a culture of death rather than a culture of life. The rights of endangered species and the rights of plant life are more protected than the right to life of babies in their mothers' wombs or the right to life of elderly persons in nursing homes. Indeed, even the injured are no longer safe because laws and legislation continue to redefine death itself. Those whose lives are diminished by disability and handicap, and those whose lives fall short of the "quality of life" standard set by medical elites and the health care industry, may find themselves dead by the hands of a doctor or other medical professional.

As a result, confusion abounds in our contemporary culture regarding the morality and justice of decisions relating to beginning-of-life and end-of-life issues. Unfortunately, these misunderstandings are not isolated to the secular world alone. Many Catholics are confused as well. Some Catholics run on "pro-choice" platforms; some Catholics vote for "pro-choice" legislators; some Catholics favorably debate doctor-assisted suicide; some Catholics tout euthanasia of the elderly; and some Catholics applaud technological advances in fertilization techniques, embryonic research, and a variety of other dehumanizing scientific developments. These are serious positions, and they are seriously flawed.

What Does the Church Teach?

As Catholics, we have the wisdom and guidance of Holy Mother Church to lead us through the quagmire of popular opinion and secular perspectives that cloud justice regarding the life issues. The *Catechism of the Catholic Church* makes it abundantly clear that contraception, abortion, and euthanasia, *for whatever reason*, are morally unacceptable. Quoting Pope Paul VI's encyclical *Humanae Vitae* (no. 14), the *Catechism* makes this statement regarding contraception:

> "Every action which, whether in anticipation of the conjugal act, or in its accomplishment, or in the development of its natural consequences, proposes, whether as an end or as a means, to render procreation impossible" is intrinsically evil.
> — CCC, NO. 2370

(It should be noted that the Catholic Church always permits abstinence from sexual activity as a means of family planning [CCC, no. 2370], and also permits the use of natural family planning, a highly effective, scientific means of spacing children, for certain legitimate reasons. The "Theology of the Body," so beautifully explained by Pope John Paul II, is must reading for all married couples who seek to understand the great gift of their fertility and its role in the plan of God.)

And there is this statement regarding abortion:

> Since the first century the Church has affirmed the moral evil of every procured abortion. This teaching has not changed and remains unchangeable. Direct abortion, that is to say, abortion willed either as an end or a means, is gravely contrary to the moral law. — CCC, NO. 2271

And finally, the *Catechism* makes this statement regarding euthanasia:

> An act or omission which, of itself or by intention, causes death in order to eliminate suffering constitutes a murder gravely contrary to the dignity of the human person and to the respect due to the living God, his Creator. The error in judgment into which one can fall in good faith does not change the nature of this murderous act, which must always be forbidden and excluded. — CCC, NO. 2277

Human life is sacred. It begins with an action of God, and it is sustained throughout its existence by God. As the *Catechism* reminds us, human life "remains for ever in a special relationship with the Creator" (no. 2258), for human life is made in the image and likeness of God. It is for the value of the human person and his immortal salvation that God sent His own Son so that whoever believes in Him might not perish but have everlasting life (John 3:16). God regards the human person with dignity and value at all stages of his life — and so must we.

But we must do more than agree with Church teaching on these issues. We must form our conscience according to them, and we must let Church teaching move us forward with faith and confidence into the public square to proclaim the truth at every opportunity. In addition, our vote must indicate our beliefs about the sanctity of life. Thus will we bring justice to the culture of contemporary man. The fourth beatitude beckons each of us to walk in its splendor and live by its light: Blessed are those that hunger and thirst for justice, for they shall have their fill.

JUSTICE: A MATTER OF THE HEART

A passage written by Father Francis Fernandez, in his *In Conversation with God* series, provides an appropriate and thought-provoking summary for our discussion on justice. We would do well to use the questions he poses at the end as part of our examination of conscience. Only through an honest evaluation of how nearly we practice the virtue of justice can we hope to experience grace in abundance for ourselves and be a conduit of that grace in the world:

> The ultimate solution for restoring and promoting justice at all levels lies in the heart of each man. It is in the heart that every type of injustice imaginable comes into existence, and it is there also that the possibility of straightening out all human relationships is conceived. . . . That is why, as Christians, we cannot forget that, when through our personal apostolate we bring men closer to God, we are building a world which is more human and more just. Moreover, our faith urges us never to avoid our personal commitment to the defense of justice, particularly in those aspects more closely related to the fundamental rights of the person: the right to life, to work, to education, to good reputation. . . .Within our personal sphere of action we must ask ourselves the following questions: Do we do perfectly the work for which we are remunerated? Do we fully pay what we owe people for services rendered? Are we responsible in the way we exercise those rights and duties that can influence the activities of institutions to which we belong? Do we make good use of our time at work? Do we defend other people's good name? Do we stand up for those who are weakest? Do we quash defamatory criticisms which may sometimes

spring up in our midst? . . . This is how we show our love for justice.

Let us pray that our hearts be forever united to the heart of Jesus Christ so that true justice can reign within us and we can bring His abundant life to the world.

WORKING THE STRATEGY

Live a Life of Justice

1. What new insight have you gained about virtue as a result of this chapter?
2. Which of the moral virtues do you most need to acquire? What convinces you that this is the one?
3. What strategy can you outline to help yourself acquire this virtue?
4. What are some of the major injustices you see in the world around you? Consider the culture, the community, the parish, and the family. Which of the four types of justice are necessary for each? What can you do to bring justice into these various areas of your life and your world?
5. Read again the quote of Father Francis Fernandez that closes this chapter. Use each of the questions contained within it as an examination of conscience. Seek the Sacrament of Penance, and make a decision to practice justice in the areas where you are remiss.

STRATEGY SEVEN

Love Your Neighbor as Yourself

ى

In the last chapter, we discovered that the virtue of justice, when infused with the grace of God, surpasses its own inherent goodness and gives way to the greatest of all virtues: love. Love is a supernatural virtue. It is a divine virtue. And as we have seen in previous chapters, true love finds its source in the life of the Trinity, the Fountainhead of Love.

The ultimate expression of love shown to us in Sacred Scripture is the gift of salvation given to us by God the Father through the passion and death of His Son, Jesus Christ. In this perfect expression of love, both the Father and the Son reveal unconditional love for man. God the Father gives His Son as the "ransom for many" (Matthew 20:28), and the Son obediently, willingly, and lovingly "[lays] down his life for his friends" (John 15:13). In the gift of redemption, love reveals its highest summit and its truest meaning — love is an act of *total* self-donation.

While the virtue of justice seeks the good of the other, love identifies with the other, and it views the other as "another self." Pope John Paul II said it succinctly: "Charity goes beyond justice, for it is an invitation to go beyond the order of mere equity to the order of love and self-giving." This is strikingly portrayed in St. Paul's Letter to the Philippians. He tells the Church of Philippi that Jesus emptied himself, took the form of a servant, was born in the likeness of men, humbled himself, and became "obedient unto death, even death on a cross" (2:7-8).

These actions of Christ were given out of love for man, not out of justice. Justice would have left man to the miserable consequences of his own sin, but Love "divinized" him instead, and incorporated him into its own Life. Love treated man as Love treated Itself. And Love commands that we do the same for one another (Mark 12:28-34).

(Note that the word "divinized" is used as it was by the Church Fathers. It does not mean that man becomes God or that man is made equal to God. This perspective is not Christian. In the Christian understanding, man and God are always separate and distinct. God is the "Creator," and man is the "created." God is the Supreme Being, and man is a human being. But through the indwelling presence of the Holy Spirit, man participates in the love of the Godhead. And through the merits of Jesus Christ, man has become an "adopted son of God," an heir, with Christ, to everlasting life.)

LOVE IN ACTION

The Golden Rule instructs us to treat others as we wish to be treated (Matthew 7:12), and Jesus tells us to "love your neighbor as yourself" (Mark 12:31). For those who are members of Christ's Mystical Body, the call is to love as Christ loves, as the Father loves, and as the Spirit loves. The call is to love with the same self-donating love demonstrated for us through Christ's redemptive act. As Christ "emptied himself" for us, so too are we called to "empty" ourselves for one another. As Christ became the perfect sacrifice for us, so too are we called to sacrifice in love for one another. And, as Christ joined His love for us to the Father's love for us, so too are we called to join our love for one another to Christ's ultimate act of love expressed upon the cross. This is the life-giving love that Jesus taught, both through His words and through His actions. And this is the essence of true charity. We are to love our neighbor as "another self." But how can we love in this way?

TO LOVE AS GOD LOVES

A passage from St. Mark's Gospel (12:28-34) provides us with the key. Here a scribe asks Jesus, "Which commandment is the first of all?" Jesus replies:

> "The first is, 'Hear, O Israel: The Lord our God, the Lord is one; and you shall love the Lord your God with all your heart, and with all your soul, and with all your mind, and with all your strength.' The second is this, 'You shall love

your neighbor as yourself.' There is no other commandment greater than these."

Jesus' words resonate within the scribe's heart, and he responds, "You are right, Teacher; you have truly said that he is one, and there is no other but he; and to love him with all the heart, and with all the understanding, and with all the strength, and to love one's neighbor as oneself, is much more than all whole burnt offerings and sacrifices." Jesus sees that the truth has been firmly planted within the soul of the scribe, and He says to him, "You are not far from the kingdom of God."

This passage reveals an important truth to us about the virtue of charity: True love of neighbor flows from true love of God. Jesus tells the scribe that the *first* commandment is to love God with the entirety of our being. *Then*, we are to love our neighbor as ourselves. The love of God is a prerequisite for love of neighbor and for every charitable action.

How, then, do we love God with the entirety of our being? A quote from Origen provides us with the answer. He says, "If we are able to love God it is because we have been loved by God." God has loved us first; and His love, active within us through the indwelling presence of His Holy Spirit, gives us the capacity to love Him in return. In loving Him, we become like Him (as St. Augustine says); and in becoming like Him, we can begin to love like Him. As we love like Him, growing in His unconditional way of love, the confines of our heart expand, and we soon discover that we are loving our neighbor as we love our very self — we have come to identify with him, to empathize with him, and to stand in solidarity with him. And like the scribe who won the approval of Jesus, we too will hear Our Lord say, "You are not far from the kingdom of God" — God's reign will already be effected in our thoughts, in our words, and in our deeds.

LIVING THE VIRTUE OF CHARITY

A profound difference exists between a humanitarian act and an act of charity. The first is inspired by human compassion and accomplished through human incentive. It is rooted in man himself, and it is effective only to the extent to which his generosity and goodwill carry it. While such an action is admirable, like its source, its benefits are limited and finite.

However, an act of charity is much more than that. As we have seen, it is rooted in God, and its source is the life of God active within the individual. Thus, the charitable act is infused with grace, and each act of charity becomes a conduit of divine life in the world. It has the capacity to infuse the situation or circumstance, the trial or difficulty, and the very heart of the recipient with a supernatural reality that yields infinite and never-ending benefits.

It is this kind of effect that our actions are called to have in the lives of others. Whether they are family members, co-workers, next-door neighbors, strangers in the grocery store, or the poor, the weak, and the disenfranchised of the world, our call as Christians is to be a channel of God's life to everyone. Three ways we can live out this holy call is through filial kindness, true friendship, and forgiveness. These three attitudes of heart, when executed with Christ-centered love, are laden with grace-filled potential. The rest of this chapter will discuss filial kindness and true friendship. Forgiveness, because it is so central to the spiritual life, will be discussed at length as our next strategy.

FILIAL KINDNESS

Every day we come into contact with other people. By year's end, literally hundreds or even thousands of individuals have crossed our path. Is there a way we can show the love of God at all times to all of the people who traverse our way? As Christians who desire to experience grace in abundance and bring that grace to others, is it possible that every personal contact becomes a conduit of God's grace in the world? Yes, not only is it possible, but it is precisely what our call as a Christian is meant to effect. How, then, can this be accomplished?

Perhaps the best way we can attain our goal to be a channel of God's life in the lives of others is through filial kindness — an attitude of heart that sees every person we meet and every person with whom we interact as a brother or sister in the Lord, and then treat them that way. This can require quite an adjustment in the way we perceive others (especially those we find particularly irksome or loathsome), and it can require quite a spiritual struggle as we work to bring our actions into conformity with our will. But in the end, we will see that our efforts have reaped a handsome yield.

Father Romano Guardini, in his book *Learning the Virtues that Lead You to God*, tells us, "Kindness means that a person is well disposed toward life." If filial kindness is to be our attitude toward others, then we must be "well disposed toward life." This requires that we see life as it truly is: a gift from God. When we see life as God's gift, then we begin to see our life, no matter the circumstance, as a gift; and, when we view our life in this way, it compels us to view every life in this way.

When we arrive at this perspective, a deep filial love for our fellow man begins to dwell in us, and this love shows itself in kindness — a kindness that cannot be suppressed but which seeks expression in our thoughts, our words, and our deeds. This disposition does much to bring the love of God to our neighbor — even in crowded airports, grocery-store lines, and church parking lots!

What, then, are the characteristics of filial kindness? While there are many, they can be summarized into three main categories: courtesy, loving words, and patient forbearance.

Courtesy

Courtesy is a virtue that is closely associated with respect. Courtesy flows from the respect that is due all men because they are created in the image and likeness of God. This certainly does not mean that all men — including us — reflect this image clearly. However, it does mean that we choose to look with supernatural eyes at the face of our brother and sister and see in them the children of God they were created to be. We treat them with the dignity that is their due by virtue of their humanity. In short, we honor and respect them.

Courtesy is the holy oil that lubricates the potential frictions of daily life. A courteous word, a kind gesture, a smile, and a well-deserved compliment all help to diffuse a difficult situation, lighten a tense moment, and mitigate an embarrassing circumstance. St. Paul speaks of courteous behavior in his instruction to the Romans. He tells them to "love one another with brotherly affection," to "outdo one another in showing honor," to "practice hospitality," to "live in harmony with one another," to "do not be haughty," to "never be conceited," to "live peaceably with all," and to "overcome evil with good" (12:10-21). When courtesy is approached in this way, it brings with it the love of God.

Father Guardini recounts in his book an incident from his own life that profoundly impressed him regarding the importance of courtesy. He writes:

> If I may be permitted, I would like to recount a personal recollection: a long time ago, when I was still attending school, a woman whom I greatly revered said to me one day, "Do not forget that there is a great love of our neighbor, but also a small one! The great one has its occasion when there is a great need to be met or when it becomes dangerous to remain loyal. But there is always an occasion for the small one, because it belongs to our everyday life. It is courtesy." I have never forgotten these words.

As this recollection so poignantly illustrates, courtesy does not belong to the magnanimous deed, but rather to the common one. But it is an act of love toward our neighbor, nonetheless, and through it the grace of God is seen. Hilaire Belloc, the great Catholic scholar, agreed. He wrote:

> Of Courtesy, it is much less
> Than courage of heart or holiness
> Yet in my walks it seems to me
> That the grace of God is Courtesy.

In our hectic world of hustle and bustle; in our world of technology and scientific discovery; in our world where the value of the human person is often reduced to a number or a statistic; and in our world where we have dehumanized classes of peoples based on race, color, gender, and abilities, we must renew the value of courtesy, and we must renew the common expressions of love. For it is from the small acts of love and kindness, inspired by the grace of God, that the truly magnanimous deeds of self-donation flow. Courtesy, the outgrowth of true respect for the human person, leads us along the path to true love of neighbor.

Loving Words

Archbishop Fulton J. Sheen once said, "A kind word gives encouragement to the despondent heart, and a cruel word makes others sob their way to the grave." How true! The words we speak have power. They can build up or they can tear down. They can restore or they can lay low. They can divide or they can bind together. Once spoken, they cannot be taken back. And once spoken, their effects can linger a lifetime. Words can bring comfort, hope, and life — or they can bring anguish, devastation, and death. Consider this story shared by a concerned mother:

> Our son was subjected to a classroom teacher who constantly berated him. He was belittled, chided, and scolded routinely. Her words and actions caused a profound change in our normally bouncy and lively child. He began to recoil at our touch. He no longer wanted for us to kiss him or show him affection. His sunny little face gave way to a somber expression, which became a permanent part of his countenance.
>
> It was long into the school year before we determined what had caused this change in our son. And, by then, much damage had been done. Even though this incident happened early on in our son's life, its effects have lingered. It has taken virtually years to restore our boy's sense of self-confidence and worth. We're still working on it some ten years later.

A Tip for Spiritual
S.U.C.C.**E**.S.S.

Empathy

*T*hat particular morning, Simeon's prophecy rang in the ears of her soul like a death knell. Many years ago, he had her told about the sword, and now that sword was piercing her heart with rapier-like precision. Jesus, her son, would be crucified that afternoon.

She had prayed to the Father and asked Him to give her a portion of her son's suffering. Though she could not alleviate His burden, she could spiritually make it her own as well. The weight of His trauma and grief had been pressing upon her since last night. How He loved those who were torturing Him! How He loved those who had abandoned Him! How He loved those who would murder Him! What pain mother and son were experiencing!

But the worst was yet to come. Today, His very life would be given for love. He would be nailed to a cross and die for love of all mankind. Yes, she would unite herself to His sufferings and let His pain become her pain; His suffering, her suffering; His love, her love. She had asked the Father, and it would be so.

She prayed in preparation for her journey to Calvary. She would be with Jesus every step of the way. She would strengthen Him with her presence. She would encourage Him with her love. She would be close by when they pounded

continued on next page . . .

. . . continued from page 175

Him to the wood. She would look strongly into His eyes as they hoisted Him up. She would stand in solidarity with Him at the foot of His cross. She would breathe with Him as He breathed His last. And when they took Him down from the tree, she would receive His body into her arms. Yes, the sword was penetrating deeply now — and though it was excruciating, she welcomed it with love.

Because of the potency of the spoken word, Sacred Scripture admonishes us to use our gift of speech with caution. Proverbs tells us that a harsh word stirs up anger (15:1), and that a perverse tongue crushes the spirit (15:4). The Letter of James says the tongue is "a restless evil, full of deadly poison" (3:8), and compares it to a tiny spark that sets a huge forest ablaze (3:5-6). St. Paul's Letter to the Ephesians instructs them to say only edifying things that will impart grace to the men who hear them (4:29). Jesus tells us we will be held accountable for every unguarded word we speak (Matthew 12:36). These admonitions remind us that the spoken word has long-reaching effects and, therefore, must be carefully chosen.

But as Archbishop Sheen's statement reminds us, just as words have the power to bring great damage, so too do they have the power to bring great good. Loving words can heal, affirm, restore, and bring life. Scripture extols the benefits of loving words. Proverbs 15:4 says, "A gentle tongue is a tree of life." Proverbs 16:24 tells us, "Pleasant words are like a honeycomb, sweetness to the soul and health to the body." And Proverbs 25:11 tells us that words spoken at the proper time are like golden apples in silver settings.

Filial kindness demands that our words speak the truth to our neighbor about himself: They must communicate to him his value, his dignity, and his worth. Even in the midst of fraternal correction, our words must shimmer with grace and bring our neighbor consolation, peace, and hope. Filled with the life of God, our words must contribute to an atmosphere of love that stirs within the heart of the individual and leads him to a deeper knowledge of his Creator. If so, in the end, our words will produce good fruit, fruit that will last, and they will do much to bring the life of God to the world.

Patient Forbearance

St. Thérèse of Lisieux writes, "True charity consists in putting up with all one's neighbor's faults, never being surprised by his weakness, and being inspired by the least of his virtues." What she so perfectly describes is the virtue of patient forbearance, the virtue that helps us to love our neighbor as we love ourselves even when they are irksome, irritable, annoying, or just plain grumpy! To be sure, this is a difficult virtue to cultivate. It requires that we die to self and choose love instead. It requires that we "reframe" the irritation and see it as a "moment of grace" to make a loving sacrifice on our neighbor's behalf. It requires that we exhibit heroic virtue and attach our own displeasure to the cross of Jesus Christ. And, it requires that we show the true face of God's love despite the battle raging within us.

An example from the life of St. Thérèse gives us good insight into how this can be done. It is helpful to know that even the great saints struggled in areas such as these, though they used God's grace to overcome their lower passions. Here is her story taken from her autobiography, *The Story of A Soul*:

> Formerly one of our nuns managed to irritate me whatever she did or said. The devil was mixed up in it, for it was certainly he who made me see so many disagreeable traits in her. As I did not want to give way to my natural dislike for her, I told myself that charity should not only be a matter of feeling but should show itself in deeds. So I set myself to do for this sister just what I should have done for someone I loved most dearly. Every time I met her, I prayed for her and

offered God all her virtues and her merits. I was sure this would greatly delight Jesus. . . .

I did not remain content with praying a lot for this nun who caused me so much disturbance. I tried to do as many things for her as I could, and whenever I was tempted to speak unpleasantly to her, I made myself give her a pleasant smile and tried to change the subject. . . .

When I was violently tempted by the devil and if I could slip away without her seeing my inner struggle, I would flee like a soldier deserting the battlefield. And after all this she asked me one day with a beaming face: "Sister Thérèse, will you please tell me what attracts you so much to me? You give me such a charming smile whenever we meet?" Ah, it was Jesus hidden in the depth of her soul who attracted me, Jesus who makes the bitterest things sweet.

What strategies did St. Thérèse employ to help her overcome her "natural dislike" for her fellow sister, and how can we adapt them to our own lives?

1. **St. Thérèse saw the truth of her situation.** She knew she was in the midst of a spiritual battle ("The devil was mixed up in it, for it was certainly he who made me see so many disagreeable traits in her."). This enabled her to rally the spiritual support she needed to address the issue head-on. She invoked the aid of charity — love of neighbor to assist her. *Strategy: Identify your most irksome acquaintance. What bothers you the most about this individual? How can you follow St. Thérèse's example?*

2. **St. Thérèse made a decision to love.** Charity, she reminds us, is not only a matter of feeling but also a matter of deeds. *Strategy: Make a decision to love the one who troubles you so. If you cannot, ask for St. Thérèse's intercession.*

3. **In love, St. Thérèse prayed for the sister.** Though her feelings had not "caught up" with her decision to love, St. Thérèse practiced the virtue of love. Out of love for God

("I was sure this would greatly delight Jesus"), every time she beheld the disagreeable sister, Thérèse prayed for her and offered to God all of the sister's merits and virtues. *Strategy: Pray for your "disagreeable sister." Enumerate her merits and virtues. Offer these to God every time you see her or she comes into your mind.*

4. **St. Thérèse engaged in acts of love.** We can almost see the positive effects Thérèse's efforts had on her own soul. Her decision to love, coupled with her prayer for her fellow nun, expanded her heart. She says that she was no longer content to simply pray for the nun. Love compelled her to do more besides. She sought out things that she could do for her, and gave her a pleasant smile whenever tempted to utter an unpleasant word. *Strategy: Be patient with yourself until you reach this point. Then act on the impulse. Begin to perform acts of kindness for the one you find so disagreeable. However, performing acts of kindness for her before you feel compelled to do so may quicken your love for her.*

5. **When the battle was too much, St. Thérèse took herself out of the near occasion of sin for love of her fellow sister.** All of us have moments when the temptation seems greater than our resources. But in Thérèse's action, we see grace in action — she flees not in cowardice or defeat, but rather in fortitude and victory. Thérèse does not give in to the battle raging within her, and the disagreeable nun never sees Thérèse's struggle. Thus, Thérèse overcomes her temptation and protects the dignity, value, and worth of her fellow sister — so much so that the sister asks her why it is that Thérèse is so attracted to her. This is humility. This is strength. This is heroic virtue. This is victory. *Strategy: Do not give in to temptation. Die to self and walk away rather than give in to your lower passions.*

6. **St. Thérèse saw Jesus in the depths of the sister's soul.** The prize is won. Thérèse has come to true love of neighbor. She sees the disagreeable sister no longer from the per-

spective of her own irritation and displeasure, but she sees her as God sees her — a person made in His image and likeness in whom His Son resides. It is Jesus in the sister who so attracted Thérèse, and He has made the "bitterest things sweet." *Strategy: Beg God to give you His eyes through which to see your troublesome acquaintance. Ask Him to reveal to you Jesus hidden in her soul. Love Jesus whom you see.*

Courtesy, loving words, and patient forbearance yield filial kindness. And filial kindness opens our heart to the possibility of true friendship, a friendship that reflects God's own love for us.

TRUE FRIENDSHIP

Webster defines "friend" as "a person whom one knows well and is fond of; intimate associate; close acquaintance." But Scripture gives us a fuller and richer definition: "A faithful friend is a sturdy shelter; he that has found one has found a treasure. There is nothing so precious as a faithful friend, and no scales can measure his excellence" (Sirach 6:14).

Such a friend was the prayerful desire of one of our daughters when she was a little girl. She was captivated by the *Anne of Green Gables* series, and of particular interest to her was the relationship between Anne and her best friend, Diana Berry. Anne referred to Diana as her "bosom friend." My little one decided there and then that she, too, wanted a "bosom friend," one who would be "a sturdy shelter," and a "treasure;" one who would be "faithful" and "precious." With faith and confidence, she set about the business of acquiring a friend just like that.

While my daughter's efforts were admirable, she soon discovered that true friendship requires more than desire. True friendship requires charity, the kind of charity we have been discussing. St. Augustine writes, "There is no true friendship unless you weld it between souls that cleave together through the charity shed in our hearts by the Holy Spirit." As we have come to see, the charity given to us through the Holy Spirit is a self-donating love that puts the other before oneself. What specifically characterizes this kind of friendship, the kind that St. Augustine says "welds" souls together?

Aristotle outlined five characteristics of such friendship: (1) willing the friend's good, (2) being glad that he is alive, (3) taking pleasure in living with him, (4) having the same preferences, and (5) sharing his griefs and joy. St. Thomas Aquinas, writing in the *Summa Theologiae*, reduces these five qualities to three. He tells us true friendship is marked by benevolence, mutual love, and community of life. What do these holy attributes mean and how do they affect a relationship?

Benevolence

Benevolence is the cornerstone of friendship and is its foundational element. Without benevolence, a relationship will collapse. Benevolence is the attribute Jesus describes to the scribe in Mark's Gospel (12:28-34). Our Lord tells him that loving our neighbor as ourselves is second only to loving God with all of our being. Because we desire only the ultimate good for ourselves, benevolence requires that we desire the ultimate good for our friend. From a Christian perspective, this means that we seek the eternal salvation of our friend as we seek our own. Thus, benevolence wills the supernatural good of our friend.

This understanding gives direction to a friendship by encouraging that which is God-honoring and routing out that which could lead to sin. Conversations, activities, types of recreation, and attitudes of heart should be wholly directed to "whatever is true, whatever is honorable, whatever is just, whatever is pure, whatever is lovely, whatever is gracious, if there is any excellence, if there is anything worthy of praise" (Philippians 4:8). In short, our friendship should be a source of grace for both parties, and the relationship should be a reflection of holiness in the world. True friendship turns our heart away from that which is temporal and fleeting, and toward that which is immortal and everlasting.

But the virtue of benevolence does more besides. Because benevolence seeks the best interests of the other, it dispels willfulness and stubbornness. It dispels envy or manipulation. It dispels selfishness and deceit. It dispels pride and arrogance. Rather, benevolence instills openness and love, faith and confidence, right judgment and joy. It takes away confusion, doubt, and despair, and brings clarity, trust, and hope. In its essence, benevolence encourages the love of God, His mercy, and His providence. Speaking the truth in love, curbing a smart retort, and performing an act of kindness all demonstrate benevolence. In responding to these moments of grace, we express love for our friend and encourage him toward sanctity and wholeness — toward conformity with God.

St. Gregory of Nazianzus beautifully expresses the benefit and impact that benevolence has in a friendship. He writes this to his friend, St. Basil:

> Come to me and revive my virtue, and work with me; and whatever benefit we once gained together, preserve for me by your prayers, lest otherwise I fade away little by little, like a shadow when the day declines.

Like Basil's influence on Gregory — and, we can be sure, Gregory's influence on Basil — so should we be a holy influence in the life of our friend, and he in ours.

Mutual love

The second characteristic of true friendship, according to St. Thomas, is mutual love. Because true friendship is a gesture of love, it requires a response. Affection and goodwill must be shared between the two individuals. A friend must be perceived as "the half of my soul," as St. Augustine says. This is the substance of mutual love.

Sacred Scripture gives some beautiful examples of mutual love between friends: Jonathan and David (1 Samuel 18-20), Ruth and Naomi (Ruth), Jesus and Lazarus (John 11:1-44), and St. Paul and St. Timothy (1 and 2 Timothy) are just a few examples that show the value and worth of mutual love expressed in true friendship. In them, we witness the selfless love friends have for each other when united by the love of God active within them. The mutual love of true friendship becomes an icon of self-donation, the ultimate reality of a God-centered friendship.

St. Ambrose provides us with keen insight and sound advice on how to live the mutual love of true friendship:

> We shouldn't change our friends the way children do, who allow themselves to be tossed about by the fickle motions of sentimentality. I will not be ashamed to protect a friend. Don't abandon him in his hour of need, don't forget him, don't deny him your affection, because friendship is the mainstay of life. Let us carry one another's burdens, as the apostle tells us. If a man's prosperity benefits all his friends, why shouldn't he count on their help in moments of adversity? Let us help our friend with our counsels, let us unite our efforts to his, let us share his afflictions.
>
> And, when the occasion arises, let us put up with great sacrifices out of loyalty to our friend. We may perhaps have to face antagonisms to defend the cause of an innocent friend, and be prepared to receive insults when we try to reply and rebut those who attack and accuse him. . . . In adversity true friendship is tested, because in prosperity everybody appears faithful.

Indeed, this type of friendship requires the virtue of love lived at a sacrificial level. How do we measure up to the demands imposed by it? A short checklist provides us with some basis for evaluation:

- Do we put our friend's needs above our own wants?
- Are we miserly with our time, or are we always ready to listen to our friend?
- Are we ready to pray with our friend, offer him counsel, or just be present to him when circumstances demand?
- Do we demonstrate concern for our friend's spiritual well-being?
- Are we willing to experience discomfort and trial for the welfare of our friend?

- Do we strive to overcome our weaknesses, failings, and sins so that we can be a better friend? Or do we make an excuse and say our friend will "understand?"

An examination of conscience according to these questions helps identify specific areas where we can grow in this second characteristic of true friendship.

Community of Life

Without fear of reprisal or judgment, friends should share with each other their innermost thoughts and feelings. St. Ambrose of Milan says, "Let us show a friend our heart, and he will open his to us. . . . A friend, if he is true, hides nothing."

"A friend," says St. Jerome, "must speak to his friend freely as to his second self." Such openness of heart is a by-product of the third characteristic of true friendship, community of life.

Essential to community of life is the concept of "togetherness." It is impossible to maintain a friendship if there is no togetherness, and togetherness implies time. It means time spent in holy conversation with each other; time spent in prayer together; and time spent in sharing joys, sufferings, hopes, and dreams. It means time spent in assistance during moments of need, and time spent in recreation and relaxation. Sometimes, it simply means time spent in each other's presence. And in the midst of the moments together, something dynamic happens. Trust is built, commonality is established, honesty is promoted, and souls "cleave together." Community of life is achieved.

Such community of life spent between friends offers the perfect setting in which to grow together in Christian fidelity and faith. It lays the foundation of mutual trust upon which can then be built the virtues of generosity, long-suffering, compassion, humility, empathy, loyalty, and fraternal correction — all indispensable to true friendship.

In the end, true friendship radiates dignity and beauty, love and joy, peace and happiness. It heals the heart, transforms the soul, and breathes life into the spirit. True friendship shines with charity, sparkles with hope, and gleams with faith. It is resplendent with benevolence, mutual love, and community of life. Ultimately, true friendship, woven into the fabric of the heart by the Holy Spirit, becomes the path by which true friends sojourn to heaven together. And that, as my daughter found out, is the stuff out of which "bosom friends" are made.

WORKING THE STRATEGY

Love Your Neighbor as Yourself

1. Filial kindness is characterized by courteous actions. How do your everyday actions toward family members, co-workers, acquaintances, and passersby reflect courtesy as defined in this chapter? In your own life, how have the courteous actions of others communicated to you God's love for you?

2. Think of a time when the words of someone had a positive effect on you. Think of a time when the words of others had a negative effect on you. What about your own words? A positive effect on someone? A negative effect? What practical steps can you begin to implement to make all of your words loving words?

3. Practice the strategies outlined under the story from St. Thérèse's autobiography. Keep track of your progress in a diary or journal.

4. Who is your "bosom friend?" Evaluate your friendship against the three characteristics of true friendship. In what areas can you improve?

5. Jesus is the bosom friend of all of us. Consider the three characteristics of true friendship with regard to your relationship with Him. In what areas can you improve?

STRATEGY EIGHT

Practice Forgiveness

In our last chapter, we saw that authentic love of neighbor compels us to become a channel of God's life to everyone with whom we come in contact. And we discovered that two of the ways we live out this call is through filial kindness and true friendship. However, one other way remains. That way is the way of forgiveness. Perhaps no other spiritual action demands more of us than forgiveness. It requires that we die to self, that we let go of emotions to which we may have a right, and that we embrace love and benevolence instead. Forgiveness is a refining fire.

I will never forget the story of Marietta Jaeger-Lane, a woman I had the privilege to interview. In my book *Living Life Abundantly: Stories of People Who Have Encountered God*, I tell her story of forgiveness. It remains one of the most inspiring testimonies I have ever heard. In brief, Marietta is a woman who lost her seven-year-old child to murder. While the family was on a camping trip in Montana, Susie was abducted from her tent and brutally killed by her kidnapper within the first week of her abduction. However, for one year, the murderer taunted the Jaegers (who were unaware of Susie's death), asking them for a ransom in exchange for the young girl's life. And so, for one year, the family held on to the hope that perhaps Susie was still alive. In the end, the kidnapper was caught, and the Jaeger family learned the truth of Susie's fate.

It is not the horrible event of Susie's abduction or the Jaeger family's grief that makes this story remarkable. Unfortunately, this same tragedy has been repeated in the lives of far too many children and their families. No, what makes this story remarkable is the heroic virtue of Marietta Jaeger-Lane, Susie's mother. You see, through her travail of that seemingly endless year, Marietta had come to forgive the man who had stolen and murdered her daughter. It was not a trite, superficial forgiveness, but rather a soul-searching, heart-wrenching, emotion-battering forgiveness, a forgiveness through which she ultimately abandoned her hatred of Susie's kidnapper in favor of beneficence — a moral love of neighbor that includes compassion, generosity, and empathy.

Marietta's successful journey from hatred to love eventually led to the capture and arrest of Susie's killer. And that same journey led Marietta to campaign tirelessly on his behalf for a sentence of life imprisonment rather than the death penalty. She says:

> Though he was liable for the death penalty, I felt it would violate and profane the goodness, sweetness, and beauty of Susie's life by killing the kidnapper in her name. She was deserving of a more noble and beautiful memorial than a cold-blooded, premeditated, state-sanctioned killing of a restrained, defenseless man, however deserving of death he may be deemed to be. I felt I far better honored her, not by becoming that which I deplored, but by saying that all life is sacred and worthy of preservation. So I asked the prosecutor to offer the alternative sentence for his crime, mandatory life imprisonment with no chance of parole. My request was honored, and when the alternative was offered, only then did he confess to Susie's death and also to the taking of three other young lives.

(The above excerpt and all others of Marietta Jaeger-Lane's story are from Robert D. Enright and Joanna North, eds., *Exploring Forgiveness*, copyright © 1998. Reprinted by permission of The University of Wisconsin Press.)

In the life of Marietta Jaeger-Lane, compassion triumphed over resentment, empathy triumphed over hatred, and love triumphed over revenge. This is what makes her story so remarkable, and this is what makes her a woman of heroic virtue.

FULFILLING OUR LORD'S COMMAND

Indeed, the story of Marietta Jaeger-Lane is a compelling one. One might ask how it was possible for her to forgive such a heinous crime, such a terrible injury. By her own admission, Marietta's journey to forgiveness started with the single step of reaching for the highest moral ground, a precept she was taught through her Catholic upbringing. She knew that Sacred Scripture instructs us to forgive. She relates:

> In both the Hebrew and Christian Scriptures whence my beliefs and values come, the God who rises up from them is a God of mercy and compassion, a God who seeks not to punish, destroy, or put us to death, but a God who works unceasingly to help and heal us, rehabilitate and reconcile us, restore us to the richness and fullness of life for which we have been created. This, now, was the justice I wanted for this man who had taken my little girl.

Marietta knew that to be true to her religious beliefs, forgiveness was the only true option. She was right. Consider these passages from Sacred Scripture:

> Then Peter came up and said to him, "Lord, how often shall my brother sin against me, and I forgive him? As many as seven times?" Jesus said to him, "I do not say to you seven times, but seventy times seven." — MATTHEW 18:21-22

> "For if you forgive men their trespasses, your heavenly Father also will forgive you; but if you do not forgive men their trespasses, neither will your Father forgive your trespasses." — MATTHEW 6:14

> "Be merciful, even as your Father is merciful. Judge not and you will not be judged; condemn not, and you will not be condemned; forgive, and you will be forgiven; give, and it will be given to you; good measure, pressed down, shaken together, running over, will be put into your lap. For the measure you give will be the measure you get back."
> — LUKE 6:36-38

Recently, I heard the testimony of another individual who forfeited hatred, bitterness, and resentment in favor of beneficence and goodwill. Lee's daughter had been killed at the age of sixteen by a drunken teenage driver. In seconds, his little girl was gone. The driver, a nineteen-year-old young man who had known the girl, was devastated by his actions. The morning following the accident, he called Lee and asked if he could come to his home to express his sorrow and to ask for forgiveness. Lee says, "I didn't want him to come to my home. I told him, 'No.' I didn't want to see him. He had been drunk, and he killed my daughter."

But the young man pleaded, and Lee relented. Lee recalls that when the young man entered his home, God's own love for the lad filled his heart. Out of that love, he extended forgiveness. This act of forgiveness had a significant impact on Lee all through his grieving process.

Sometime after the death of Lee's daughter, the Lord called on him to forgive yet again. Several years before his daughter died, Lee's brother had been murdered. He had been beaten to death. The murderer had been tried, convicted, and was doing time in prison. Lee believes that the Lord was asking him to visit his brother's killer and extend forgiveness to him. Trusting in God's providence, he made the necessary arrangements.

"I arrived at the prison," Lee recalls. "A police officer frisked me, and a desk clerk asked me my relationship to the prisoner: Was I a family member, a relative, or a friend? I told her I couldn't answer because I had never met the man. She chose to write down that I was a friend. When she did that, an indescribable joy flooded through me."

Lee continues, "I went into the room, and the police officer there pointed to a big man leaning against a desk. I am a smaller man, and the prisoner looked to be about six feet two inches, and to weigh about two hundred fifty pounds. The officer opened the door, and I walked in. It was only through the power of the Holy Spirit that I could walk through that door. The policeman locked the door behind me. I asked the big man his name. He was the right person."

Lee recounts that he told the man that he was the brother of the person the man had killed. "I've come to forgive you," he said. With that, the big man reeled. "There I was," says Lee, "a little man, helping this big man to a chair. He was about to fall down from the words I spoke."

They had talked together for about fifteen minutes when the prisoner put his head into his hands and began to cry. He told Lee that he had just been rejected for parole. Lee asked the man if he would like to pray with him. If so, Lee would pray that God would intervene on the man's behalf the next time he was eligible for parole. The prisoner nodded his head. Lee recalls, "With the power of God's love and God's grace, I took into my hands the very hands that had beaten my brother to death, and I prayed with him that God would intervene on his behalf the next time he came up for parole, and that God would help him. It was a moment I will never forget."

For Lee, as well as for Marietta, the journey to forgiveness began with the recognition of the Gospel mandate to forgive. Though it was but a first step, it was a step that ultimately led to wholeness and hope, freedom and new life. Like Christ our Lord, who forgave His betrayers, torturers, and crucifiers from the cross, so too are we called to forgive those who have hurt, injured, and persecuted us. It is a path made holy by the footsteps of Our Lord, and it is a path to which He beckons us who go by His name. Why? What is it about forgiveness that makes it so important? What happens when we don't forgive?

THE DEVASTATING EFFECTS OF
LACK OF FORGIVENESS

In my book *Full of Grace: Women and the Abundant Life*, I recount the story of a thirtysomething man who approached me at a day of recollection I was giving for people involved in parish ministry. He was troubled, though convicted, by something I had shared.

"You really got me with what you just talked about," he said. "I've listened all day waiting to hear that special word you said Our Lord would speak to each one of us, and I think I've just heard it."

He shared with me the story about a family member who had caused great difficulty for him and for others in the family. He confided to me that he had not forgiven the individual for the heartache or the harm the individual had caused. The thirtysomething man continued, "I lose my temper with him, and I'm stressed out most of the time. I'm developing blood pressure problems, and my anger is affecting my work. You said God says we must forgive. I don't think I can do it, but I want to try."

I could certainly see the pain in the young man's face. He was sincerely troubled by the prospect of forgiving the wayward family member, but he was also convinced that it was something he had to do. It is a fact of life that all of us, in time, will face the daunting task of forgiving someone who has wounded us to the core. Each of us will experience some misunderstanding, ridicule, or mockery. We may be humiliated, betrayed, or manipulated. Some will become the subject of rumor, calumny, or detraction. Still others may know the degradation of abuse. And then there are those, like Marietta and Lee, who will know violence, treachery, and injustice.

The difficulty to forgive is proportionate to the degree of injury, hurt, or offense. The deeper the wound, the harder forgiveness comes. And our anger may be justified. A wrong was committed against us, so why should we forgive? Why would God ask us to do such a thing?

The reason is simply this: Lack of forgiveness blocks the grace of God in our lives. It brings death — spiritually, emotionally, and often, physically. It is the very opposite of what Jesus desires for us: "I came," Jesus says, "that they may have life, and have it abundantly" (John 10:10). Our will — freely choosing to hold on to anger, bitterness, resentment, and hostility — becomes an impenetrable fortress preventing God's life from entering our heart, which, through the privation of grace, becomes stony, hard, and cold. This interior reality eventually affects all aspects of our being. Let's take a look at the physical and emotional ramifications of unforgiveness first.

THE PHYSICAL AND EMOTIONAL EFFECTS
OF AN UNFORGIVING HEART

The story of the thirtysomething man at the day of recollection sheds some light on the effects of unforgiveness. He told me that he was developing blood pressure problems from stress, and that the quality of his work was suffering. He also had complained to me about memory problems, irritation, and a "short fuse." Clearly, his resentment and bitterness were having deleterious effects on his physical health, and they were beginning to affect his emotional health as well. It wasn't until the day of recollection, however, that he began to see a connection between his health problems and his lack of forgiveness.

In addition to the problems our thirtysomething friend was experiencing, others have had trouble with ulcers, gastrointestinal disorders, nervous conditions, heart problems, and insomnia. Irritability, agitation, short-temperedness, sadness, and fatigue can also be caused by bitterness, anger, and resentment. Like our friend, many people fail to associate these health issues with a failure to forgive. However, once an individual begins to engage the forgiveness process, symptoms and problems often go away.

This has led many researchers, medical doctors, and mental health professionals to begin to study the physical, emotional, and psychological effects of anger and lack of forgiveness. What they are discovering is nothing short of amazing. Take clinical depression, for example. Researchers have discovered that this mental health problem is largely caused by pent-up anger. The pent-up anger sets off a chemical chain reaction within the brain. In *Happiness Is a Choice*, Drs. Paul Meier and Frank Minirth outline the chemical effects of pent-up anger. They write:

> The pituitary gland . . . releases such hormones as ACTH (adrenocorticotropic hormone), growth hormone, luteinizing hormone, prolactin, and thyroid stimulating hormone. . . . The pituitary gland is actually controlled by the nearby hypothalamus. . . . The hypothalamus secretes releasing factors, which cause the pituitary to release the above-mentioned

hormones. It is further known that these releasing factors from the hypothalamus are controlled by biogenic amines such as norepinephrine. Of course, this is a chemical, along with serotonin, that is known to be depleted in cases of depression. Thus, if there is a disturbance in the biogenic amines in the brain, depression results, and there also may be an endocrine abnormality. This has indeed proven to be the case. It has been found that in cases of depression there is an elevation of cortisol (stress hormone) levels in the blood. One possible scenario is as follows. When cortisol levels are increased, lymphocytes (certain white blood cells) are suppressed. Lymphocytes produce antibodies. With fewer antibodies, the individual becomes more susceptible to nearly all physical illnesses. In other words, pent-up anger results in decreased norepinephrine, which results in increased ACTH releasing factor from the hypothalamus, which results in increased ACTH from the pituitary gland, which results in increased cortisol release from the adrenal gland (near the kidneys), which results in decreased lymphocytes, which results in decreased antibodies, which results in susceptibility to nearly all infectious diseases. Pent-up anger is probably the leading cause of death.

The connection between pent-up anger, clinical depression, and death brings new light to the wisdom of St. Paul when he advises: "Be angry but do not sin; do not let the sun go down on your anger" (Ephesians 4:26). God tells us to forgive because it can mean the difference between physical and emotional life, or physical and emotional death.

THE SPIRITUAL EFFECTS OF AN UNFORGIVING HEART

But as disastrous as the physical and emotional effects of lack of forgiveness are, they pale in comparison to the spiritual damage an unforgiving heart creates. This is why God mandates us to forgive. In Matthew 18:18, Jesus says, "Truly, I say to you, whatever you bind on earth shall be bound in heaven, and whatever you loose on earth shall be loosed in heaven."

We remember these words as the words Our Lord spoke to His apostles the evening He rose from the dead. He used these words to institute the Sacrament of Penance, a sacrament of forgiveness. While they apply in a special way to the apostles and their ministry of binding and loosing sin (and "loosing" grace to flow into our souls as well), they also apply in a general way to each baptized Christian. For us, they convey a great spiritual principle regarding the giving or the withholding of forgiveness.

Jesus emphasizes the importance of His statement by using the word "truly." In His day and time, rabbis used such an emphasis as a "rhetorical signal" to communicate to the listener that what was coming next was of utmost importance. "Wake up and listen carefully," it announced. This rhetorical signal again cries out for us to sit up and take notice. And for good reason. Jesus' statement tells us that lack of forgiveness has serious spiritual implications.

Through lack of forgiveness we hold ourselves in bondage to the sinful incident, and we hold ourselves in bondage to the offending party as well. This is serious business, indeed. Our refusal to forgive is a chain that holds us captive to the very event from which we wish to heal, and binds us to the one who caused our pain! What is more, Jesus' statement tells us this miserable situation can be ours into eternity!

One could sink to despair if it were not for the fact that we also hold the key that releases the chain. When we forgive, the harm committed against us loses its power over us. Anger flees, and with it go hostility, hatred, resentment, and bitterness. We are set free — and so is the person who, in some mysterious way, has also been held in spiritual bondage by the fetters of our unforgiveness. The incident can be put to rest. To paraphrase St. John Chrysostom, an injury is either sustained or destroyed — not by the disposition of those who injure, but by the disposition of those who bear it.

But there is more besides. Now that our anger and its attending responses are gone, we can see clearly. We are "free" to see the offending party through new eyes — eyes informed by the grace of God once again active within our soul. We can see him as a person "beyond" the horrific incident, as a person bigger than that one event. And through grace, we can begin to extend empathy, compassion, and goodwill toward him. We have willfully abandoned our resentment, and instead we have assumed beneficence and moral love. Our disposition, our attitude, our heart, and our soul have been transformed. We are experiencing grace in abundance.

Consider this illustration. A gentleman is closing his store in the early evening when two gunmen enter, knock him on the head, steal the money out of his cash register, and flee. The storeowner is left in a pool of blood and is later found to be in critical condition. He is whisked away to the hospital whereupon it takes him several months to recover. During his time of recuperation, his anger and hostility toward the two gunmen festers and grows. Rage seethes within his heart, and inwardly he begins to plot his revenge.

However, other things have now begun to grow in him as well. A sense of foreboding begins to haunt him. Anxiety wells up within him whenever he thinks about the store. On Fridays, the day of the week the incident took place, he frequently breaks out in a cold sweat for no apparent reason. And whenever he tries to resume his work at the store, a panic attack sends him to his home and to his bed.

These severe reactions cause the storeowner to stay inside his house. As his phobia widens, his sphere of activity narrows. All the while, the man rages inwardly at the gunmen who so dramatically changed his life. His blood pressure soars, and he begins to develop chest pains. His doctors are concerned that he may be headed for a stroke or a heart attack.

His compromised health causes him more stress. He rails at his wife and children, his miserable behavior chases his friends away, and he swears at God whom he holds responsible for his misery. The storeowner is in bad straits. He has stopped going to church, and he has stopped receiving the sacraments. Prayer has become a distant memory. He drinks to excess in an attempt to medicate his fears, and he has begun to entertain suicidal thoughts.

It is clear that the man's attack has come to dominate his life. In fact, it has come to define his very existence. While he is obviously suffering from trauma, his situation is exacerbated by the fact that he has not forgiven. Like a fly caught in the web of a spider, the man is caught in the web of his experience. It clings to him and lives on. He cannot let go of the pain, and he cannot forgive. He is physically, emotionally, and spiritually bound to the horror of his event.

But the grief of his situation does not end there. The man has given over to his attackers the very power he so longs to recover. He has permitted them to "control" his thoughts, his emotions, his behavior, his relationships — his life. Thus, not only is he chained to the experience, but he is also chained to the men who attacked him as well. There is no room for God or anyone else in this prison of misery. He is locked tight in his trauma and bitterness. How can he loosen the grip? What can set him free?

According to many therapists, forgiveness is the key that can free him. He must forfeit bitterness and hatred in favor of beneficence and goodwill if he is to regain his life and save his soul. Again, an injury is either sustained or destroyed — not by the disposition of those who injure, but by the disposition of those who bear it: The store owner's present disposition is sustaining (keeping alive) the injury; he must change his disposition and choose to destroy the effects of the injury instead.

St. Paul's advice to the Ephesians admonishes us not to sin in our anger. This presupposes that we will experience anger in our lives, often justifiably so. But we must not hold on to it. We must not let it take root in us. Like the store owner's story so clearly illustrates, if we do, it becomes a poisonous growth that wraps around our heart and chokes off the life of God within us. The physical and emotional effects of unforgiveness are devastating; but the spiritual effects are everlasting. Like a cancer feeds on its host, so too does our anger feed upon our soul until it languishes and dies. Forgiveness is the key that sets us free and brings us new life.

WHAT IS FORGIVENESS?

Forgiveness at this level is not easy. It is only through God's grace active within us that it is possible at all. However, many individuals reject the prospect of forgiveness because they hold erroneous thoughts about what forgiveness is. Writing in their work, *Helping Clients Forgive: An Empirical Guide for Resolving Anger and Restoring Hope*, psychologist Robert D. Enright and psychiatrist Richard P. Fitzgibbons state that common misperceptions about forgiveness include confusion of forgiveness with reconciliation, equating forgiveness with forgetting, equating forgiveness with condoning and excusing, and equating forgiveness with moral weakness. In short, forgiveness does *not* mean:

- We condone or excuse hurtful behavior.
- Our pain doesn't matter.
- We "forgive and forget."
- We pretend everything is okay.
- We should allow ill will toward us to continue.
- We should allow ourselves or those we love to stay in a potentially harmful or abusive situation.
- We have "moved on."
- No retribution is necessary.
- We "feel" forgiveness.
- We are weak or a "patsy."
- Forgiveness is a quick fix.

Such misconceptions will stultify our ability to forgive and keep us chained to past events and past injuries.

Addressing therapists, psychologists, psychiatrists, and mental health counselors, Enright and Fitzgibbons use philosopher Joanna North's definition of forgiveness for advancing their work in forgiveness therapy. They define forgiveness as follows:

> People, upon rationally determining that they have been unfairly treated, forgive when they willfully abandon resentment and related responses (to which they have a right), and

endeavor to respond to the wrongdoer based on the moral principle of beneficence, which may include compassion, unconditional worth, generosity, and moral love (to which the wrongdoer, by nature of the hurtful act or acts, has no right).

By the words "rationally determining," Enright and Fitzgibbons mean that the person does not rush to a hasty judgment of the offender; that the forgiver is free of mental defect whereby he or she does not distort reality; and that the forgiver sees that the other has done a moral wrong. "Willfully abandon" is used to mean that the person is actively engaging in changing the response of resentment. They remind that forgiveness is not a passive activity but one filled with struggles and challenges. Enright and Fitzgibbons use the words "responses" and "respond" to mean the feelings, thoughts, and behaviors that accompany resentment, on the one hand, and beneficence, on the other hand.

At the heart of the definition used by Enright and Fitzgibbons is the movement from a stance of anger toward the perpetrator, albeit justified, to a position of beneficence instead. This movement, by their definition, is a renunciation of resentment and its responses in favor of an embracement of goodwill and moral love.

How does one make this move, especially in light of the painful and difficult emotions that flood the heart of the injured party? How does one move from resentment to beneficence, from revenge to goodwill, from hatred to love? How does one face the horror of his own situation and give the offending party the opportunity to begin again? Enright and Fitzgibbons outline the process for us, and Marietta's story shows us the way.

ENTERING THE PROCESS OF FORGIVENESS

Perhaps the first thing to understand about forgiveness is that it is a process. Mental health counselors and spiritual advisers agree that this is a work — it requires patience, consistency, perseverance, and hope. In addition, it requires fortitude and long-suffering. Marietta Jaeger-Lane, in describing her own experience, explains it this way in Robert Enright and Joanna North's book *Exploring Forgiveness*:

> I've heard people say that forgiveness is for wimps. Well, I say then that they must never have tried it. Forgiveness is hard work. It demands diligent self-discipline, constant corralling of our basest instincts, custody of the tongue, and a steadfast refusal not to get caught up in the mean-spiritedness of our times. It doesn't mean we forget, we condone, or we absolve responsibility. It does mean that we let go of the hate, that we try to separate the loss and the cost from the recompense or punishment we deem is due.

C. S. Lewis, the great Christian apologist, wrote, "There is no use in talking as if forgiveness were easy. We all know the old joke, 'You've given up smoking once; I've given it up a dozen times.' In the same way I could say of a certain man, 'Have I forgiven him for what he did that day? I've forgiven him more times than I can count.' For we find that the work of forgiveness has to be done over and over again."

However, both Marietta Jaeger-Lane, and I am sure C. S. Lewis, too, would agree that the effort is well worth the reward. Forgiveness sets us free from the consequences of the sins against us and helps us to once again experience the abundant life of Jesus Christ. According to Enright and Fitzgibbons, forgiveness implies transformation. It makes a qualitative difference in a number of areas: forgiveness changes previous responses toward the offender; the forgiver's emotional state may make a change for the better; and the relationship between the offending party and the offended party may improve. These changes are echoes of what Scripture tells us will occur when we forgive:

> "Forgive, and you will be forgiven; give, and it will be given to you; good measure, pressed down, shaken together, running over, will be put into your lap. For the measure you give will be the measure you get back." — LUKE 6: 37-38

How then, do we enter that process?

In their watershed work, *Helping Clients Forgive*, Enright and Fitzgibbons outline "The Phase Model of Forgiveness." Basically, this model is comprised of four phases, though Enright and Fitzgibbons are quick to add that these phases are not necessarily consecutive, nor do they always correspond exactly for each patient or client. However, they are a good guideline for what most people experience. They also caution that there is no way to predict how long the forgiveness process will take. As mentioned earlier, the difficulty to forgive is often proportionate to the degree of injury, hurt, or offense: The deeper the wound the harder it may be to forgive. Enright and Fitzgibbons list the four phases of forgiveness as Uncovering, Decision, Work, and Deepening. Let's look at each of these in turn and see how they relate to Marietta Jaeger-Lane's experience.

The Uncovering Phase

In this phase, the individual begins to see precisely how the injustice and subsequent injury have affected his life. He may see these offenses through the lens of the psychological and emotional impact of the event, as well as the physical implications he may have been left with. He may recognize the potential permanence of the injury, or he may see the offenses through other adverse affects not so long-lasting. In either case, these insights can bring with them a host of emotions including anger and hostility. And even if the injury took place years before, the new clarity with which the individual views the event can produce an emotional response as strong, if not stronger, than his initial reaction.

In Marietta's case, the Uncovering Phase began the moment she saw that Susie was missing from the tent. Fear, anxiety, worry, and concern flooded through her as she and her family, law enforcement officers, and volunteers scoured the campgrounds in search of her daughter. Desperation set in as their efforts proved futile. And when the river was dragged in a search for Susie's body, terror coursed through Marietta each time the boat would stop. Marietta describes this time and her subsequent anger:

I watched the toll this terrible time was taking on my family, and I began to seethe with rage at this man who had done this to us. As an adult, I rarely expressed anger verbally, but while I prepared for bed that night, very consciously and very deliberately and with much premeditation, I said out loud to my husband, "Even if the kidnapper were to bring Susie back, alive and well, this very moment, I could still kill him for what he has done to my family." I believed I could have done so with my bare hands and a big smile on my face, if only I knew who he was.

These are powerful emotions, indeed. And if they are not dealt with through forgiveness, the potential for physical, emotional, and spiritual damage is clear. However, it is important to admit that they exist. Many people feel guilty about recognizing they have been hurt or injured in some way. As long as this anger remains below the surface, it exerts a power over us that is difficult to control, and it will often come out "sideways" in passive-aggressive behavior, for example. Admitting the anger is there helps to loosen its grip on us.

Two suggestions can help us through this phase. The first is to identify or name the emotion(s) or hurt(s) involved. Ask the questions, "What loss did I experience?" or "What negative effect have I experienced because of the offense?" The answers to these questions point the direction to healing, and they help to identify what needs to be resolved. Is it a loss of fidelity, a loss of security in a relationship, the negative effect of rejection, a loss of good name, or the loss of a child as Marietta experienced?

Secondly, once the emotion or hurt has been identified, express it. Write it out in a journal. Talk with a friend, confessor, spiritual director, or mental health counselor. The important thing is to get the emotion or hurt out into the open.

Other aspects of the Uncovering Phase outlined by Enright and Fitzgibbons include admitting shame (common with cases of incest or rape); depleted emotional energy; "obsessional thinking" or "preoccupation" with thoughts of the offender; comparing the self with the offender (your diminished capacity or loss with his full capacity and intact status); and having an altered sense of the world (from safe to unsafe, fair to unfair, kind to cruel).

The Decision Phase

Enright and Fitzgibbons underscore the fact that the emotional pain experienced in the Uncovering Phase can serve as a catalyst to continue the process. The lack of comfort produced by sustained anger, the deep psychic pain caused by the effects of the injury, and the change in life often precipitated by the offense work together to lead the individual to resolution.

Often, this phase comes after a period of seeking revenge, harboring animosity, and expressing anger. When these strategies prove useless in resolving the pain, a "change of heart" can occur whereby the individual seeks another alternative to his misery. For Christians, this moment often comes after prayer, soul-searching, and a fundamental acknowledgment that such behaviors and attitudes are in opposition to Christ's mandate to love our enemies and pray for our persecutors.

Certainly, the grace of the sacraments, especially Penance, works to move the individual to this stage. Recognizing that he, too, is a sinner in need of God's mercy, accepting God's mercy for his own sins and failings, and then looking to extend God's mercy to others often lead the individual to consider forgiveness as an option. Ultimately, the person makes the decision to forgive.

Marietta's own intensity of anger and hostility alerted her about the direction she was heading. She knew that to cultivate her bitterness and rage was against her Catholic faith and her religious principles and values. She also knew that hatred was not healthy psychologically or emotionally, and that if she permitted her rage to engage her mind, it would drain her of the energy she needed to help her family, cope herself, and care for Susie should she come home. However, Marietta was still "utterly furious." She states:

> I felt absolutely justified in my desire for revenge, believing I'd have some input about what should happen to the

kidnapper whenever he was apprehended. I knew the death penalty could be an option, and I was unabashedly convinced that this person should get "the chair." Susie was an innocent, defenseless little girl; I had every right to avenge whatever had happened to her. And so, round and round I went, wrestling with the worst and the best of myself.

In the end, it was the "best" of Marietta that prevailed. After much interior agonizing and struggle, and through God's grace, she made a decision to forgive, all the while acknowledging that the decision alone did not mean that she had accomplished her goal. Much work would be needed for that to take place. However, she began to notice an immediate effect. She recounts:

> Finally, because I had been well taught always to reach for the highest moral ground, I surrendered. I made a decision to forgive this person, whoever he was. Yet, so saying, I clearly understood that this was not an accomplished feat by any means. The best I could muster was to choose to begin to make a serious effort to measure up to the call of my conscience. My choice seemed to lift an enormous burden from my heart, and for the first time since Susie had been taken, I actually was able to sleep soundly and felt rested in the morning.

Marietta made the decision to abandon her resentment and to work toward beneficence to the extent that she could.

Two things are important to mention at this point. The first is that just as forgiveness itself is a process, so too is the decision to forgive. This process of decision can be quite laborious and extend over a long period of time. Often the pain is so deep, or has been buried for such a long time, an individual doesn't want to forgive and can't ever imagine doing so. However, this negative response does not justify his anger according to the law of God. For the Christian, forgiveness is not an option. How then, can we overcome this resistance to forgive?

First, we must pray for the grace to enter the forgiveness process. Then, pray for the "desire" to forgive. If that is still too difficult, pray for the "desire to desire" to forgive. And if even that causes us to bristle with indignation, pray for the "desire to desire to desire" to forgive. Go back as far as necessary and begin there, moving forward one "desire" at a time.

Secondly, our emotions may in no way match our decision to forgive at this point. But this should not deter us from our goal. Our emotions are gifts from God that give us important information about that which is stimulating them. But our emotions are not to rule us. We, by exercising our will, are to rule them. In Marietta's case, she was still "utterly furious" with the kidnapper. However, she rose above the emotion, exercised her will, and made a decision to forgive in spite of how she "felt." While we need to admit our emotions, they should not ride herd over our will. Of course, it needs to be said that our will is to be subordinate to our conscience, and our conscience is to be formed according to the laws of God and the teachings of His Church.

The Work Phase

Marietta admits that making the decision to forgive is not the same as forgiving. In order to accomplish the goal of forgiveness, work needs to be done. However, Marietta did make a commitment to forgive. And the work of forgiveness must begin with that commitment in tact. Throughout the course of the work process, there is much temptation to give in, to resort back to old ways of thinking, to lapse into the anger and hostility that once shaped our attitudes and behaviors. Enright and Fitzgibbons point out that "the work ahead is difficult but can pay dividends for emotional relief and possibly even reestablish relationships."

The Work Phase can be the most challenging step in the process of forgiveness because it represents a move away from our own pain in order to explore the reasons for the behavior of the other. Psychologists call this step "reframing." Essentially, reframing is choosing to reappraise what has happened by considering other factors that we may initially have ignored. For example, it is hard to forgive someone if we perceive his action as only malevolent and unloving. But it may be easier to forgive him if we see his actions as a result of his own deprived circumstances and personal limitations.

Reframing causes us to look at the situation with a fresh perspective, and to begin to view the offender as a human being rather than the personification of evil. Enright and Fitzgibbons encourage us to ask and answer questions such as "What was it like for the offender as he or she was growing up?" and "What was it like for the offender at the time of the offense?" and "Can I see him or her as a member of the human community?"

A point of clarification must be made here. Reframing is not meant to provide an excuse for the offensive behavior of the person who has injured us. In no way is it an attempt to blame behavior on social conditions, economic class, poor family background, or the injuries and offenses the perpetrator may have experienced in his own life. Rather, reframing is an attempt to broaden our perspective of the offender and to try to see him as a person created by God and a person whom God loves unconditionally.

Though it may take time, reframing will eventually move us along the continuum of forgiveness, and it will eventually take us to empathy and compassion for the one who has hurt us. Only through empathy and compassion can we approach our "enemy" with Christlike love. And only through empathy and compassion can we extend that love to our offender and call him "friend." This, indeed, is forgiveness at work. This, indeed, is the call of the Christian.

Bearing the Pain and Giving a Moral Gift

Two other aspects of the Work Phase are *bearing the pain* and *giving a moral gift*. Bearing the pain refers to the ability of an individual to mature as a person by accepting what happened. It does not mean that the individual should live with debilitating emotions but rather he should admit those emotions and move forward with his life by absorbing his loss into the framework of his day-to-day existence. Marietta indicates that she had begun this process when she said that she was able to "sleep soundly" and feel "rested in the morning." By quietly bearing, Marietta was able to bring some semblance of balance back into her life. She felt stronger and more in control of herself again.

Enright and Fitzgibbons point out that "bearing the pain is not a passive step. It involves waiting, but with the expectation that the suffering will pass as forgiveness deepens." The sacraments of Penance and the Eucharist are invaluable in helping us to bear the pain of injuries and hurts no matter how devastating or how slight. And our assurance that God wants to heal us is a great consolation as we bear the effects of the injustice committed against us.

Ultimately, the Work Phase brings us to the point of expressing our forgiveness. In the nomenclature of forgiveness therapy, this is called "giving a moral gift." Remember that part of the definition of forgiveness is willfully abandoning resentment in favor of beneficence or goodwill. At some moment, this goodwill must be shown or expressed. However, this moment should not be rushed nor should it be feigned: It must come from real healing and sincerity of heart. For many, this moment also signifies the completion of the forgiveness process. For others, it is a goal that may never be attained this side of purgatory. For all, it is the point of true freedom.

The demonstration of beneficence is completely unique and individual to the persons involved and the situations in which they find themselves. Beneficence can be shown in small ways like a handshake, a smile, a friendly note, or the sending of flowers. For other situations, goodwill is shown in a more dramatic way. Lee's invitation to pray with his brother's murderer gives us an example of a dramatic display of goodwill. If the offending party is deceased, visiting the grave, having a Mass celebrated for him, or praying for his soul in other ways all demonstrate a desire to show him beneficence.

Marietta tells us much about the Work Phase of her forgiveness process. She states that once she made the decision to forgive and be committed to it, she strategized a plan for herself. For example, she consciously reminded herself that no matter how she felt about the kidnapper, God loved him unconditionally. She knew that no matter his actions, the man who had taken her daughter was a child of God, and therefore he had dignity and worth. In addition, Marietta determined that she would not permit anyone to speak to her negatively about him, nor would she speak about him unkindly. She knew this would only add fuel to the fire of her rage. Instead, she chose to pray for him.

Marietta began to consider what circumstances in his life could possibly have influenced him to do such a horrible thing. Obviously, he must have experienced much himself. Therefore, he needed God's mercy, not her hatred. Authentically, Marietta began to desire the best for him. None of this was easy. It continued to pull from her the "best" of herself, and at times her heartache all but crushed her. However, by cooperating with the grace of God, she persevered. And in the end, her perseverance won the prize — at a crucial moment, Marietta was able to demonstrate to him the goodwill that had begun to grow in her heart. And that demonstration led to his capture. Marietta recalls the night she received his telephone call:

> He woke me from a sound sleep, but I knew who he was immediately. It quickly became clear he was calling to taunt me: "You wanted to talk to me? Well, here I am! Now what are you going to do about it? Because no one is ever going to find out who I am, and I am the one who is calling the shots. So, what does it matter if you get to talk to me or not?"
>
> To my own amazement, as smug and nasty as he was being, something utterly unforeseen began to happen to me. From that time a year before, in Montana, where I had surrendered my rage and desire for revenge, I had truly tried to cooperate with moving my heart from fury to forgiveness . . . and when I heard this man's voice in my ear for the first time, all that I had been working for was there — and neither of us was expecting it.

He was taken aback, backed off from his taunts, gentled down, and stayed on the phone for over an hour, even though he repeatedly expressed fear that the call was being traced and he'd be caught speaking to me. When I asked him what I could do to help him, he lost control and wept. Finally, he said, "I wish this burden could be lifted from me." I certainly knew the possibilities of what "this burden" could be, but I couldn't get him to elaborate. However, that's when I really understood the transformation that had happened in me. As desperate as I was for Susie's return, I realized I also wanted to reach and help this man.

Marietta's concern about "what 'this burden' could be" was justified. That telephone call, through which she was able to show Christlike compassion and true goodwill, led to the capture and arrest of Susie's kidnapper and killer. But Marietta's concern for this man did not end there. When she had the opportunity to meet him face-to-face, she again extended forgiveness to him, and she told him she hoped he would confess and receive the help he needed. And as we have already seen, Marietta asked that he be given life imprisonment instead of the death penalty, a request that was granted. Marietta completes her story by stating:

Anger, hatred, resentment, bitterness, revenge — they are death-dealing spirits, and they will "take our lives" on some level as surely as Susie's life was taken. I believe the only way we can be whole, healthy, happy persons is to learn to forgive. That is the inexorable lesson and experience of the gospel of Marietta. Though I would never have chosen it so, the first person to receive a gift of life from the death of my daughter . . . was me.

The Deepening Phase

The Work Phase of the forgiveness process brings us to the point of beneficence. What, then, can be left?

A Tip for Spiritual
S.U.C.C.E.**S**.S.

Service

*T*he Blessed Mother has shown us that empathy requires a desire to enter into our neighbor's emotions, thoughts, and feelings. Empathy makes us a compassionate participant in our neighbor's suffering rather than a sympathizing on-looker. For those aspiring to a life of holiness, empathy should characterize our service to others. How, then, do we serve in this way? Mother Teresa of Calcutta tells us that we must serve in love: "Love cannot remain by itself — it has no meaning. Love has to be put into action, and that action is service." True Christian service, then, begins with love.

To serve in love, we must lay aside preconceived notions or ideas, all prejudice, bias, bigotry, and hate. We must look for Jesus in each person and love each person with our love for Him. We must look for the "hidden treasure" in each human heart and help to "mine" that treasure for the sake of all. We must subordinate our wants to our neighbor's needs, and we must be willing to carry his burdens. Mother Teresa says:

> At the end of life we will not be judged by how many diplomas we have received, how much money we have made, how many great things we have done. We will be judged by "I was hungry and you gave me to eat, I was naked and you clothed me, I was homeless and you took me in." Hungry not only for bread, but hungry for love. Naked not only for

continued on next page . . .

. . . continued from page 209

clothing, but naked of human dignity and respect. Homeless not only for want of a room . . . but homeless because of rejection. This is Christ in distressing disguise.

When we serve our neighbor with the love of God, we serve Jesus himself, and grace in abundance comes into the world.

For the individual who has been injured through the actions of another, it is important to find meaning in the suffering. Our fourth chapter, on embracing the cross, helped to develop the purpose, value, and meaning of suffering in light of the passion of Jesus Christ. We saw that through the incarnation of Jesus Christ, and through His suffering and death, man's misery and pain were redeemed and given worth and value. The theology of suffering, so beautifully developed in Catholic teaching, reminds us that by uniting our sufferings to the passion and death of Jesus Christ, our own injuries and trials can become conduits of grace in the lives of those we love and in the world at large. Such a perspective toward suffering infuses value and worth into the heartache of the injury sustained. It reminds us that God has a plan in all things and works all things to the good.

It is also during the Deepening Phase that the individual sees he is not alone. Suffering is part of the human condition. Others have suffered in the past, and others are suffering now. Still others will suffer in the future. We live in a broken and fallen world inhabited by broken and fallen people. In a sense, we all stand in solidarity with one another as members of a "suffering community." However, in the midst of it all, God is with us, and He gives us the grace we need.

Coming together with others who have experienced a similar tragedy or injury is helpful at every stage of healing. During the Deepening Phase, a sense of community can help us make the necessary choices to move forward with our lives. These gatherings can be formal — such as a support group or church group — or they can be informal — getting together with a trusted friend over a cup of coffee. In all cases, coming together with others can help us shake off the isolation and loneliness that are always a part of the pain.

Finally, it is in the Deepening Phase of forgiveness that an individual often feels called to "give back what he has learned." Not only is this a loving and compassionate decision, but it is a cathartic one as well. It helps to reinforce the meaning and value of our suffering, and it also encourages us to let our suffering be a source of consolation for others. This may come soon after the Work Phase, or it may come years later. Whenever it comes, it beautifully fulfills St. Paul's words to the Corinthians:

> Blessed be the God and Father of our Lord Jesus Christ, the Father of mercies and God of all comfort, who comforts us in all our affliction, so that we may be able to comfort those who are in any affliction, with the comfort with which we ourselves are comforted by God. For as we share abundantly in Christ's sufferings, so through Christ we share abundantly in comfort too. — 2 CORINTHIANS 1:3-5

Marietta Jaeger-Lane has "deepened" her process of forgiveness by "giving back" what she has learned for the past twenty-four years. What is more, her testimony has been a beacon of hope and a light of faith illuminating the way to forgiveness through Christlike love and compassion. Marietta has worked with victims and their families all over the world, expressing what she has so poignantly learned: that only through forgiveness does true liberation come; that only through forgiveness can we experience grace in abundance; and that only through forgiving can we be a channel of God's grace for others.

WORKING THE STRATEGY

Practice Forgiveness

1. Is there someone whom you need to forgive? What might hold you back from extending forgiveness to this person?
2. Have you seen any of the negative effects — physically, emotionally, or spiritually — from your lack of forgiveness?
3. Do you hold to any of the common misconceptions about what forgiveness is? If so, what are they? How can you help to adjust your thinking?
4. Can you make a decision to enter the forgiveness process? Why or why not? Are you at a place where you can make a plan for the Work Phase of forgiveness? What would this plan look like?
5. Often, we think of forgiving others only if they have committed a major offense against us. However, even the slights, injuries, and hurts we consider "ordinary" or "small" can create serious spiritual and emotional problems for us. Whom may you need to forgive for these kinds of offenses? Is there someone from whom you need to seek forgiveness? In what practical ways can you go about doing this? How will the Sacrament of Penance aid you in your quest?

STRATEGY NINE

Seek Forgiveness From Others

&

On March 12, 2000, in a ceremony at St. Peter's Basilica in Rome, Pope John Paul II knelt before God and implored divine forgiveness for the faults of all the faithful, past and present. This was truly a monumental day for the people of God and for all mankind. Seven categories of sin marked his pleas for pardon: sins in general; sins committed in the service of truth; sins that have harmed the unity of the Church, the body of Christ; sins against the people of Israel; sins committed in actions against love, peace, the rights of peoples, and respect for cultures and religions; sins against the dignity of women and the unity of the human race; and sins in relation to the fundamental rights of the person.

This courageous and edifying act of reconciliation was a powerful example of what Pope John Paul II calls a "purification of memory." Through it, the Holy Father sought to free the Church from the sins of the past so that she might move forward with apostolic zeal into the new millennium.

However, this was not the first time the Holy Father publicly asked forgiveness for the sins of the people of God. Seeking reconciliation has been a customary part of his visits to nations the world over and, in the estimation of some, provides the key to his unprecedented pontifical travel. He has asked forgiveness on behalf of the Church from Native American Indians, from women, from the Jewish people, from our separated brethren, and from the Muslims. He has asked forgiveness in the United States, Germany, Australia, the former Czechoslovakia, and Switzerland. He has asked forgiveness for incidents related to the Crusades, the Inquisition, racism, and religious oppression. In these cases and all of the other cases unmentioned, Pope John Paul II has revealed his pastoral love for the peoples of the world, as well as his personal humility as the Vicar of Christ entrusted to lead the world's people to all truth.

The Holy Father's public act of reconciliation on March 12, 2000, carried with it an exhortation to the Catholic faithful. In addition to seeking pardon for the past and present offenses caused by members of the Church, Pope John Paul II encouraged each member of the faithful to join him in seeking pardon for their personal sins and to extend forgiveness to everyone who has sinned against them. "Let us forgive and ask forgiveness!" he exhorted. "The acceptance of God's forgiveness leads to the commitment to forgive our brothers and sisters and to be reconciled with them." With fatherly counsel and wisdom, his exhortation reminds us that to be released from the chains of the past we must both forgive and seek forgiveness. Our duty to do so, he tells us, comes from the divine pardon we have received.

Thus far, our discussion about forgiveness has focused on the need to forgive. But what about those times when we need to ask for forgiveness? Given the reality of our condition — that though we are striving for holiness, we remain a broken and sinful people — it is obvious that we ourselves have often been the ones who have injured, offended, perpetrated, and maligned. My guess is that even though we try to justify our behavior and rationalize it away from time to time, the truth of our situation often glares at us from deep inside our memory.

Why is it so difficult to seek pardon from others for our transgressions against them? For many, the very thought is almost incomprehensible. Pride prevents us from ever admitting a wrong to another — and if we do, it is always couched in defensive terms. For still others, a fundamental disregard for our neighbor prevents us from asking him for forgiveness. He has ceased to matter to us for any number of reasons. And, for still others, poor self-observation prevents us from seeing just how hurtful our comments or behaviors really are. Finally, there are those who refuse to ask forgiveness because they are plainly stubborn. An iron pole rides along their spine making them inflexible, rigid, and set in their ways. No matter the reason, many people have difficulty in asking for forgiveness.

However, our lack of enthusiasm in seeking pardon in no way excuses us. Jesus tells us, "So if you are offering your gift at the altar, and there remember that your brother has something against you, leave your gift there before the altar and go; first be reconciled to your brother, and then come and offer your gift" (Matthew 5:23-24). These words do not give us the option of backing out of asking for pardon because it is uncomfortable, awkward, distasteful, or hard to do. In every case, Jesus commands us to seek reconciliation.

Now, we cannot govern our brother's response. He may choose not to forgive us, and in that case, reconciliation will not be achieved. Nonetheless, we will have benefited greatly, both emotionally and spiritually, in complying with the Gospel command to show love.

ASKING FOR FORGIVENESS

What then is required when asking for forgiveness? Whether we are reconciling with God or with one another, the same fundamental principles apply. We read in Psalms, "Create in me a clean heart, O God, and put a new and right spirit within me. . . . The sacrifice acceptable to God is a broken spirit; a broken and contrite heart, O God, thou wilt not despise" (Psalm 51:10,17). Here the psalmist identifies two of the characteristics necessary for true contrition: a broken heart and a contrite heart.

A Humbled and Contrite Heart

By a broken heart, the psalmist is talking about a heart that sees itself as it truly is: incomplete, lacking, wanting, and poor. It is a heart humbled by the truth of its condition and a heart humble enough to admit its condition. It is a heart pained at the loss of relationship with God and others. It is a heart burdened and strained by the weight of its transgression. It is a heart willing to lay its imperfections at the feet of Jesus and beg to be healed. And it is a heart that sees the consequences of its actions and is ashamed by what it sees. Such is the humility of heart a penitent needs.

But the psalmist also tells us our heart must be "contrite." One might ask how the heart could be anything but contrite once it sees the truth of itself. But to see the truth is not enough. We must be truly sorry about the truth we see. We may feel the weight of our sin, and we may feel the strain of our sin, but we may not be sorrowful for the sin we committed. To a greater or lesser extent depending upon the sin, all sin wounds our relationship with God and with others, and it can even break our relationship with both. We must be truly sorry about the effect our sin has on our relationship with God. We must be truly sorry about the effect our sin has on our relationship with others. And we must be truly sorrowful about the effect our sin has had on ourselves as well.

In addition, we must be truly sorry about the contribution our sin has made to the corporate effect of sin in the world at large. In other chapters, we have talked about the social nature of sin — that no sin is strictly personal and individual, but that every sin has repercussions on the family of man. It should sadden us deeply that our sin adds to the "burden of sin" that plagues the world. Sin, both personally and corporately, has devastating effects. True contrition or sorrow for our sin and all of its damaging effects is the second principle in asking for forgiveness.

Knowing Our Sin

We live in a day and time when sin has been expunged from the social consciousness. The seeds of relativism, carefully planted in the days of the Enlightenment, have come to full blossom in the twenty-first century. Culturally, we believe that we can determine our own morality based upon a principle of "political correctness" and "social tolerance." And though we may fight against it, most of us have been affected by this "silence on sin" in some way. Our conscience has grown weak, and our ability to see sin has diminished.

For this reason, it is essential that we cooperate with grace to "re-sensitize" and "re-form" our conscience according to the Judeo-Christian understanding of morality, good and evil, right and wrong. The best way to do this is by a daily examination of conscience, a time set aside each day to evaluate our thoughts, words, and deeds in light of Sacred Scripture and the teachings of the Catholic Church.

This assumes, of course, that we have knowledge of both scriptural teaching and Church teaching. While we will spend more time on this topic in the next chapter, suffice it to say that this means we must read Scripture and we must study Church teaching. A good translation of the Bible (Revised Standard Version, Catholic edition, is recommended) and the *Catechism of the Catholic Church* are indispensable tools in helping us form our conscience properly. In addition, numbers of booklets are available that will help us examine our conscience according to the laws of God and the precepts of the Church. We should make use of all these aids because, as Pope St. Gregory I stated, "A sin that is not quickly blotted out by repentance is both a sin and a cause of a sin." Failure to admit our faults, first to God and then to one another, keeps us entrenched in error and locked in the misery of our situation. It also sets us up to sin again.

How do we know from whom we need to ask forgiveness? A daily examination of conscience according to the categories of sin outlined by Pope John Paul II in his act of repentance in March 2000 is a good way to evaluate from whom we need to seek pardon. Have we committed a sin against another through thoughts, words, or deeds that are opposed to love, peace, the rights of peoples, and respect for cultures and religions? Have we committed a sin against charity toward another by treating him without dignity or worth, value, or esteem? Have we sinned in relation to the fundamental rights of the person — his right to life, his right to a living wage, his right to his good name, his right to love? Have we sinned against another in the normal course of our duties and responsibilities — a failure to do our fair share at home, at work, in the parish, in our community? Have we sinned against another through slander, calumny, detraction, or rash judgment? Have we offended our neighbor through prejudice or bigotry? These questions help us reflect on our recent thoughts, words, and deeds, and to probe our memory for past thoughts, words, and deeds for which we need to ask forgiveness.

Acknowledging Our Sin and Confessing Our Sin

If an examination of conscience is as far as we go, it has been an exercise and nothing more. Our examination of conscience, coupled with a broken and contrite heart over the sins we have discovered, should lead us to a sincere acknowledgment of our offenses. First, we should take our sins to the Sacrament of Penance, and then we should seek the forgiveness of those whom we have offended. This indeed can be difficult. But the grace given to us in the sacrament, received by us through the sacrament and working in us because of the sacrament, has the power to heal our broken relationship with God and with others.

We all have seen this grace at work. How many families have been reunited through the admission of an offense? How many friendships have been restored through a simple act of forgiveness? How many marriages have reconciled when a husband and wife own up to their hurtful behavior toward each other? Acknowledging and confessing our sin, first to God and then to one another, brings the very life of God into the circumstance. It releases His love in us and acts as a cord of grace uniting us to Him and to one another once again.

What should characterize our behavior when we ask for pardon? As we have already mentioned, humility and contriteness of heart are essential. These attitudes should guide our actions. We must purge ourselves from defensiveness and the desire to rationalize or justify. Additionally, our goal is to cooperate with God's grace to heal the relationship. Therefore, we should not rehash the argument, lest the argument swell again. Finally, we should place no expectations on the reaction we will receive. We cannot force or coerce the offended party to forgive us. We are simply called to seek reconciliation and surrender the outcome to God.

More Than Just Words

A popular expression applies to the next requirement when asking for forgiveness. We must not only "talk the talk," but we must "walk the walk." Someone once said that words are cheap — everybody has them. Our sincerity regarding forgiveness is displayed in our actions. To quote the act of contrition, we must have "a firm purpose of amendment." This means that our behavior needs to change. Saying "I'm sorry" but continuing to do the very thing we say we are sorry for is insincere at best and dishonest at worst.

The depth of our sorrow is measured by the length we go to avoid the sinful action in the future. A man who routinely ridicules his wife in public is not truly sorry if such behavior continues. However, he proves his sorrow by not only treating her respectfully in public, but also by cultivating respect for her privately.

In addition to "a firm purpose of amendment," true contrition compels us to make up for the "loss" we have caused. If we have stolen, we must make restitution. If we have ruined a good name, we must work to restore it. If we have slighted a friend, we should perform an act of kindness to make up for it. This is the nature of repentance. It shows that we are truly sorry, and that we want to fill the gap our injury has caused.

One way to encourage humility of heart, word, and deed, and to "walk the walk," is to incorporate a penitent attitude into our life. Such a disposition becomes a constant reminder of our need for God's mercy, our need to extend God's mercy, and our need to ask for mercy and forgiveness from others. A penitent attitude causes us to look for sacrificial offerings we can make throughout our day. These should not be flamboyant sacrifices that draw attention to our activity, but rather quiet sacrifices that are seen only by God. Every day offers us countless opportunities to practice little acts of penance for the glory and honor of God, and for the benefit of those we love. Though simple, they become an outward commitment of our decision to begin again, to join our sufferings to the sufferings of Christ, and to die to self as we seek to live for God and one another.

St. Josemaría Escrivá de Balaguer exhorts us to a penitent life when he writes:

> We need to smooth off the rough edges a little more each day — just as if we were working in stone or wood — and get rid of the defects in our own lives with a spirit of penance, with small mortifications. . . . Jesus Christ will later make up for whatever is still lacking.

Our sacrificial acts, no matter how small, work to smooth our "rough edges," all of which then eases the friction between others and us. Their yield is a softened spirit tempered by patience and humility.

SEEKING PARDON: SPECIAL SITUATIONS

Of course, there are times when it is not possible to seek the forgiveness of another in the traditional sense. We may remember an incident from our past and may have lost touch with the party long ago. It may be that we remember an offense we committed against someone who is now deceased. We may have slighted a complete stranger — a motorist on the road, a clerk in a store, a waiter or waitress, or a fellow shopper in a grocery line. And then, there may be those who could pose a serious threat to us if we sought their forgiveness. What do we do about these situations? Though we may not be able to seek pardon from someone directly, we are still called to ask forgiveness. How can this be done?

If We Have Lost Touch

If we have lost touch with the party we offended, we can still ask for forgiveness from them spiritually. Remembering the incident, acknowledging our fault, "confessing" our fault to God, and asking Him to release the party we injured from the consequences of our offense is a valuable prayer exercise for this situation. We may wish to remember this person in our prayers for a period of time, trusting that God is at work within them. It is true that in this life we may never see the effects of our prayer in the person we offended, but the release we feel within our own heart will testify to the power of the prayer we have prayed.

If the Person Is Deceased

Losing a family member is always a painful and grief-filled moment. But when we lose someone before we have patched up a difference, reconciled a quarrel, or sought reconciliation, the loss is excruciating. No one knows the day or the hour when our life, or the life of a loved one, will be taken from us. Therefore, we should never put off seeking pardon and reconciliation for any length of time. St. Paul's admonition to resolve our differences before the sun goes down is excellent advice. But the unfortunate reality is that far too few heed it, and family members do die estranged. Is it possible to seek pardon from someone who is deceased? The answer is "yes."

Remember that we all are united in the Mystical Body of Christ. This unity is called the "communion of saints." Three categories define the communion of saints: the Church Triumphant, consisting of all the saints in heaven; the Church Suffering, comprising all the souls in purgatory; and the Church Militant, consisting of all of us still living. Because we are one in Christ, though death may separate us physically, we remain united spiritually. Speaking to this, the *Catechism of the Catholic Church* quotes *Lumen Gentium* (no. 49), a document from the Second Vatican Council, which states:

> "When the Lord comes in glory, and all his angels with him, death will be no more and all things will be subject to him. But at the present time some of his disciples are pilgrims on earth. Others have died and are being purified, while still others are in glory, contemplating 'in full light, God himself triune and one, exactly as he is.' " — CCC, NO. 954

It continues:

> "So it is that the union of the wayfarers with the brethren who sleep in the peace of Christ is in no way interrupted, but on the contrary, according to the constant faith of the Church, this union is reinforced by an exchange of spiritual goods." — CCC, NO. 955

One "exchange of spiritual goods" that is possible through the unity of the communion of saints is the spiritual good of asking pardon and extending it if necessary. The death of the party we offended need not put to death our opportunity to ask for forgiveness.

By no means is this the best-case scenario. As was already mentioned, we must strive to resolve all differences in this life. But it can bring peace, comfort, and consolation to know that forgiveness can be sought and given to those who are no longer living.

But how can we show contrition and true repentance to a deceased person? The *Catechism* gives us the answer. It states:

> "In full consciousness of this communion of the whole Mystical Body of Jesus Christ, the Church in its pilgrim members, from the very earliest days of the Christian religion, has honored with great respect the memory of the dead; and 'because it is a holy and a wholesome thought to pray for the dead that they may be loosed from their sins' she offers her suffrages for them." Our prayer for them is capable not only of helping them, but also of making their intercession for us effective.
> — CCC, NO. 958, QUOTING *LUMEN GENTIUM*, NO. 50

Thus, in an attitude of contrition and penitence, brotherly love and compassion, we should augment our request for pardon of the deceased by praying for him. We can have a Mass celebrated for the person we offended, pray a Rosary for him, or make a donation to the poor in the person's memory. These are acts of love and true Christian charity, and through them we live out our life of faith. "For if we continue to love one another and to join in praising the Most Holy Trinity — all of us who are sons of God and form one family in Christ — we will be faithful to the deepest vocation of the Church" (CCC, no. 959, quoting *Lumen Gentium*, no. 51).

If We Have Slighted a Stranger

We may be surprised to discover that we need to seek pardon from someone we offended even though we have no ongoing relationship with him. However, nothing in Scripture gives us permission to be uncharitable to strangers. In fact, it shows us just the opposite (see Luke 10:25-36). Our Christian witness is meant to be a source of inspiration and grace for all of those whose paths we cross. When we are rude to a salesclerk, huffy with a waiter or waitress, irritable with a telephone solicitor, impatient (or worse!) with a fellow motorist, grumpy with a delivery boy, or quick with a customer, we sin against charity and we sin through poor example. How do we seek pardon, especially when we may never see or talk to that person again?

First, let us hope we catch ourselves in midstream and make an apology on the spot. This may not be possible in the midst of traffic, but it certainly is in most other situations. If we lack the where-withal to immediately ask forgiveness, then we should take the incident into our prayer time and spiritually ask for pardon. Our repentance can be shown by going out of our way to be kind to individuals we meet who are in similar capacities, asking Our Lord to apply the grace of our charitable action to the person with whom we are currently interacting and to the person we had offended. Of course, we should offer a prayer on behalf of the individual we slighted — a Hail Mary, a Glory Be, or an Our Father may be the "words" we use to "ask" him for forgiveness. In addition, we should examine ourselves regularly to see if our "casual" behavior speaks to our Christian faith. The way we conduct our life and our daily example should be a light leading others to Jesus Christ.

If the Person Poses a Threat

There are some circumstances when an injury we have caused has been so serious or so severe that the party we offended may seek some kind of emotional or physical retaliation. Common sense and prudence, then, must guide our interaction with him. Perhaps in these situations, it is best to ask for pardon spiritually, and then have a Mass celebrated for him. We do not want our desire for pardon to be a source of temptation for the other party. We may well be acting more charitably by keeping our distance than by seeking his forgiveness in a traditional way.

As we come to the close of this chapter, we would do well to prayerfully consider the words of Pope John Paul II that opened it: "Let us forgive and ask forgiveness! . . . The acceptance of God's forgiveness leads to the commitment to forgive our brothers and sisters and to be reconciled with them."

May these words be a constant source of inspiration and guidance for us as we strive to live the grace in abundance that Jesus Christ came to bring to us.

WORKING THE STRATEGY

Seek Forgiveness From Others

1. What is your attitude toward asking for the pardon of others? What part of it is most difficult for you? Take this difficulty to your time of prayer, and ask the Holy Spirit to reveal what sin or imperfection this difficulty may be rooted in. Take that sin to the Sacrament of Penance.

2. Is there a person from your past from whom you need to seek forgiveness? Are you willing to do so? Why or why not? Given current circumstances, how can you best achieve this goal?

3. Is there a person currently in your life from whom you need to seek forgiveness? To what extent is your heart broken and contrite? To what extent are you willing to acknowledge and confess your sin? What would stop you? How can you show your sincerity and repentance?

4. Review the reasons for living a penitent life. Do they hold a value for you? Why or why not? Develop a strategy to implement small acts of mortification throughout your day, and check yourself on them each night. Over the course of a month, what effect have your acts of penitence had on your relationship with God and with others?

5. From whom do you need to seek pardon that fits into the "special situations" category? Make a list. Develop a strategy for each and engage the process. Look for the effects of your actions in your spiritual and emotional life. What does this tell you about the power of forgiveness — seeking it and extending it?

6. What practical strategies can you implement to live a life of forgiveness as encouraged by Pope John Paul II?

STRATEGY TEN

Know and Share Your Faith

❧

As we come to this last chapter, let us cast a glance back at where we have been and what we have learned. We have discovered that God has chosen each one of us to have life at this time. In His divine providence, He knew that this particular time in the history of man was precisely the right moment for us. Everything about it would help us achieve our fundamental vocation and mission: to be holy, to be blameless, and to be full of love.

But in His omniscience, God knew something more. He knew that not only was this time for us, but also that we were for this time as well. We were precisely the people who could most benefit mankind at this particular moment in history. By virtue of our life in Him, He chose us to be the ones who would bring His love to the world in this particular day and age. Speaking to the European bishops, Pope John Paul II tells us:

> We need heralds of the Gospel who are experts in humanity, who know the depths of the heart of many today, who share in his hopes and joys, his worries and his sadness, and at the same time are contemplatives, in love with God. For this, new saints are needed. The great evangelizers . . . have been saints. We must implore God to increase the spirit of holiness in the Church and to send us new saints to evangelize today's world.

Here, the Holy Father is talking about us! Indeed, God has given us life at this time to be those heralds, to be those experts in humanity. He has given us life at this time to share the hopes and joys, worries and sadness of others. He has given us life at this time to be those contemplatives who are in love with Him. And He has given us life at this time to be the "new saints" and the "new evangelizers" who will proclaim His love to the world. What, then, is needed to fulfill this awesome mission?

Our strategies have helped to answer this question. We need to believe the truth about ourselves: that we have been chosen by God, and that this is, indeed, our call; that we need a consistent prayer life and fervent reception of the sacraments; that we need to embrace the cross of Jesus Christ as it is presented to us in our daily lives; that we need to have hope that God is in the midst of all circumstances, and that He is greater than all circumstances; that we need to live our lives with justice, and that we need to love our neighbor as we love ourselves; that we need to forgive others for their sins against us, even as we seek pardon for our sins against them; and, finally, that we need to step boldly into the culture of the day and fulfill our evangelization mission "in season and out" (2 Timothy 4:2).

But before we can *preach* the Gospel, we have to *know* the Gospel. Unfortunately, the various ideologies flooding the marketplace of ideas in today's culture does not always make this easy. What are these ideas and from whence did they come?

THE TURBULENT DECADE AND BEYOND

I came of age in the 1960s. It was a time of self-discovery and self-fulfillment. The main quest was to find the purpose and meaning of life and how that purpose and meaning related personally, socially, and politically. While an exploration of the existential questions is part of the coming-of-age experience for most generations, there was a decided twist for sojourners of the "now" generation. Their time was unlike any other.

The culture was in a state of rapid change and revolution. The Judeo-Christian worldview, upon which the society had been built, was giving way to moral relativism and situational ethics. Secular humanism, coupled with psychology's "human potential movement," was doing a good job of convincing academia and the public at large that the answers to life's questions could be found within the human person, whose power and potential was unlimited. In this scheme of things, man was at the center of the universe, and he was the arbiter of all things. God simply didn't figure in. In fact, He and His laws were antiquated carryovers from a less enlightened time.

Besides, should God exist, who needed Him? Medical science was eradicating disease and prolonging life. Technology was shrinking the world and expanding the universe. Electronics was decreasing labor and increasing leisure. Mass communication was shaping public opinion and forming popular mores. The computer age, still in its infancy, had already begun to transform business and inform the masses. And, in charge of it all, was man. Perhaps he was his own god.

The convergence of these prevailing ideologies became a weighty force that sought to push aside the "restrictive view" of the Judeo-Christian ethos and replace it with an "open and free" ethic wherein all of man's appetites could be indulged and liberated as he sought to discover his own unlimited potential. "If it feels good, do it," "It's your thing, do what you want to do," "Turn on, tune in, drop out," and "Make love, not war" were the mantras of the time. This mind-set, along with all of the other cultural influences and the popularization and availability of consciousness-altering drugs, created a noxious environment in which to investigate the deeper realities of life. Few "seekers" remained entirely unscathed.

Writing in *Apostolicam Actuositatem* (Decree on the Apostolate of the Laity), in 1965, at the heart of the cultural revolution, the fathers of the Second Vatican Council called the lay faithful "to be more diligent in doing what they can to explain, defend, and properly apply Christian principles to the problems of our era in accordance with the mind of the Church."

"In our own times," they continued, "new problems are arising and very serious errors are circulating which tend to undermine the foundations of religion, the moral order, and human society itself" (no. 6).

The Council Fathers urged the laity to use their "own gifts of intelligence and learning" and to "work vigorously in order that men may become capable of rectifying the distortion of the temporal order and directing it to God through Christ."

"The laity," they continued, "must take up the renewal of the temporal order as their own special obligation"(no. 7). And they wrote, "The member who fails to make his proper contribution to the development of the Church must be considered useful neither to the Church nor to himself" (no. 2).

The Council Fathers pointed to holiness of life as the way to restore the temporal order and the way to eternal happiness and true fulfillment. They instructed the laity to conform their lives to their faith, to practice honesty in all their dealings, to exercise fraternal charity, and to "complement the testimony of life with the testimony of the word" (no. 13). They encouraged the lay faithful to "make progress in holiness in a happy and ready spirit, trying prudently and patiently to overcome difficulties"(no. 4). And they reminded the laity that their success "depends upon the laity's living union with Christ, in keeping with the Lord's words, 'He who abides in me, and I in him, bears much fruit, for without me you can do nothing' (John 15:5)" (no. 4).

With these words and instructions, the Council Fathers sought to exhort the lay faithful to imbue the contemporary culture with the truths of Sacred Scripture, the teachings of the Church, and the love of Jesus Christ.

How helpful St. Paul's words to the Ephesians would have been at this important juncture in the maturation and personal development of a generation had it not permitted the Word of God to be drowned out by so many other voices: "[God] chose us in him before the foundation of the world, that we should be holy and blameless before him" (1:4). At once, these words answer the existential questions, "Who am I and why am I."

Here, as we have already seen, we discover that we are the "chosen people of God," whom He determined to have life prior to His first creative act. And here we also discover why we have life: to be holy and blameless in the sight of God and to be like Him — full of love. This holiness and love become for us the way to eternal life — a life that continues on the other side of the veil, a life spent with God himself.

How much sin, suffering, and senseless musing could have been avoided had these truths been explored and accepted by the "now" generation. They would have discovered that Jesus Christ is the answer, and that His Church is the key. Here is the Source of personal liberation. Here is the Source of true freedom. Here is the Source of love, peace, and joy. Herein is the abundant life. And herein is the way to experience grace in abundance.

But for a large number of people, that was not to be. Instead, the pseudo-philosophies and secular mores of the day enticed their hearts and minds. The bewitching notion of man as the center of the universe enchanted them just as seductively as it had Eve in the Garden of Eden. And, like her, they fell victim to its spell.

TWENTY YEARS HENCE

These young people carried their ideas and philosophies into the institutions of the day. What once had been intellectual speculation now became mission statement and strategy, policy and legislative decision, curriculum and lesson plan. The "fringe" had moved to the center, and what had been the center — the Judeo-Christian ethos upon which Western civilization had been built — was now viewed as the "unenlightened radical right." Secular humanism, coupled by a spirituality infused with neo-gnostic ideas and concepts, now shaped the public consciousness. From boardrooms to classrooms, from classrooms to "rec" rooms, from "rec" rooms to bedrooms, from bedrooms to research labs, the new ideology had taken root in the mind and heart of contemporary man, and it had taken root in the way he made the most fundamental decisions about his life.

And so, writing twenty years later, Pope John Paul II, echoed the prophetic words of the Council Fathers. As had they, he too, beseeched the Catholic lay faithful to read the signs of the times and to respond. However, his tone was even more urgent. He wrote:

A new state of affairs today both in the Church and in social, economic, political and cultural life, calls with a particular urgency for the action of the lay faithful. If lack of commitment is always unacceptable, the present time renders it even more so. *It is not permissible for anyone to remain idle.* — CHRISTIFIDELES LAICI, NO. 3

The "new state of affairs" within the Church and within the culture of man that made this time so urgent was the secularization of Western culture. The Holy Father continued:

How can one not notice the ever-growing existence of *religious indifference* and *atheism* in its more varied forms particularly in its perhaps most widespread form of *secularism*? Adversely affected by the impressive triumphs of continuing scientific and technological development and above all, fascinated by a very old and yet new temptation, namely, that of wishing to become like God (cf. Gen. 3:5) through the use of a liberty without bounds, individuals cut the religious roots that are in their hearts; they forget God or simply retain him without meaning in their lives, or outrightly reject him and begin to adore various "idols" of the contemporary world.

The present-day phenomenon of secularism is truly serious not simply as regards the individual, but in some ways as regards whole communities. . . . At other times I myself have recalled the phenomenon of de-Christianization which strikes long-standing Christian people and which continually calls for a re-evangelization. — CHRISTIFIDELES LAICI, NO. 4

The Holy Father's portrayal of the state of the culture in 1988, the year that he wrote these words, is sobering. He stated that even Christian people of long-standing had come under the spell of secularist ideas and concepts. He could see how Western culture had been radically impacted by secularist tenets, and he knew that the worse was yet to come, unless the marketplace of ideas was once again infused with the Judeo-Christian ethos. Secularism was leading man to the edge of a moral, ethical, cultural, and spiritual abyss. It was leading him to death.

ANOTHER TWENTY YEARS HENCE

As had been the case with the words of the Council Fathers, for the most part the words of John Paul II were ignored. And, the deaf ear that turned to his urgent plea led to what he now calls the "culture of death."

It would be impossible to list all of the alarming effects the ideology of secularization has had on Western culture. The disintegration of the family; the unprecedented explosion of venereal disease, including AIDS; the exploitation of women and children through pornography; the increase in child sexual abuse; crime of all stripes; an increase of mental illness, especially in disorders related to depression — all are but some of the bitter fruits of the secularist ethos. But one area stands out among the others: the change in attitude toward life itself.

Today, the contemporary culture's divorce from the Judeo-Christian ethos has led to some of the most grizzly scientific practices and experiments since the regime of the Third Reich in Nazi Germany. Not only has abortion been legal since the *Roe v. Wade* decision in 1973, but it is legal through all nine months up to the moment of birth. Partial-birth abortion, for example, is performed on late-second and third-trimester babies who are almost fully delivered.

A painful, brutal process, partial-birth abortion is performed by the doctor turning the baby into the breech position, pulling the child into the birth canal by grabbing her legs with forceps, delivering all of her except for her head, and then jamming scissors into her skull. The doctor opens the scissors to enlarge the hole in the child's skull, and then removes them. He inserts a catheter into the hole and sucks out the baby's brains. The child's skull collapses, and the doctor removes the dead baby. Grizzly? Yes. Legal? Yes (as of this writing). Moral? No. God-honoring? No.

Other examples loom large before us. Infanticide, euthanasia, stem cell research using embryos, frozen embryos, and cloning are all practices already in process. One can only imagine what is on the near horizon. Our culture is awash in a sea of ideologies, spiritualities, and philosophies that are far removed from a Christian understanding of who God is, who man is, what the world is, what man's problem is, what the solution to man's problem is, and what his final end will be. Acceptance of these erroneous beliefs has become the cultural standard, and it is pushing the world as we know it to the brink.

Indeed, this "new state of affairs" renders it "not permissible for anyone to remain idle." By virtue of our baptism, we all have a duty, responsibility, and obligation to communicate the Good News of Jesus Christ. We have been given life at this time to do exactly that, and we have been given every grace and "spiritual blessing in the heavenly places" (Ephesians 1:3) to do just that. It is imperative that we respond to the call. It is entirely possible that the destiny of mankind depends on it. We must evangelize. What does this mean and how do we do it?

EVANGELIZATION: OUR HOLY CALL

Evangelization. The word itself conjures up all kinds of ideas: mission fields in far-flung places; preachers atop soap boxes on big-city corners; teams of two knocking on suburban doors; people on television exhorting from Bibles; and well-meaning souls passing out pamphlets. While these are all ways of evangelizing, we may or may not be able to see ourselves doing any one of them. And yet, the call for each of us remains the same: We are to share the faith with others. The tenor of the times makes our call urgent. How do we do this within the day-to-day circumstances of our lives?

Perhaps my own witness will serve as an example. I had been a high school English teacher for a number of years but then decided I wanted to go into the insurance industry. To do so, I needed to acquire a state license by attending insurance school and passing an extensive examination. As I prepared to register for the course, I learned that a woman I knew was making the same plans. We decided to carpool together.

My friend was distraught about her marriage. She was going through an unwanted and difficult divorce. Her story was painful, and as we drove the twenty miles to class, she would pour her heart out to me. I ached for her, and many mornings our tears washed the miles. Though it was clear my friend was in emotional pain and facing an uncertain future, something about her intrigued me. Despite the fact that she was confronted with a tragic and life-changing situation, she was certain that God had a plan for her in the midst of it. Never before had I seen such faith operative in a person's life.

My friend's trust in God stood in stark relief against the backdrop of my own faith life. I had been born and raised a Catholic and had twelve years of parochial education. The Vincentian Sisters of Charity and the Dominican Sisters taught me, and as a child I even imagined myself dressed in one of those habits. But when I graduated from high school and made my way to a university, I lost my faith amid the campus turmoil and ideologies that marked the time.

In 1973, my husband and I were married, and within the next few years I gave birth to three children. Each child had been baptized at the local Catholic parish, but neither of us was practicing the faith. Now it was 1981, and I was still a non-practicing Catholic for the most part. That was the state of my spiritual life when I began carpooling with my friend. Intrigued by her faith? You bet! And one day I asked her how a person "got faith" like she had.

My friend had been waiting for this question. She shared with me about Jesus, who He was in her life, and who He wanted to be in mine. Like living water flooding the landscape of my soul, her words brought me new life. They were the catalyst for my "coming home." I thank God for my friend, without whom I may never have returned to Christ and His Church. And for her words and witness I will be eternally grateful.

My friend's example fits perfectly into the Catholic Church's understanding of evangelization. Because the essential mission and purpose of the Church is to bring all of God's people into relationship with Him through the saving merits of His Son, Jesus Christ

(CCC, no. 850), each of us baptized into His Church is called to share the faith with others according to our state in life. This sharing of the faith is what we mean by evangelization.

The *Catechism of the Catholic Church* defines evangelization as "the proclamation of Christ and his Gospel by word and the testimony of life, in fulfillment of Christ's command" (CCC, Glossary). And Vatican II states that "a true apostle looks for opportunities to announce Christ by words addressed either to non-believers with a view to leading them to faith, or to the faithful with a view to instructing, strengthening, and encouraging them to a more fervent life" (*Apostolicam Actuositatem*, no. 6).

My friend's sharing of the faith illustrates this perfectly. Her words, coupled with the testimony of her life, made a compelling statement about God, Jesus Christ, Christianity, and Catholicism. Like a "true apostle," when the opportunity came for her to "announce Christ" she made use of it by "instructing, strengthening, and encouraging" me to come back home to the Catholic Church. Through my friend, I was evangelized.

In *Evangelii Nuntiandi*, Pope Paul VI gives the true test of evangelization – that the evangelized go on to evangelize others. He states, "It is unthinkable that a person should accept the Word and give himself to the kingdom without becoming a person who bears witness to it and proclaims it in his turn" (no. 24). What, then, are the essentials of evangelization? These three help to comprise the list: the witness of a Christian life, the proclamation of the Good News, and the new apostolate of evangelization springing from the evangelized. Let's take a look at each in its turn.

The Witness of a Christian Life

In the documents of Vatican II we read, "On all Christians . . . is laid the preeminent responsibility of working to make the divine message of salvation known and accepted by all men throughout the world" (*Apostolicam Actuositatem*, no. 3). One of the chief ways through which this is accomplished is the witness of our lives. The document continues and states that "the success of the lay apostolate depends upon the laity's living union with Christ. . . . The laity must make progress in holiness in a happy and ready spirit, trying prudently and patiently to overcome difficulties" (no. 4).

As the relationship with my friend grew and I got to know her better, it became obvious to me that she had a deep and abiding relationship with Jesus Christ. Daily prayer, reception of the sacraments, a conscious reference to God in her daily activities, and drawing upon His strength in her hour of need convinced me that her life of faith was authentic. It also convinced me that it was the source of her hope. In the final analysis, it was the witness of my friend's life that attracted me to the faith first and foremost.

To be evangelizers of Jesus Christ through the witness of our lives, we must ask ourselves some fundamental questions:

- Who is Jesus Christ to me?
- Do I reflect His presence?
- Am I actively pursuing a life of holiness through the usual means: daily prayer, frequent attendance at the Holy Sacrifice of the Mass, fervent reception of the sacraments?
- Do I evaluate life's events from the perspective of faith?
- Have I developed a balanced attitude toward the acquisition of temporal things in light of eternal life?
- Do I unite my own difficulties and trials to the cross of Christ?
- Do my actions and reactions reflect hope and trust in God?
- Does the Holy Spirit, the love of God, and a true concern for others animate my life?
- Have I sought healing for those areas within me that have been wounded through personal sin, the sins of others against me, or the circumstances of life?
- Do I forgive?

These questions help us determine to what extent our lives witness to the truth of who Jesus Christ is. Those areas where we have made progress should encourage us. And those areas where progress has yet to be made should inspire us to move forward with holy vigor.

The Proclamation of the Good News

But the work of evangelization often requires more than the witness of life. Most typically our witness must be accompanied by words. Pope Paul VI says:

> The Good News proclaimed by the witness of life sooner or later has to be proclaimed by the word of life. There is no true evangelization if the name, the teaching, the life, the promises, the kingdom and the mystery of Jesus of Nazareth, the Son of God, are not proclaimed. — *EVANGELII NUNTIANDI*, NO. 22

This proclamation of the faith is called *kerygma*, which means "preaching" or "catechesis" — and St. Paul tells us it is the usual means by which the faith is communicated (Romans 10:17).

Step One: Know the Faith

How, then, do we effectively communicate the Catholic faith to others? First, we must know our faith. This does not require us to attain a degree in theology, nor does it require us to become Scripture scholars. Rather, it means we must be informed Catholics: faithful sons and daughters who have a good understanding of the precepts of our faith and who know Church teaching on various subjects and issues.

Religious education is not meant to end with elementary school, high school graduation, or Confirmation class. As Catholics, we are called to an ever-deepening experience of faith that comes about through prayer, study, and holy reading. Participating in Bible study, reading faithful Catholic literature, attending spiritual-enrichment classes, studying the lives of the saints, and spending quiet moments in prayer all lead us to maturity of faith. In most cases, my friend was ready with an answer for my questions — and when she wasn't, she knew where to go to get them. Through prayer, study, and holy reading, she had grown to an adult understanding of her Catholic faith.

Many aspects of the age in which we live — the explosion of the electronic media to convey images and ideas in lightning speed;

the proliferation of non-Christian (and often anti-Christian) concepts and philosophies in every aspect of popular culture; the saturation of secularist ideologies in curricula from kindergarten through graduate studies; the onslaught of pagan practices encroaching on business seminars, medical institutions, children's games, prime-time television, so-called Catholic retreat houses, and the very real message of a moral code devoid of God — point to the absolute need to separate truth from fiction. We need to evaluate what is presented to us from the vantage point of our Catholic faith. As St. Paul says, "For the time is coming when people will not endure sound teaching, but having itching ears they will accumulate for themselves teachers to suit their own likings, and will turn away from listening to the truth and wander into myths" (2 Timothy 4:3-4). That time is now. "As for you, always be steady, endure suffering, do the work of an evangelist, fulfill your ministry" (2 Timothy 4:5).

The chart on pages 238 and 239 offers a thumbnail comparison between Catholic teaching on the essential issues of faith and the ideology of the secularistic humanists and cosmic (New Age) humanists. We must study it and know it well. St. Paul's words to the Romans apply very well to us today: "Do not be conformed to this world but be transformed by the renewal of your mind, that you may prove what is the will of God, what is good and acceptable and perfect" (Romans 12:2).

Step Two: Expect to Evangelize

Secondly, we must *expect* to evangelize. A guest I once interviewed said that he starts his morning prayer by asking God to send him people to evangelize throughout the day. Imagine what this world would be like if all the Catholic faithful prayed this prayer — and then followed through on it! The world would be transformed.

If we *expect* to evangelize, it means that we are prepared. St. Peter tells us, "Always be prepared to make a defense to any one who calls you to account for the hope that is in you" (1 Peter 3:15). One of the best ways to have our "defense" ready is to pre-

CATHOLICISM AND SECULAR/COSMIC HUMANISM

Criteria	Catholicism	Secular Humanism	Cosmic Humanism
Who Is God?	God is personal, relational, a triune being who created the universe. He is all-knowing, all-powerful, and ever-present.	There is no God. Faith in a God is outmoded. Creedal religions are dangerous to society.	God is an impersonal life force or cosmic energy that pervades the universe (monism).
What Is the World?	The world is God's creation. It reflects His majesty and glory. He sustains it. It was made for man.	The world is self-existing and not created.	God and the world (nature) are one. There is no distinction. God is everything, and everything is God (pantheism).
Who Is Man?	Man is the summit of God's creation. He is not God and never will be, but he is made in God's image and has free will and the gift of reason. Man is created in two sexes — male and female. Man was separately created by God.	"Humanism believes that man is a part of nature and that he emerged as a result of a continuous process" ("Humanist Manifesto I"; from *www.jcn.com/ manifestos.html*).	Because God is all things, and all things are God, man is God.
Man's Problem	Sin is man's problem — original and personal sin. Man needs a Savior.	Man's problem is that the humanist message has not permeated all sectors of society and its institutions.	Man's problem is his ignorance of his true potential to be God.
Man's End	Man will die once, be judged individually, and experience heaven, hell, or purgatory.	Man has no immortal soul. There is no eternal life. Man's potential must be realized now. Ideas about immortal salvation are "illusory" and destructive to society.	Death is only an illusion because man is reincarnated.

Ethics and Morality	Truth is knowable. There are moral absolutes. These moral truths lead to real freedom and happiness.	Man establishes his own moral truth. Ethics are autonomous and situational. "We strive for the good life, here and now" ("Humanist Manifesto II"; see above).	There are no moral absolutes. Everything is subjective. Ethics are situational.
Who Is Jesus Christ?	He is the Second Person of the Blessed Trinity, the Redeemer, and the Savior of mankind.	A historical figure who is a non-issue to the future of man.	A person who, after several incarnations, realized his own god-consciousness (divinity).
How Man Attains Salvation	Salvation is attained by the merits gained through the passion and death of Jesus Christ.	There is no salvation. Man must make the best life in the here and now through personal and corporate achievement.	Man attains salvation through knowledge (gnosticism).
What Is History?	History is a chronicle of man's events, experiences, and interactions marked by the passage of time. God has always been engaged in it.	An evolutionary process of man's emergence (Darwinian theory).	A cyclical process of death-rebirth-death, which continues until man discovers his own divinity.

pare our testimony. Our testimony is simply our own personal story of God's action in our life. Through it, we "declare the wonderful deeds of him who called [us] out of darkness into his marvelous light" (1 Peter 2:9).

This same guest shared that the perfect way to form our testimony is to divide it into three parts: how we were before we knew Jesus or before God's action in our life; what happened when we got to know Jesus or when God intervened; and finally, how we are now. Or simply: "I was," "Jesus did," and "I am."

My friend's story of her personal walk in faith during a traumatic time inspired me to invite Jesus into my life as well. Now I make it a point to share my own story of faith at every opportunity. Pope Paul VI asks the question, "In the long run, is there any other way of handing on the Gospel than by transmitting to another person one's personal experience of faith?"(*Evangelii Nuntiandi*, no. 46). Personal testimony remains the most effective means of evangelization. Through it we inform, instruct, and inspire others with the truths of Sacred Scripture and the teachings of the Catholic Church.

Step Three: Be Patient

Finally, to effectively evangelize, we must be patient. The Letter of James says, "Be patient, therefore, brethren, until the coming of the Lord. Behold, the farmer waits for the precious fruit of the earth, being patient over it until it receives the early and the late rain. You also be patient. Establish your hearts, for the coming of the Lord is at hand" (5:7-8).

My friend never imposed the faith on me. Instead, she proposed it through her testimony and the example of her life. Patiently, she sowed the seeds of truth into my heart, watered them with prayer and friendship, and waited for them to take root. This process can take time. She was willing to invest the time, confident that the Lord's work would be accomplished in the end.

The Apostolate of Evangelization

It is our holy mission to be a "sign of contradiction" in our world today, to be like the Blessed Virgin Mary, who always points back to Jesus Christ. He is the Way, the Truth, and the Life. And no man comes to the Father except through Him (John 14:6). Our call is to evangelize man to this truth, and to penetrate and perfect the temporal order through the spirit of the Gospel (*Apostolicam Actuositatem*, no. 2). Pope Paul VI stated:

> It is a question not only of preaching the Gospel to ever wider geographic areas or ever greater numbers of people, but also of affecting and as it were upsetting, through the power of the Gospel, mankind's criteria of judgment, determining values, points of interest, lines of thought, sources of

A Tip for Spiritual
S.U.C.C.E.S.**S**.

Sacrifice

The "spiritual essentials" we have discussed thus far leave us asking but one question: How far are we willing to go for love of God and love of neighbor? This is a good question. Not only does our answer reveal much to us about our interior life, but it causes us to look seriously at our Christian call.

Writing in *Incarnationis Mysterium*, Pope John Paul II tells us that a sign of the truth of Christian love, ageless and powerful, is the call to martyrdom. He continues and says:

> The believer who has seriously pondered his Christian vocation, including what Revelation has to say about the possibility of martyrdom, cannot exclude it from his own life's horizon. The two thousand years since the birth of Christ are marked by the ever-present witness of the martyrs.
>
> — *Incarnationis Mysterium*, no. 13

These are stunning words. They force us out of religious sentimentality and make us look at our fundamental call as "Christian": to be "another Christ." From the apostolic age to the present day, imitators of Christ have given their lives for the truth of His Name. Would we be willing to count ourselves among them?

continued on next page ...

... continued from page 241

The Holy Father prays so. In the same document, he encourages us to let our admiration for the martyrs grow so great that we might "desire to follow their example, with God's grace, should circumstances require it" (no. 13). Are we willing to pray for this call if it be God's will for us? Would we make the ultimate sacrifice?

May the Virgin Mary, Mother of Mercy, ever docile to the Holy Spirit, pray and intercede for us today and always.

inspiration and models of life, which are in contrast with the Word of God and the plan of salvation.

— *Evangelii Nuntiandi*, no. 19

The work of evangelization is a great work, and it is a comprehensive work. Through the power of the Holy Spirit operative in us, we are to imbue all of society and culture with the Gospel message. We are to infuse a Christian spirit into the customs and mores of the social milieu. We are to establish Gospel principles as the standard against which laws and ethics are weighed. We are to advance all of society's values that are God-honoring, and to eliminate those that are not. We are to bring a Christian perspective to public affairs, to mass media, to professional duties, and to domestic life. We are to infuse our schools, our parishes, our communities, and our social activities with the life of Jesus Christ. In a word, we are to transform the world in which we live. How, then, do we accomplish such a mission?

This mission is accomplished to the extent that each one of us is committed to our own daily conversion; to sharing the faith with others when given the opportunity; to speaking the truth with love in every event; to openly and publicly declaring the truths of the faith when a situation requires it; to exercising our civic duties with an informed mind and conscience; to infusing our particular vocations and careers with the Gospel standard; and to becoming involved in the social and political affairs of mankind.

To the extent that each of us is willing to be a "first ripple" that makes an impact in the sea of contemporary culture, to that extent will the world of man be transformed. My friend was willing to be a "first ripple." She shared her faith with me. The question we must ask ourselves is not "*How* will the mission of evangelization be accomplished?" but rather "Am I willing to accomplish it?"

The answer lies with us. Will we respond to God's call and move with faith and confidence to the task at hand? Will we be a "first ripple" in the lives of others? If we say "yes," we are certain to experience grace in abundance and to bring that abundant grace to so many others. May we today have the courage to move forward with faith and confidence inspired by the One who gives us "every spiritual blessing in the heavenly places" (Ephesians 1:3).

As we come to the close of this book, let us promise to make use of the strategies it contains. Let us focus our hearts and minds on Jesus Christ and the will of the Father. Let us promise to aspire to holiness of life. And let us pray that through our witness and our word many others will come to experience grace in abundance. To this end, let us seek the intercession of our Blessed Mother, asking her to intercede on our behalf and on behalf of the whole world.

May God bless you and may the abundant life of Jesus Christ be yours!

WORKING THE STRATEGY

Know and Share Your Faith

P.A.S.S. I.T. O.N. — Eight Tips to Share the Faith
The Holy Father has encouraged all Catholics to "put out into the deep" and enter the hope-filled waters of the New Evangelization.

Here are eight ways you can prepare yourself to share the Catholic faith with others. Prayerfully read each one and then plan a personal strategy to implement it in your daily life. Through the grace of God, we can work together to infuse the world with the Truth who is Jesus Christ.

1. **P**RAY. Mother Teresa of Calcutta said, "Everything begins with prayer." Prayer leads us into a more intimate union with God, helps us become conformed to His holy will, heals us of interior wounds, and prepares us to be channels of grace in the lives of others. As we have discussed, our life of prayer should include a personal prayer time, the Holy Sacrifice of the Mass, fervent reception of the sacraments, and faithful participation in other holy devotions such as the Rosary.

2. **A**CCEPT THE CALL. By virtue of our baptism, each Christian has an apostolic mission. Therefore, the great commission that Jesus gave to His disciples applies to us as well. Before ascending into heaven, He told them, "Go into all the world and proclaim the good news to the whole creation" (Mark 16:15; NRSV). Ask God to give you the grace to see the many evangelistic opportunities in your daily life.

3. **S**TUDY. St. Peter tells us to be ready to give an answer for the hope that we have received (1 Peter 3:15). Knowing our faith and being able to share it with others require study. Our study materials should include Sacred Scripture, the *Catechism of the Catholic Church*, and other good resources that are faithful to Church teaching. They help us know our faith better.

4. **S**ACRIFICE. To be effective evangelizers, we must know how to sacrifice. Some sacrifices will be passive, coming to us through the circumstances and events of daily life. Other sacrifices should be active — a conscious decision to mortify ourselves for the spiritual well-being of others. Fasting, almsgiving, and self-denial are ways we can empower our evangelization efforts.

5. **INTERCESSION.** Intercessory prayer is essential for evangelization. We must ask God to send us people to evangelize. We must pray to communicate to them effectively. And we must pray for them once we deliver the salvation message. Our petitions should be accompanied by expectant faith and gratitude.

6. **TEACH BY EXAMPLE.** St. Francis of Assisi is quoted as saying, "Preach the Gospel, and use words when necessary." Our everyday lives speak volumes about our life of faith. A daily examination of conscience helps us see what message we are communicating to others.

7. **ORGANIZE YOUR TESTIMONY.** A most effective means of evangelization is sharing our own story of God's action in our lives. Structure your story around three parts: (1) what your situation was like before God's intervention, (2) what God did for you in your life, and (3) how you are now. Having your story ready to tell is great preparation, and it helps us make use of every opportunity.

8. **NO EXCUSES.** If we pray, accept the call, study, sacrifice, ask for intercession, teach by example, and organize our testimony, we should be ready to share the faith with others. Therefore, no excuse is acceptable! Be ready for excitement, joy, and holy surprises as you take your faith and **PASS IT ON!**

Notes

Notes

Notes

Notes

Notes

Our Sunday Visitor . . .
Your Source for Discovering the Riches of the Catholic Faith

Our Sunday Visitor has an extensive line of materials for young children, teens, and adults. Our books, Bibles, booklets, CD-ROMs, audios, and videos are available in bookstores worldwide.

To receive a FREE full-line catalog or for more information, call **Our Sunday Visitor** at **1-800-348-2440**. Or write, **Our Sunday Visitor** / 200 Noll Plaza / Huntington, IN 46750.

Please send me: __ A catalog
Please send me materials on:
__ Apologetics and catechetics   __ Reference works
__ Prayer books   __ Heritage and the saints
__ The family   __ The parish
Name_____
Address_____Apt._____
City_____State_____Zip_____
Telephone (   ) _____

A29BBABP

Please send a friend: __ A catalog
Please send a friend materials on:
__ Apologetics and catechetics   __ Reference works
__ Prayer books   __ Heritage and the saints
__ The family   __ The parish
Name_____
Address_____Apt._____
City_____State_____Zip_____
Telephone (   ) _____

A29BBABP

OurSundayVisitor

200 Noll Plaza
Huntington, IN 46750
Toll free: **1-800-348-2440**
E-mail: osvbooks@osv.com
Website: www.osv.com

What does God ask from a woman?

In exploring answers to this question, radio and TV host Johnnette Benkovic guides women into a deep and rewarding walk with the Lord by providing a unique combination of Scripture passages, insightful quotes, and her own penetrating insights and heartfelt prayers. This is a book to be savored and treasured by women of all ages, in all situations.

Grace-Filled Moments, 0-87973-899-5, **(899)** hardcover, 256 pp.

Our Sunday Visitor

200 Noll Plaza, Huntington, IN 46750
Toll Free: 1-800-348-2440
E-mail: osvbooks@osv.com
Website: www.osv.com